THE PLANT-BASED DIET MEAL PLAN

THE PLANT-BASED DIET

MEAL PLAN

A 3-Week Kick-Start Guide to Eat & Live Your Best

HEATHER NICHOLDS, CHN

FOREWORD BY TESS CHALLIS

Photography by Nadine Greeff

ROCKRIDGE PRESS

For general information on our other products and services or to obtain technical support, please contact our Customer Care Department within the U.S. at (866) 744-2665, or outside the U.S. at (510) 253-0500.

Rockridge Press publishes its books in a variety of electronic and print formats. Some content that appears in print may not be available in electronic books, and vice versa.

TRADEMARKS: Rockridge Press and the Rockridge Press logo are trademarks or registered trademarks of Callisto Media Inc. and/or its affiliates, in the United States and other countries, and may not be used without written permission. All other trademarks are the property of their respective owners. Rockridge Press is not associated with any product or vendor mentioned in this book.

Photographs © Nadine Greeff, 2018
Author photo courtesy of Heather Nicholds

Illustrations © Tom Bingham, 2018

ISBN: Print 978-1-93975-456-1
eBook 978-1-93975-457-8

Dedicated to every single person who wants to go plant based but isn't sure how to make it happen. I was in your shoes many years ago, and I hope this makes the journey easier.

CONTENTS

Foreword ix

Introduction xiii

PART ONE

the plant-based diet primer   xvi

1: Plants and Your Health   1

2: The Plant-Based Diet   11

3: The Food Lover's Plant-Based Kitchen   31

PART TWO

the plant-based meal plans   42

4: Week One   45

5: Week Two   53

6: Week Three   61

PART THREE

the recipes   72

7: Smoothies and Breakfasts   75

8: Soups and Salads   105

9: Main Dishes   137

10: Snacks and Sides 189

11: Desserts   209

12: Homemade Basics, Sauces, and Condiments   225

13: Drinks   245

Appendix A: The Dirty Dozen and the Clean Fifteen 257

Appendix B: Conversion Sheet 258

Appendix C: Blank Shopping List 259

Appendix D: Blank Meal Planner 260

Resources 262

References 264

Recipe Index 267

Index 269

FOREWORD

As a nutritionist, I've felt a kinship with Heather's approach for years now. When it comes to a plant-based diet, Heather focuses on making the food delicious and delightful because she knows that this is the only way it can be "doable." Also, she doesn't force extreme diet practices simply because they never end up working. We believe in the same fundamentals when it comes to food and nutrition, which is why she and I have been champions of each other's work for so long. We both see tremendous value in balance. Far too many diets don't focus on the food first, leaving most people frustrated and discouraged, because how long can you keep going when you feel deprived? Like Heather, I have encountered far too many clients who feel overwhelmed at the prospect of implementing a plant-based diet. They've watched a documentary (or found out they have high cholesterol) and are motivated to make a change, but they don't know where or how to start—and they've become increasingly frustrated with the popular programs available, due mainly to recipes that aren't appetizing or accessible.

The Plant-Based Diet Meal Plan is different; instead of a typical diet that restricts foods, it *is* a celebration of food. The food in Heather's meal plan is life changing, because it shows that eating plant based is about discovering a new and delicious world of options, where you don't have to give up flavor or substance to get the results you want. The collection of recipes in this book are a far cry from the bland meals that most people envision when they hear the word "plant-based diet." Instead of steamed broccoli over millet (and a side salad with vinegar), you'll be treated to sumptuous dishes like Vietnamese Summer Rolls, Moroccan Aubergine Salad, Miso Coconut Dragon Bowl, and even tasty desserts like Mint Chocolate Chip Sorbet.

Along with being delicious, Heather's meal plans are clear, practical and easy to follow. She provides daily menus for the first three weeks of your journey and weekly shopping lists to help you stay focused and on track. Finally, whether you decide to continue with the plant-based diet or simply want to integrate more plants into your omnivore diet, she offers essential and valuable information on preparing and cooking plants intuitively, so that by the end of the third week, you'll have enough knowledge to build your own tasty and satisfying meals.

This kick-start guide is effective because, at its core, it is truly balanced and it was developed by a caring expert—a package that is hard to find!

Heather is the real deal, and she gives you everything you could possibly need to begin your own plant-based journey to greater health and happiness in a way you can—joyfully—maintain for a lifetime. You can do this!

—Tess Challis
Author, vegan chef, and One Degree Coach

INTRODUCTION

For me, a perfect lunch is something delicious, easy, and of course plant based, like a Miso-Coconut Dragon Bowl: quinoa, red peppers, and mushrooms in a creamy coconut-miso broth and topped with fresh greens and sliced almonds. I love food, and these plant-based bowls are the types of meals I enjoy, but I didn't always eat like this. Once upon a time, I was an omnivore, and meals often revolved around the main entrée, which was some type of meat from a regular rotation of animal-based protein. It wasn't until I started eating mostly plants that I discovered how rich and diverse food could be. Eating a plant-based diet made me the foodie I am today.

Growing up, my favorite foods were made by Mom: spaghetti Bolognese, salmon patties, roast chicken. As a kid, I was a really picky eater and didn't like too many vegetables, so I imagine my mom is amused nowadays when she sees me digging into a big kale salad.

I didn't start developing an interest in cooking until after university, during which I subsisted on standard cafeteria food and sub sandwiches. I started buying cookbooks and experimenting with recipes—many of which were disasters. The more I created meals for myself, the more I wanted to know about making them healthier. I started on the path to more wholesome meals while I was still an omnivore, gradually steering away from meat-centric dishes.

My tipping point was when I learned about the environmental impacts of industrial food production. Animal agriculture creates 18 percent of our greenhouse gas emissions, which is more than what all the cars and trucks on the world's roads emit. Eating more plant foods and fewer animal foods was the single biggest action I could take on behalf of our planet. But the next step begged the question: What do I eat? Being a meat-eater all my life, I didn't have a clear answer or plan.

Like most people who switch to plants, I wondered if the food would be filling enough. I was also concerned that I would find plant-based food uninspiring and limiting, especially because of the notion that plant based meant eating boring, bland salads. So, I put in a little work to learn how to make healthy, plant-based foods taste amazing. I took a chef training course for intuitive plant-based cooking, which entails learning to cook based on your intuition as a chef, without using recipes. Also, because I wanted to make sure I was getting everything my body needed to thrive, I went back to school to study holistic nutrition, focusing on a natural approach to healthy living.

I've never had as much fun cooking and eating as I do now. I never feel restricted or deprived; in fact, quite the opposite. I feel liberated, exploring endless possibilities with new flavors and new flavor combinations and constantly adding exciting new foods and meals to my list of go-to recipes. After shifting to a plant-based lifestyle, I have more energy; I lost weight without trying; and I don't experience the chronic gas or digestion issues that I had in the past. I didn't realize how bad I felt until I felt better.

This was how my path to plants unfolded, but I know that each path is different because our food experiences are different. The way we eat is so personal. Food not only fuels our bodies, it has the power to make life more enjoyable. Food is intimately intertwined in cultures and in our social lives, and our taste buds compel us to find happiness and satisfaction in the foods we consume. It can be hard to maintain a plant-based lifestyle in a meat-centric and convenience-oriented society. Most people are daunted by the idea of giving up their comfort foods and of learning to prepare new and strange foods they know little to nothing about—and sometimes can't even pronounce. And if eating plants doesn't come naturally, it's hard to be excited about the countless vegan and plant-based diet cookbooks and blogs out there.

That's where this book is different. The meal plan and recipes in this book were developed with the goal of teaching you how to make the best plant-based meals so that the food itself becomes the incentive. Because no matter your reason for switching to plants—whether it's simply to get more vegetables into your diet, lose those stubborn ten pounds, look more svelte for that special occasion, make long-term health changes as recommended by your doctor, find relief from chronic illness and symptoms, or, like me, shrink your carbon footprint by reducing your meat and dairy consumption—the reality is that if the taste of the food you eat doesn't excite you, then there is no way you will be able to maintain this way of eating, not even for three weeks.

I decided to arm myself with a culinary nutrition education, but you don't need to go that far to be successful with this diet. Using knowledge and techniques that have helped me and my many clients, I've carefully developed these recipes so that you can explore different foods through quick and easy meals that are practical to make after work or on a busy weeknight. I've also taken inspiration from cuisines around the world so that you can discover that new favorite food, meal, or recipe, expanding your food vocabulary and experiences. Plus, the three-week meal plan includes daily menus and shopping lists to show you exactly how to make this diet work for you and help you stay on track. You'll find clear guidance and a solid action plan to transition to a fully nourishing plant-based diet, with a constant focus on delicious and wholesome foods. You might even make some meals that the meat-eaters in your life will fall in love with.

Finally, the amazing thing about eating and enjoying plants is that in three weeks, you will start to see and feel their healing powers. Your complexion will look more radiant, your digestion will improve, you'll have more energy, you'll think more clearly, and you'll sleep better. If you stick with this diet for the long term, you should find that your immune system is more resilient, your moods are more balanced, your waistline is slimmer, and your mind is more at ease with the choices you make.

Being a food lover doesn't have to mean feeling guilty about the foods you love. And eating to nurture your health and body doesn't mean giving up the foods you love. Being a food lover can also mean carefully choosing foods that your taste buds will love and that your body needs and craves. Plants are natural healers that, when prepared with thought and care, are fulfilling and delicious, delivering daily doses of health and happiness. By choosing plants, you are taking the first step to finding that necessary balance to eat your best, live your best, and be your best. By choosing plants, you will change your life.

PART ONE

THE PLANT-BASED DIET PRIMER

Before we jump into the balanced meal plans and delicious recipes, let's take some time to get to know and understand the principles and science behind the plant-based diet. You may be eager to get going, but it's helpful in the long run to learn the whys and hows behind what we're doing. It will also help you save time, as you'll begin to understand how to put together a balanced and delicious meal, rather than having to always follow plans and recipes. In the first chapter, we'll look at the link between a plant-based diet and your health; then we'll move on to a breakdown of balanced nutrition from plants; and then I'll give you plenty of tips and tricks for setting up your plant-based kitchen.

chapter 1

PLANTS AND YOUR HEALTH

Chronic diseases, like cancer and heart disease, are unfortunately all too common in the United States. There's good evidence that changing how we eat can help prevent chronic disease and that a diet rich in meat and dairy is linked to some major health complications, including heart disease and diabetes. Several compounds in meat and dairy (such as casein, nitrites, saturated fat, cholesterol, heme iron, and arachidonic acid) are implicated as potential culprits for this link.

All of this has sparked a growing public interest in a plant-based diet for health reasons, since plant foods are rich sources of nutrients and compounds that help protect us from these same chronic diseases. Before we discuss what to eat to support this new lifestyle, it's important to take a closer look at the role eating plants plays in managing weight loss and promoting a healthier you.

Plants as Medicine

One of the most important choices you can make for your health is to eat more fresh fruits and vegetables, whole grains, beans, nuts, seeds, herbs, and spices. Incorporating more of those foods into your life has powerful effects.

Plant-based diets are higher in dietary fiber, magnesium, folic acid, vitamins C and E, iron, and phytochemicals. They also tend to be lower in calories and are lower in saturated fat and cholesterol than other diets. Vegetarians generally have a lower risk of cardiovascular disease, obesity, type 2 diabetes, and some cancers.

Cardiovascular Disease

Heart disease is the number one cause of death for Americans. The dietary recommendations for those at risk for cardiovascular disease are to reduce saturated fat, cholesterol, refined carbohydrates, and sugar, and to increase fiber, antioxidants, omega-3s, and monounsaturated fats. A plant-based diet—eating vegetables, whole grains, nuts, seeds, legumes, and fruits—is the best way to achieve this.

In studies, vegans consistently have lower markers for cardiovascular disease than meat-eaters or even vegetarians: low blood pressure, low LDL cholesterol (the bad kind), low triglycerides, low serum total cholesterol and apolipoprotein B concentrations (lipoproteins carry cholesterol through the bloodstream, and apolipoproteins are a component of many lipoproteins that are involved in atherosclerosis and cardiovascular disease), lower systolic and diastolic blood pressure, as well as a lower prevalence of hypertension.

Vegetarians generally have a lower incidence of high blood pressure, most likely due to a high potassium intake from vegetables, fruit, whole grains, and legumes. Blood pressure is related to the ratio of sodium to potassium in your body. Although a common recommendation for people with high blood pressure is to reduce salt intake, that alone hasn't been shown to have a significant impact on blood pressure control. Increasing the potassium side of the ratio is the other key to this equation. The average intake for a typical American is 2:1, meaning they eat twice as much sodium as potassium. The ideal ratio is 1:5, so decreasing salt (sodium chloride) doesn't take it far enough. You need to eat more plant foods to boost the potassium side of the scale.

A plant-based diet dramatically increases the intake of protective nutrients (such as antioxidants) and phytochemicals (compounds in plants that are beneficial to us), while minimizing the intake of risky compounds that have been implicated in several chronic diseases. This doesn't mean vegans are immune to disease—heredity and other environmental and lifestyle factors also come into play. But a plant-based diet offers the best chance of avoiding risk and helps build a strong immune system to deal with any challenges that are beyond your control.

Cancer

Cancer is the second leading cause of death in the United States. Whole plant foods—that is, foods that are as close to their natural state as possible—are full of powerful cancer-fighting antioxidants and immune-boosting nutrients and are naturally low in saturated fat and high in fiber. Plant-based eaters get significantly more legumes (seeds, peas, and beans), more total fruit and vegetables, more fiber, and more vitamin C than do omnivores. Those foods and their nutrients are ones that have been shown specifically to be protective against cancer. A plant-based diet also reduces foods associated with increased cancer risk, including dairy, eggs, red meat, and processed meats.

Stroke

The risk factors for strokes are similar to those for cardiovascular disease: elevated cholesterol, high blood pressure, and obesity. Since a plant-based diet tends to improve all three of those, it's a good way to offset the risk.

Alzheimer's Disease and Dementia

While the onset of Alzheimer's and dementia is mostly determined by heredity, eating a nutrient-dense plant-based diet gives our bodies the best chance to stay healthy as long as possible. One of the factors that can speed the onset of dementia is oxidative stress—an imbalance between the level of free radicals in the body and the ability to neutralize their harmful effects through antioxidants. (Free radicals damage cell membranes and other structures, including DNA.) Plants are the richest dietary source of antioxidants, and they can help slow that damage.

Recommendations for delaying the onset and slowing the progression of Alzheimer's often include eating fish and seafood, for the omega-3 fatty acids. However, studies also show that toxins and heavy metals damage nerve cells and contribute to neurodegeneration. Since fish and seafood are unavoidably rich in mercury and other toxins that pollute our oceans, such as plastic, it makes more sense look to nonpolluted plant sources of omega-3s, like flax and chia seeds.

One of the first questions I ask when people mention that their parents are starting to show signs of dementia is whether they are getting enough vitamin B12 and folic acid. A deficiency in either of those nutrients creates symptoms that mimic dementia. Folic acid is easily obtainable from plant foods, but our diets don't always prioritize the nutrient-density needed to maintain healthy bodies and minds. As older adults' metabolisms slow, they need more of these nutrients, not fewer. As we age, our bodies are less able to extract vitamin B12 from our food, so government recommendations are that adults over 50 take a B12 supplement, regardless of whether they eat animal foods.

Diabetes

The main dietary recommendations for diabetes include decreasing the glycemic load (the overall potential of a food to raise blood sugar) and saturated fat intake, increasing fiber intake, and using cinnamon, which has been studied for possible benefits to blood sugar control. This can be easily achieved through a plant-based diet. Many prediabetics and people with type 2 diabetes find their blood sugar levels much easier to control when eating a plant-based diet.

PLANTS AND JOINT INFLAMMATION

Studies on the link between arthritis and diet have shown that those observing a plant-based diet have a significant decrease in morning stiffness, joint pain, swelling, and inflammatory compounds in their blood. This is likely because a plant-based diet increases your intake of anti-inflammatory foods and decreases your intake of inflammatory compounds from animal foods. There may also be a link with bacteria called *Yersinia*, found in contaminated pork, that can lead to chronic inflammation. To cap it off, vegans tend to have a lower body weight on average than meat-eaters, putting less stress on joints.

Meat, fish, and eggs are rich sources of arachidonic acid, which is a precursor to inflammatory compounds (prostaglandins and leukotrienes). A diet low in arachidonic acid has been shown to help relieve symptoms of arthritis. Advanced glycation end products (AGEs) are inflammatory toxins that appear when foods are heated, grilled, fried, or pasteurized. They're created mostly in animal foods, since the reaction is triggered by proteins and saturated fats. They're also produced in our bodies when we eat too much refined sugar and flour. Dairy is one of the most common triggers of arthritis pain because it contains a protein that can irritate the tissue around the joints.

Whole plant foods are are naturally rich in anti-inflammatory compounds like fiber, water, and antioxidants and naturally devoid of all the inflammatory compounds listed to the left. The top anti-inflammatory foods are high-carotenoid yellow, red, orange, and dark green leafy vegetables, like spinach, kale, and collards, nuts rich in mono-unsaturated fats like almonds and walnuts, omega-3-rich flax or chia seeds, fruits like anthocyanin-rich strawberries, blueberries, tart cherries, and bromelain-rich pineapple, turmeric (for its curcumin content), and ginger (for its gingerol compounds).

Plants for Weight Loss

So many weight-loss diets focus on avoiding, losing, reducing. This makes you feel deprived and shortchanged. Negativity and self-deprecation will raise your stress levels and affect your health and quality of life.

Despite the dedication to counting calories, tracking steps, going to the gym, and diets that eliminate everything we love or add a "miracle" supplement, our society is increasingly afflicted with obesity and the diseases that result from it. Deprivation dieting isn't a successful long-term strategy, and calorie restriction slows your metabolism, making it harder to maintain any weight loss.

A simpler and more effective way to approach weight loss is to think of foods in terms of nutrient density and calorie density. To lose weight, you increase your proportion of nutrient-dense foods and decrease your proportion of junk foods. The magic of this approach is that it flips the focus to the positive of creating health for yourself by eating more of the delicious, satisfying good stuff.

Nutrient-dense foods have a high amount of vitamins, minerals, and antioxidants for their volume. Vegetables, fruit, whole grains, beans, herbs, and spices are all nutrient-dense foods. Calorie-dense foods have a high amount of calories for their volume. Some examples are oils, sugars, dairy, eggs, oily fish, meat, and fried foods.

There are some foods that are both nutrient and calorie dense, like nuts, seeds, and avocados. You want to eat those foods because they have important minerals and other nutrients, and small amounts can help you feel full. You just need to eat them in smaller portions than you do other nutrient-dense foods.

Some foods are lacking in nutrients, even though they add calories to your day. These are called empty-calorie foods. They leave your body still craving nutrients, even though you've added calories to your day. White rice, white bread, refined oils, and refined sugar are examples.

Going plant based and focusing on choosing whole foods over processed or refined versions boosts nutrient density while lowering calorie density. It will also increase your water and fiber intake, both of which boost your metabolism and improve your digestion.

Use small bowls and plates. On a large plate or bowl, most people will take larger portions just to visually fill the space. Use roughly the same size plates and bowls for all your meals, so that you know how to fill them with the portions that will fuel your day without overindulging.

Use only two or three flavors. Our taste buds and our brain process our sense of the different flavors in a meal and want to experience a certain amount of each one before they feel satisfied. If we have too many different dishes and flavors all at once, we'll generally eat more than we need, just to get a good taste of each. A textbook example is Thanksgiving dinner. So, if we make a meal with just two or three different dishes, we'll be satisfied before we wind up stuffed.

Eat with chopsticks. It slows (most of) us down, and makes for smaller bites, which gives us a better chance to feel our body's satiety cues before we've eaten too much.

Swallow between each bite. This is harder than it sounds! Give it a try, and see if it makes you more conscious of chewing. It also slows you down a bit to let the satiety cues catch up.

Brush your teeth between meals. This is a great idea for dental hygiene in general, and it also makes you less likely to randomly snack between meals. Planned snacks for fuel and nutrients are of course a fine idea, but it's best to minimize mindless munching.

Change the calorie density of foods. By cooking brown rice with an extra cup of water, you decrease the calorie density. It will come out the same, you just need to cook it a bit longer. You can also do this with morning porridge, so you get more hydration to start your day; plus it's easier to digest.

Dilute your juice or soda. One of the most effective ways to drop some pounds with one single change is to replace juice or soda with water. You can drink a lot of sugar-even in 100 percent natural fruit juice-without realizing how many calories you have added to your day. Can't go cold turkey? Start by diluting your drinks with water or club soda. Diluting them by half cuts your sugar intake in half. You can gradually try diluting further, until you only need a splash of flavor in your carbonated or uncarbonated water.

All the elements of the diet work together to satisfy and nourish the body on a deep level, so you thrive while you naturally lose weight. Over time, you'll find that those intense cravings you used to have for junk foods just fall away, as you feel the energy and health you're building. You're adding and expanding, not denying and taking away, so you feel abundant, happy, and fulfilled.

Plants and Other Benefits

There are lots of other potential health benefits to eating more plants. Here are some that people have found when switching to a plant-based diet.

Energy boost. As they shift to plant foods full of nutrients that fuel energy levels, and away from refined sugars and grains that cause the blood sugar to spike and inevitably crash, many people find they have more sustained energy levels throughout the day.

Clear complexion. Dairy is one of the most common and clearly linked acne trigger foods. Sugar is also a common trigger, so as you reduce refined sugars and move to whole-food sweetness, your skin will likely become clearer.

Immune boost. The nutrients your immune system needs to be strong are plentiful in plants. Focus on the dark green, red, and orange fruits and vegetables, plus seeds for zinc.

Better digestion. With a massive boost in fiber, most people find their digestion improves. Many of my clients find that their pants fit better simply from a less bloated stomach.

Soothed stomach. Eating too much meat, dairy, processed foods, and fatty foods, not chewing enough, and being under stress can all cause your stomach to act up and may be the culprit in heartburn and indigestion.

Faster recovery after workouts. Athletes, runners, and bodybuilders on plant-based diets report that they recover faster after workouts, meaning they can fit in more training than their omnivorous counterparts. This may be due to increased antioxidants, vitamins, potassium, or a decrease in the inflammatory compounds found in meat and dairy.

The bottom line: If you can be healthy and adequately nourished on a plant-based diet, reduce your risk for debilitating degenerative diseases, help the planet, animals, and humans affected by animal agriculture, plus eat interesting, varied food that tastes amazing—what's left as a reason to not make this change?

chapter 2

THE PLANT-BASED DIET

Planning nutritionally balanced plant-based meals isn't nearly as hard as it's made out to be. A few key nutrients are well known to be associated with animal foods, such as protein and iron, and a lack of knowledge about which plant foods provide them might scare some people away from changing their diet.

If you eat a variety of healthy, whole plant foods, you'll get enough of most of the nutrients you need to be perfectly healthy, including protein, vitamins, and minerals like iron and calcium. The only nutrients missing from plant foods are vitamin D and vitamin B_{12}, which you can easily get from supplements.

It does take some awareness and knowledge to get started on a healthy plant-based diet, but once you learn the basics, you can easily and quickly make healthy and balanced meals every day. You get this wonderful feeling of empowerment when you understand how to nourish yourself properly and how to listen to your body's feedback.

In the first chapter we examined the crucial role that eating plants plays in maintaining your health and weight. Now let's take a closer look at what the plant-based diet looks like.

What Is It?

First, let's go over exactly what each term means.

Vegetarians eat no animal flesh (beef, fish, poultry, pork, lamb, and so on) and may not use products that involve the death of animals (such as leather).

Vegans eat no animal products of any kind (a vegetarian diet, plus no dairy, eggs, gelatin, or honey) and don't use products that involve the death of, cruelty to, or suffering of animals (such as leather, wool, or any products that have been tested on animals) as much as practical and possible.

Plant-based adherents focus on whole plant foods and on a healthy lifestyle, avoiding heavily processed and refined foods and those with lots of processed oils and refined sugars.

Pescatarians eat fish, but no other animal flesh. Many do eat dairy or eggs.

Flexitarians eat mostly vegetarian but are flexible in social situations.

Whether the motivating factor is mostly environmental, ethical, or health-related may determine the choices each individual makes about what they buy and eat. Personally, I am vegan and plant-based. I'm driven by all three motivational factors of the vegan trifecta, and I focus on whole foods.

However, what's more important to keep in mind, and what this book focuses on, is enjoying a wide variety of nutrient-dense foods and eating a large portion of your diet as fresh vegetables and fruit. And you can make this all taste phenomenal, so you'll never feel like you're missing out.

Some people's perception of a plant-based diet is that it's all about eating salads and not enjoying food for the rest of your life. If you're scared or guilted into a diet with only your personal health as motivation, it's very hard to maintain long term, especially if the food is boring. A lot of clients come to me after trying to go plant based but getting so bored with the food that they need help making it more balanced to sustain long term.

While I certainly don't think of oils and sugars as health foods, there is an overall benefit in using them judiciously to enhance flavor and encourage long-term enjoyment of a healthy diet. If a pinch of salt gets people eating more carrots, or a drizzle of oil gets people eating more squash, I take that as a win. Being hyper-focused on health and missing out on flavors is a shame, because they can work so beautifully together. Also, the motivation of improving your health can work perfectly in tandem with improving the health of our planet and with reducing suffering of animals. It turns out that the trifecta can serve to strengthen your motivation even further, so it truly becomes a lifestyle rather than a diet.

The Plant-Based Food Groups

At first glance, people often assume that a plant-based diet is extreme and restrictive. The truth is, I actually eat a wider variety of foods now. There are vegetables, fruits, seeds, and spices I'd never heard of before—and cooking with and eating them is so much more fun! I never feel restricted or deprived; more like liberated into an exciting and flavorful new world full of options. Let me introduce you to the abundant world of plant foods waiting for you to explore.

Vegetables are the place to start; they are so important that they should make up the largest portion of your diet. They include all the leaves, roots, bulbs, stems, vines, and flowers listed here. Vegetables can be eaten in large quantities because much of their bulk is water and fiber. They are full of vitamins and minerals, and are an important source of potassium. Potassium is a mineral that, in proper ratio to sodium, works to regulate blood pressure. Getting enough potassium is just as crucial for those with high blood pressure as lowering sodium intake.

Leaves

Leaf vegetables, or greens, are one of the most nutrient-dense foods you can eat. They contain plenty of vitamins (especially K, A, C, and folate) and minerals (like iron, magnesium, and potassium), as well as lots of chlorophyll, which is cleansing to the human system, particularly the liver. If you feel maxed out on salads, try adding some greens to a fruit smoothie or a soup. Puréed greens shrink quite a bit. The wide variety of leaves includes lettuce, kale, spinach, cabbage, Swiss chard, mizuna, arugula, bok choy, collard greens, mustard greens, dandelion greens, endive, escarole, watercress, sorrel, and tatsoi.

Roots

Root vegetables are generally made up of complex carbohydrates and starches. This is why they are usually cooked before being eaten, since cooking breaks down the starch molecules into easier-to-digest forms. However, carrots and radishes are commonly eaten raw in North America. The many root vegetables include carrot, beet, parsnip, rutabaga, turnip, sweet potato, potato, celeriac, and radish. Many root vegetables, such as beets, radishes, and turnips, also have very tasty leaves.

Bulbs

This group includes onions, leeks, and garlic. Garlic's claim to fame is boosting cardiovascular health; it's been shown in many studies to reduce cholesterol, inhibit platelet aggregation (when platelets in the blood stick together, which is how clots form), and reduce blood pressure. Onions are also recommended for cardiovascular health, since they have sulfur compounds similar to the ones that make garlic so powerful.

Stems

Stem vegetables include asparagus, celery, and kohlrabi. They are all very nutritious green vegetables with very few calories. Kohlrabi is a relative of cabbage and broccoli, so it contains the powerful cancer-fighting and anti-inflammatory compounds of this family of vegetables.

Vines

Although some of these vegetables are botanically considered fruit, when it comes to nutrition and cooking they are in the vegetable category. These vegetables have a high water content and will shrink considerably when cooked. Because this category includes a variety of vegetables, they have very different nutritional profiles, but vine veggies are generally rich in carotenoids and vitamin C. Vine vegetables include zucchini, squash, eggplant, cucumber, peas, okra, tomato, and bell and hot peppers.

Flowers

Yes, flowers can also be vegetables! This group includes broccoli, cauliflower, and artichoke. Broccoli, as a dark green vegetable, is packed with nutrients and antioxidants. Although cauliflower has no color, it has similar nutrients and is just as good for you as broccoli.

Mushrooms

Mushrooms are not actually plants (they're fungi), but nutritionally they get lumped in with vegetables. The difference with mushrooms is that they eat organic matter and do not use photosynthesis like plants. Since they are a totally different organism than other vegetables, they have value in our diet by bringing in different nutrients, such as selenium and copper, as well as powerful anti-inflammatory, cardioprotective, cancer-protective, and immune-supportive compounds. Mushrooms are high in minerals and protein per calorie and are also a good source of B vitamins.

Some of the mushrooms you might find in your local markets include chanterelle, shiitake, oyster, cremini, button, morel, and puffball. There are also many other types of edible mushrooms, including mushrooms used for their healing powers in Chinese medicine—some powerful enough to combat cancer.

Fruits

Like vegetables, fruit also has high water and fiber content and lots of vitamins and minerals. Fruit is an important source of quick energy, as it is digested and used by your body the fastest of any food group. Fruits contain concentrated antioxidants, and because they're sweet they're often more enjoyable than vegetables—particularly for kids.

Tree fruit is available in the summer and fall and includes apples, pears, plums, and peaches. Citrus fruit is best in the winter and includes oranges, grapefruit, lemons, and limes. Pure juice from citrus fruits can be used to flavor many plant-based recipes, including those using vegetables. Summer fruits include berries, grapes, and melon. Tropical fruits include bananas, pineapple, mango, and kiwi.

Nuts and Seeds

Nuts and seeds are a great source of concentrated nutrients, particularly minerals, and contain healthy fats to help your body absorb and fully utilize those minerals. Studies consistently show that people who eat nuts are at lower risk for cardiovascular disease than those who don't eat nuts. It's good to get a variety of all the different kinds of nuts and seeds, since they all have different nutrients. Popular ones include almonds, walnuts, pistachios, cashews, pecans, pumpkin seeds, sesame seeds, and flaxseed.

Legumes

Legumes are plants that bear their fruit in pods; typically, we eat the fruit or seed. They are an important source of the amino acid lysine, are rich in fiber, vitamins, and minerals, and are low in fat. They are a healthier protein than animal products, as well as a cheaper one per gram of protein. The most well-known legumes are peas, beans, lentils, peanuts, and alfalfa.

Whole Grains

Whole grains contain complex carbohydrates for sustained energy and are a source of fiber, protein, vitamins (especially the B vitamins and vitamin E), minerals, essential fatty acids, and antioxidants. They are very difficult to digest raw so are generally cooked. Some have tough outer husks, while others have a shell with a soft whole grain inside. Always opt for whole grains, which have all their nutrients intact, as opposed to white, refined, or polished grains, which are left with just the starch cells. There is an exciting array of whole grains available these days, with different textures and flavors. They include rice, millet, buckwheat, oats, quinoa, farro, barley, and amaranth.

Spices and Herbs

 Spices and herbs are not only a way to add rich flavor to your dishes but they also have small amounts of important nutrients. A study of vegetarian males eating an Indian diet showed that they got between 3.9 and 7.9 percent of their essential amino acid requirements, along with about 6 percent of calcium and 4 percent of iron, just from the seasonings in their food.

Many spices have protein, and although it doesn't amount to much in terms of grams, it provides a source of some of the amino acids that may be low in plant foods. Popular spices that will add a world of flavor to your food include cumin, coriander, cinnamon, paprika, and nutmeg.

Herbs like parsley, cilantro, mint, ginger, and basil pack loads of nutrients, and are most beneficial and flavorful when you eat them fresh. Parsley gives women 22 percent of their daily vitamin C recommendation, and men 27 percent, in just 4 tablespoons. All fresh herbs, like leafy greens, have a high antioxidant and chlorophyll content, providing energy and helping your body neutralize free radicals.

Nutrients in the Plant-Based Diet

Foods are made up of a mix of macronutrients (carbohydrates, fats, and proteins) and micronutrients (vitamins and minerals). The largest component of your daily intake should be carbohydrates. Fat makes up the next largest section, followed closely by protein. Since fats give you twice as much energy for the same volume, when looking at the portion size, fat and protein should be about equal.

Most people should aim for 60 to 70 percent carbohydrates, 20 to 30 percent fat, and 10 to 15 percent protein in their daily diet, with up to 20 percent protein for elite athletes. If your energy needs are about 1,500 calories, which I find to be the average of my clients, that works out to 225 to 263 grams of carbohydrates, 33 to 50 grams of fat, and 38 to 56 grams of protein per day. The specific percentage that works for you may be at the higher or lower end of those ranges, but the ranges are appropriate for about 98 percent of the population. Where you fall within the ranges may change a bit throughout your life and throughout the

There are so many fad superfoods buzzing around the news on any given day. They're fun because they're new and exotic. What might surprise you is that a lot of the foods you see every day are packed full of superfood-level nutrients. So let's give these everyday super-heroes the recognition they deserve.

1. Parsley

- High in iron, which the body uses to produce energy and transport oxygen.
- High in vitamin C, which boosts your immune system and helps aid the absorption of iron.
- Incredibly high in vitamin K, which is part of healthy bone structure, prevents blood clots, and keeps your nails strong.
- High in vitamin A, which keeps your eyes functioning well, maintains your immune system, and has a skin-clearing effect for acne, eczema, and psoriasis.

2. Chia Seeds

- One of the best sources of omega-3 fatty acids.
- Have a mix of both soluble and insoluble fiber to maintain healthy gut function.
- High in calcium, which helps maintain strong bones, minimize muscle cramps, and aid sleep.

3. Quinoa, Amaranth, and Teff

- High in protein, a good alternative to beans if they give you gas.
- Higher levels of quercetin and kaempferol than other foods-both compounds that help limit the inflammatory response to allergens.
- A good source of manganese (which supports healthy bones, skin, and blood sugar levels), magnesium, folate (which helps support a healthy brain, cardiovascular system, and pregnancy), zinc, and vitamin E.

4. Buckwheat

- A good source of rutin, a plant pigment that can prevent blood clots, thyroid problems, memory loss, osteoarthritis, and varicose veins.

- High in B vitamins for energy and fat metabolism.
- High levels of antioxidants, which fight free radicals that cause signs of aging, cancer, atherosclerosis, and other problems.
- Contains a compound called D-chiro-inositol, which helps balance blood sugar.

5. Blueberries

- Incredibly rich source of antioxidants (go organic or wild for a superdose), which counter cell damage, and the ones found in blueberries are particularly helpful for maintaining memory.
- Low glycemic index (40 to 50; with under 50 being low) and shown in studies to improve blood sugar regulation.
- High in manganese, which helps maintain bone and skin health as well as balance blood sugar.
- Some women swear they help reduce hot flashes.

6. Squash

- High in vitamin A, which supports healthy eyes, skin, and the immune system.
- High in all the carotenoids (plant pigments responsible for bright red, yellow, and orange), including alpha, beta, lutein, zeaxanthin, and beta-cryptoxanthin, which are antioxidants and have anti-inflammatory and immune system benefits.
- Their starch comes from polysaccharides, which include special compounds called homogalacturonan that have antioxidant, anti-inflammatory, antidiabetic, and insulin-regulating properties.

7. Avocados

- High in potassium to balance sodium for healthy blood pressure.
- Contain healthy fats, which help the body absorb vitamins A, D, and E, K, and minerals. The fat from avocados is mostly monounsaturated, which are shown to lower the risk of heart disease, reduce blood levels of LDL cholesterol (the bad kind), and lower levels of oxidative stress in the bloodstream.
- Good source of B vitamins, vitamin A, and vitamin K.

8. Chickpeas

- High in manganese, folate, iron, and zinc.
- Complex carbohydrates for energy, as well as a protein source, which helps muscles, digestion, hormones, neurotransmitters, genes, blood pressure, energy, and detoxification.
- Have a specific type of fiber that results in better blood fat regulation, lower levels of LDL cholesterol, total cholesterol, triglycerides, blood sugar and insulin secretion, and are metabolized by bacteria in the colon to produce compounds that act as fuel to the cells that line your intestinal wall, lowering risk of colon cancer.

9. Brazil Nuts and Sunflower Seeds

- High in zinc, which helps boost the immune system and maintain healthy skin and male reproductive organs.
- A good source of selenium, which maintains the immune system, detoxifies the liver, supports thyroid function, prevents certain types of cancer, and maintains healthy hair, skin, and nails.
- High in vitamin E, which is an antioxidant that helps protect the cardiovascular system.

10. Ginger

- Aids in digestion, boosts metabolism; has anti-inflammatory and immune-boosting effects.
- Gingerols may inhibit the growth of colorectal cancer cells and induce cell death in ovarian cancer cells.

seasons of the year, so listen to your body. Despite some popular diet guides, there's most likely no benefit in going outside of these ranges. Even the biggest bodybuilders never need more than 20 percent protein, and it can in fact be harmful to your kidneys and general metabolism.

If you're like most people, though, you don't look at foods as carbohydrates or fats—but as rice or avocados. The cool thing about plant foods is that they're much more nutritionally balanced than animal foods, so it's easier to stay within the normal ranges listed earlier without having to meticulously track what you're eating. Let's look at the proportions of macronutrients in whole plant foods.

Carbohydrates

Some people worry about consuming too many carbohydrates by eating plant foods. Carbohydrates are your body's main source of energy and are completely healthy if you eat them in the form of whole foods (such as whole grains, vegetables, and fruit), since they contain lots of vitamins, minerals, antioxidants, water, and fiber. Fiber is also a carbohydrate, but its role is to facilitate digestion rather than give energy.

Whole grains and fruit have the highest levels of carbohydrates, with about 70 to 90 percent carbohydrate content. Eating a banana is an instant energy boost. The best food sources of fiber are psyllium or flaxseed and leafy green vegetables.

Protein

It's not nearly as hard as people think to get enough protein from plant foods. All whole plant foods have some protein in them. If you eat enough calories from a balanced and varied diet, and include legumes regularly, you should get more than enough protein and all the essential amino acids (which are the building blocks of protein). You do not have to combine different foods in a single meal to get the essential amino acids all together—a common misconception. If you eat different foods within 48 hours, the amino acids will get together to do their job.

Legumes, including beans, have the highest overall protein content of plant foods at about 18 to 25 percent; they are also important in plant-based diets because they provide enough of the amino acid lysine. Dark green leafy vegetables have a high proportion of protein at 40 percent, spices add tiny but important amounts of amino acids, and whole grains add a fair amount of protein to an overall balanced diet at 8 to 12 percent.

Fats

Your body needs enough dietary fat to function, maintain metabolism, and absorb and utilize minerals and certain vitamins. People with cold hands and feet, amenorrhea (missed menstrual periods), or dry skin, hair, or throat may need more fats in their diet, and particularly saturated fats like coconut oil. To be clear, eating healthy fat in reasonable amounts doesn't make you fat.

The best source of healthy fat is whole plant foods—avocados, nuts, and seeds (including nut and seed butters). These average about 80 percent fat. Whole grains and beans also have some healthy fat, and there are even small amounts in fruits, vegetables, spices, and pretty much every food. Oats, for example, are about 15 percent fat.

Oils are 100 percent fat and aren't something you necessarily need to eat, but they are great for carrying rich flavor and mouthfeel in a dish, particularly when you're transitioning to a healthier diet. If you use oils, it's best to keep them minimal and use unrefined oils like olive, coconut, sesame, and avocado. (Refined oils include canola, soy, sunflower, and corn oil.) You can easily sauté vegetables for two people with just a teaspoon of oil.

That doesn't mean you should never eat oils, though, and some people can actually benefit from concentrated fats. For example, flax oil or concentrated DHA might be necessary for someone with issues digesting and utilizing omega-3 fatty acids.

Nutrition Guidelines to Stay Strong and Focused

As a holistic nutritionist, I believe you must step fully onto the path of healthy living if you want to thrive and find the energy and health you're looking for. That path includes what you eat, what you don't eat, what you do during the day, and most importantly, the attitude you bring to the table.

But I don't believe you have to do everything at once. And I definitely don't believe you have to be perfect. I am living proof, as are the hundreds of clients I've worked with, that a gradual and nondogmatic approach to changing your diet can work wonderfully. What's most important is just to get started. Then, stay focused each day by making food you enjoy and celebrate your successes. Here are some tips and motivation to stay strong on this path.

Eliminate Meat and Seafood

Replace hamburgers with veggie burgers. Meat contains an inflammatory compound called arachidonic acid, along with saturated fat and cholesterol. Cows produce 150 billion gallons of methane per day—a major contributor to global warming. One pound of beef requires 2,500 gallons of water.

Replace fish with flaxseed. Seafood contains heavy metals like mercury, as well as microplastics from our polluted oceans. About 90 million to 100 million tons of fish are taken from the ocean every year, and for each pound of fish there is up to 5 pounds of bycatch. (That's fish that are caught up unintentionally in nets.) We could see fishless oceans by 2048.

Eliminate Dairy and Eggs

Replace dairy with almond milk and coconut yogurt and all the other non-dairy options. Dairy is one of the most common triggers of food allergy intolerance and a common trigger for acne. One pound of cheese requires 900 gallons of water. One gallon of milk requires 1,000 gallons of water.

Replace eggs with flax or chia seeds. Or try the Chickpea Scramble in chapter 7 (page 100). It takes 477 gallons of water to produce just one pound of eggs. While the debate over whether eggs are healthy rages on, they're not adding any nutrients we can't get elsewhere, and for people with diabetes they may increase the risk of heart disease.

Avoid Processed and Refined Foods

Processed foods are those whose form has been changed. Any time we cook or purée food, we process it. Nut butters and bean dips are processed foods that are healthy because they still contain all their natural nutrients and have little or nothing removed or added. Unhealthy processed foods are the ones that have been made with added unhealthy ingredients, like potato chips and frozen dinners.

Refined foods are ones that have had parts taken away, removing key parts of their nutrition as well. White flour and white sugar are refined, as are white rice and oils like canola. When foods are refined, they lose fiber, protein, vitamins, and minerals. The part of a grain that's left after refining is mostly starch, with trace amounts of a few nutrients. That's why they're called empty calories. They leave your body still craving nutrients, but they have added calories to your day.

Focus on Whole Foods

Whole foods are as close to their natural form as possible. Fresh vegetables, fruit, whole grains, beans and legumes, and nuts and seeds are all whole foods. By eating mostly whole foods, you maximize nutrient density from all the vitamins, minerals, and antioxidants in these foods. You also minimize calorie density, since these foods have lots of fiber and water, so they fill you up without excess calories.

Chew Your Food

Not only does this slow you down a bit to enjoy your meal, so you can more easily sense when you're full, but it's also the crucial first step in digestion. Without proper chewing, carbohydrates won't be broken down fully and can cause gas or indigestion later in the day.

Avoid Large Portions

Restaurant portions are so often way more than what you need to eat for a meal (unless you're at a fancy restaurant that serves bite-size eye candy). Get back in touch with appropriate portions by trying the recipes and meals in this book. The recipes tell you how many servings each one makes. Take those numbers seriously, divide up the dishes, and see how you feel when you eat a regular-size serving. Chew slowly, and start tuning in to your body's hunger and satiety cues. That's the best way to know how much you need to fuel—but not overfeed—your body.

Have a Fun Food Night

Most nutrition tips and healthy meals are boring. Keep things fun and keep your taste buds happy by making fun food. Yes, it can still be healthy. Try out one of the pizza or veggie burger recipes in this book, or have a Mexican night with build-your-own burritos, tacos, or fajitas.

Take Some Supplements

Vitamin B_{12} supplements are necessary when eating a completely plant-based diet, and for adults over 50 regardless of diet, as well as anyone with digestive issues. If someone suggests eating eggs or other animal foods as a better or more natural way to get vitamin B_{12}, keep in mind that B_{12} isn't created by animals; it's generated by bacteria in animals' digestive tracts. Older adults, and people with digestive issues, aren't able to extract B_{12} from animal foods, so supplements are the more effective way to get B_{12}.

The US recommended daily allowance (RDA) for vitamin B_{12} is 2.4 micrograms per day for most adults and 2.8 micrograms for pregnant or nursing women. More recent studies put the ideal intake higher, at 4 to 7 micrograms per day. Since

SPICES
SEASONINGS
SWEETENERS
OILS

WATER

FRUITS + VEGETABLES

WHOLE GRAINS

HEALTHY PROTEINS + FATS

The Ideal Plant-Based Diet Plate

Let's get visual and look at how a balanced meal would look on a plate. Fruits and vegetables should make up about half of your plate. The other half should be made up of equal parts whole grains and healthy proteins and fats. Spices and seasonings are important for flavor and nutrition. Sweeteners and oils help make healthy meals tastier but should be used sparingly. Finally, don't forget to drink plenty of water. Most people need roughly 1.5 liters per day, but you may need more or less depending on your size and lifestyle.

B vitamins stimulate energy and the nervous system, it's better to take them in the morning and early afternoon so that you don't get wired before going to sleep.

Without vitamin D, you won't be able to absorb and use calcium properly, and the lack of both calcium and vitamin D will weaken your bones. Researchers are also starting to link vitamin D deficiency with all kinds of health problems and diseases, including asthma and cancer. Meat-eaters should be just as concerned here. The results of a 2009 study showed that the majority of both vegetarians (59 percent) and meat-eaters (64 percent) do not have sufficient blood levels of vitamin D.

There's no vitamin D in plant foods, but our bodies produce it naturally when our skin is exposed to the sun. It's a hard thing to measure and rely on, though, since we produce different amounts depending on skin color and other factors. In the winter, we usually don't get as much sun exposure as we do in the summer. The farther north you are, the more winter will affect your vitamin D levels, and if you're really far north you may not get any in the winter. The baseline RDA is 600 IU a day, but for optimal health, supplementation in the range of 1,000 to 2,000 IU daily has been shown to be a good level for most people. Up to 4,000 IU is safe for most adults.

The cause of calcium deficiency isn't always low intake, and plant sources are often a better choice than dairy, since they come with magnesium to help absorb the mineral. However, since calcium is such a large nutrient, it's hard to get enough from food alone without consuming excessive calories. The average through food intake is about 700 mg per day, and the recommendation for adults is 1,000 mg (up to 1,300 mg for older adults). That means a supplement to add that extra 300 mg can help.

Our bodies also need two specific fatty acids from our diet: omega-3 and omega-6. The others can be produced in our bodies if we eat enough fat in general. The tricky part is that our bodies need a certain ratio of omega-3 to omega-6. Most food sources have too much omega-6, which creates a relative deficiency of omega-3. The most potent food sources of omega-3 fatty acids are ground flax, flax oil, chia seeds and oil, and sacha inchi oil, which is derived from a tree native to the Amazon. Ground flaxseed is fantastic, but it can be difficult to digest and absorb. If you want to be sure you're getting enough omega-3 fatty acids, oils made from flax, chia, and sacha inchi (also known as Inca peanut) are great ways to do that.

There's a specific type of omega-3 called DHA, which is important for brain and nerve function. Your body converts omega-3 to DHA but isn't always efficient at it. Taking a 200mg to 300mg DHA supplement is often the best way to get this nutrient. People who need more long-chain n-3 fatty acids, such as pregnant and lactating women, children, and anyone with digestive tract or nervous system problems, would benefit from DHA-rich microalgae supplements.

Digestive enzyme and/or probiotic supplements may be helpful in the transition to a plant-based diet if your body is having difficulty digesting beans. Incomplete digestion is one of the top reasons for nutrient deficiencies and for food allergies and intolerances. Probiotics are also crucial after any course of antibiotics, to repopulate healthy gut flora.

chapter 3

THE FOOD LOVER'S PLANT-BASED KITCHEN

To succeed and make yourself accountable, you have to shape your environment to match your goals—starting with what you bring into your kitchen and put into your body. If you make sure you have a variety of healthy foods in your kitchen, you can always pull together a balanced meal. Even if you don't have exactly what a specific recipe calls for, you should have the components you need for substitutions. Let's give your kitchen a makeover.

The Pantry

Let's toss the refined flours, sugars, and oils, and opt instead for wholesome, unrefined versions. Stock up on whole grains, beans and legumes, and dried fruit.

- Whole grains (brown rice, quinoa, buckwheat, millet)
- Beans and legumes (chickpeas, kidney beans, lentils)
- Dried fruit (raisins, dates, dried apricots, cranberries)
- Unrefined oils (olive, coconut, toasted sesame)
- Vinegars (apple cider, balsamic, wine)
- Whole-grain flours (whole wheat, spelt, oat, buckwheat)
- Unrefined sweeteners (whole unrefined cane sugar like sucanat, coconut sugar, maple syrup, molasses, pure stevia)

- Sea salt
- Spices (ginger, cumin, coriander, turmeric, paprika, cinnamon)
- Dried herbs (basil, oregano, thyme, dill, herb mixes)
- Nutritional yeast

The Refrigerator

Let's toss the meats, cheeses, milk, eggs, and packaged meals. Stock up on fresh produce, nuts and seeds, and non-dairy choices.

- Leafy greens (lettuce, kale, chard, spinach)
- Fresh herbs and spices (parsley, basil, mint, garlic, ginger)
- Green/non-starchy vegetables (cucumber, bell peppers, green beans, broccoli, mushrooms)
- Starchy vegetables (carrots, beets, sweet potato, winter squash)
- Onions (sweet, red, yellow, green)
- Fruit (apples, oranges, plums, grapes, melon)
- Nuts and seeds (almonds, pecans, sunflower seeds, chia seeds, flaxseed)
- Nut and seed butters (peanut, almond, cashew, sunflower)
- Non-dairy milk (almond, soy)

The Freezer

Time to ditch the TV dinners, French fries, frozen waffles, ice cream, frozen pies, and cakes. Stock up on fresh-frozen produce and homemade stuff.

- Frozen berries, mango, melon
- Frozen ripe bananas for smoothies and creamy sorbet
- Frozen edamame beans, peas, corn, broccoli, spinach, and other fresh-frozen whole vegetables

- Food you cook in big batches and freeze in single servings (soups, stews, chili, tomato sauce, veggie burgers)
- Healthy desserts (whole-food brownies, muffins, cookies, fruit pies)

Cooking Equipment

Healthy eating doesn't require any special equipment, but there are some things I use regularly and think you will be glad to have on hand when you make my recipes. However, there are ways to get around most things, so I'll tell you what you really need, and what would just be nice to have.

Essential Items

Good knives. No way around this one. One of the absolute best kitchen tools you can have is a good knife. They make such a huge difference in the speed and control you have in food prep. I'm always reminded of that when I travel and have to use cheap and/or dull knives. If you're short on cash, just buy one good chef's knife and one paring knife. They'll cover most jobs, and are much more useful than a full set of cheap knives.

Cutting board. Wood or bamboo are best to prolong the life of your knife. Flavors get trapped in them, so you may get a hint of garlic or onion with your mango, unless you have two cutting boards. Plastic (bonus if it's recycled) is a good way to minimize flavor combinations but doesn't offer much protection for your knife, so layer plastic on top of wood or bamboo for the best of both worlds. The bigger the surface area, the better.

Pots and pans. Just a few good ones will do: one big soup pot and one smaller pot for cooking rice, both with lids, and one big sauté pan or skillet. You'll also need a baking sheet, a pie pan, and an eight-inch or nine-inch square baking pan. I like stainless steel or tempered glass for pots, stainless steel or cast iron for skillets, and glass for baking dishes. Ceramic coatings are a good nonstick option for skillets.

Measuring cups and spoons. Get a stainless steel or ceramic set rather than plastic.

Sometimes we don't have time to follow recipes. For those days, I've made you a sketch outline of a balanced meal, so you can throw it together with whatever happens to be in your kitchen.

Smoothie Builder

Build a perfect nourishing smoothie to start your day and fuel you to lunch. You'll need:

- Cup and straw: sipping from a reusable straw minimizes contact with your teeth for better dental health, and using an insulated cup or travel mug keeps your smoothie cool through the morning.
- Creaminess: banana (frozen makes it like ice cream), avocado, nut butter or non-dairy milk.
- Omega-3s: 1 tablespoon flax or chia seeds.
- Protein: a handful of rolled oats or quinoa flakes, or a scoop of plant-based protein powder.
- Fruit: about 1 cup of berries, melon, grapes, cherries, apple, whatever you like.
- Vegetable boost: greens such as spinach, sprouts, or kale; vegetables such as cucumber or carrots; fresh herbs such as mint or basil.
- Superfood boost: fresh ginger, greens powder, matcha powder, probiotics, goji berries or powder, cocoa nibs.

creaminess
+
omega-3s
+
protein
+
fruit
+
vegetable
boost
+
superfood
boost

Bowl Builder

Build a perfect bowl for lunch or dinner that gives you all the nutrients and fuel you need for the rest of the day. You'll need:

- Bowl: get a couple that are the same size to keep your portions consistent.
- Leafy greens: grab a handful or two, as much as you want, of lettuce, arugula, spinach, kale, chard, parsley, or other greens.
- Starchy vegetables and/or whole grains: about 1 cup of sweet potato, winter squash, brown rice, quinoa, farro, soba noodles, rice noodles, and so on.
- Beans or legumes: about ½ cup of chickpeas, black beans, lentils, edamame, or other legumes.
- Other vegetables: about 1 cup of raw vegetables such as cucumber, bell pepper, tomato, and avocado; grilled such as zucchini, eggplant, and mushrooms; or steamed such as broccoli, carrots, and beets.
- Nuts or seeds: a small handful, either whole (pumpkin, cashews, almonds) or nut butter, which you can use as the base for the sauce.
- Sauce: a long, generous drizzle. Try the recipes in this book, like Toasted Sesame Miso Dressing (page 237), Green Goddess Dressing (page 235), or Creamy Balsamic Dressing (page 236), or check the ingredients to see if you can find a whole-foods variety in the store.

sauce

nuts or seeds

beans or legumes

other vegetables

starchy vegetable
or whole grains

leafy greens

Cooking utensils. There are lots of little things, like a stirring spoon, ladle, flipper and spatula that you'll find you need in the course of your budding kitchen adventures.

Nice-to-Have Items

Immersion or hand blender. This is the best way to purée soup and mashed potatoes. You can use a blender or food processor if you have one, or simply eat soups loose instead of puréed. You could even get away with a potato masher if you're okay with a chunky soup.

Blender and/or food processor. Use a blender to make smoothies, soups, and sauces. You don't need to spend $400; the $20 blenders are perfectly adequate for most functions. Food processors are much more versatile, so if you can only have one appliance, I'd suggest a food processor. They do tend to cost more than blenders, though. If you need a low-cost option, try a thrift store; they often have used food processors fairly cheap.

Garlic press. A garlic press pulverizes garlic cloves, which will meld the garlic flavor more smoothly into your dishes. Crushing also activates the antioxidants in garlic.

Bonus Items

Citrus zester. A zester takes the very outside of a citrus peel, which contains a huge amount of flavor and antioxidants. Once you start adding orange, lemon, and lime zest to your cooking, you won't be able to look at a citrus fruit without thinking of what you can put that zest into. Many people also use Microplanes (very fine graters) instead of a zester. I love the visual of the thin curls that come from my zester, and I bought it for a dollar at a thrift store, so I stick with that. But if you already have a grater for zesting, there's probably no need to get another tool for the same purpose.

Ginger grater. This enables you to grate a piece, and squeeze the juice from it. It gives your meal a nice ginger kick, but in a smooth and even way. You can do this with a normal grater or a Microplane, but a ginger grater does a better job of ripping the ginger into pulp and keeping it all together so that you get more of the juice.

Sprouting jars. Sprouts (like alfalfa or clover) are full of nutrients, and making your own at home offers maximum nutrition. You can use mason jars topped with mesh held on with an elastic band for sprouting, but the sprouts made in a sprouting jar are usually better quality because they have better drainage and airflow. They also make it a lot easier to rinse the sprouts, so I'm more likely to do it when I'm supposed to. If you compare the jar to the cost of buying sprouts from the grocery store, it's well worth it.

Oil sprayer. Not the aerosols but the kind you fill up with your own choice of oil and then pump to build up pressure and spray. They're fantastic for getting a fine mist of oil on veggies (rather than drizzling too much) for roasting, or seasoning your cast iron pan.

Seasonings

One of the top complaints I hear when people start eating healthier is that they feel like their meals are bland. But most of what people taste in any dish (from sausages to veggie burgers) is the seasoning. Herbs, spices, vegetables, and fruits are the major source of flavors in most recipes.

Most people (including restaurant chefs) fall into the bland meal trap when they cook with grains and beans. On their own, grains and beans don't have much flavor. Try eating a plain kidney bean out of a can; it tastes like bland, mushy starch. But then think of a hearty chili and how spectacularly flavorful it is. The secret is in the spices and flavors you add.

By adding things like chili powder, garlic, onions, and tomatoes to your kidney beans, plus salt to bring all the flavors together, you have something delicious— and the great part is that seasonings are healthy, too! Fresh spices like garlic and ginger, as well as dried spices and herbs, add lots of nutrients to your meal, so don't shy away from using them in anything and everything.

Certain spices, like ginger and cinnamon, help stimulate your digestive system and get your metabolism going so you can efficiently process the foods you eat.

Cayenne can work as an appetite suppressant. You may find that if you add a bit of spice to your tomato sauce, you need to eat less to feel satisfied. Turmeric has been shown to have beneficial effects not only on fat metabolism but also regulating blood sugar levels and reducing inflammation.

Keep in mind that cooked grains and beans absorb flavors slowly, so if you leave them to marinate in a sauce or dressing for an hour or longer, they will be much tastier.

Seasoning Combinations

The art of seasoning is one of the most treasured skills of a good chef. It's the secret to any good dish and can make all the difference when you want to make a truly amazing meal. Seasoning is about knowing the rules but not being afraid to break them to find innovative taste combinations.

The best way to learn how to combine seasonings to create flavors that you enjoy is to figure out which recipes you really like, then look at the ingredients and see which herbs and spices they use. Here are some tried-and-true flavor combinations you can start with.

    Asian cuisine flavors like tamari or soy sauce, toasted sesame oil, and ginger are great with broccoli, mushrooms, and dark green leafy vegetables like kale and bok choy.

    Basil, oregano, and marjoram are classic herbs to perfectly season tomato sauce.

    Dill, onion powder, and nutritional yeast are tasty mixed into a creamy dressing with some fresh garlic and tossed with brown rice and steamed veggies.

    Thyme, parsley, and bay leaves add rich flavor to mushroom gravy or squash risotto.

    Cumin, coriander, ginger, turmeric, and cayenne make a simple curry powder that's great with chickpeas, sweet potato, apple, and lime juice.

    Cayenne, cumin, and allspice are the base of a great chili with tomatoes, kidney beans, mushrooms, and zucchini.

Cinnamon, nutmeg, allspice, ginger, and molasses perfectly flavor ginger-bread or porridge.

Once you get confident with your seasoning senses, you can always add a little bit of an individual spice to make your dish taste different—like a pinch of cardamom or cinnamon with curry powder. I love to add paprika and/or cumin to almost anything, and a small pinch of nutmeg always adds a lot of flavor and dimension.

Salt

Don't be afraid to cook with salt. Sodium (the main component of salt) is not inherently bad for you. Some sodium is necessary for your body to function properly; the absolute minimum is half a gram a day, but standard recommendations put it at 1 to 3 grams per day. The problem is that the average American diet contains about 3 to 6 grams of sodium per day. This breaks down to about 30 percent from naturally occurring salt in food, 40 percent from processed foods, and 30 percent from adding salt in cooking or at the table.

If you take that average and do the math, someone eating 6 grams of sodium per day can cut back to 3.6 grams just by eliminating the 40 percent coming from processed foods. Of course, not everyone will fit neatly into these average numbers, but it's a pretty good incentive to move from processed foods to cooking your own healthy meals with whole foods.

What's more, it turns out that it's even more effective for our cardiovascular health to increase our potassium intake than to reduce sodium intake. Our blood pressure is regulated by the ratio of sodium to potassium, so both sides of the equation are important, and recent studies are finding that improving the potassium side has more impact overall. What are the best sources of potassium? Plant foods—particularly vegetables and fruit. So, if cooking with a pinch of salt means you'll eat more carrots, that's a win.

The recipes in this book call for sea salt, because it's less processed than table salt, which also includes an additive to prevent clumping and, often, iodine. If you prefer regular table salt, go for the uniodized version, since it's still less processed than iodized salt.

Buy Fresh

Buy produce that's as fresh as you can get, grown locally and organically when possible. If you can, grow your own. Sprouts and herbs are easy to grow on your windowsill. If you don't use up things like whole grains and spices in your pantry, replace the older stuff after about a year. If you start with fresh, quality ingredients, your meals will naturally taste better.

Choose Foods You Like

Most of the time, pick the vegetables and other foods you enjoy most. Get variety by throwing in a new one every now and then, but it doesn't have to be all the time. Some foods are naturally tastier than others for most people. The natural sweetness of butternut squash, sweet potato, red pepper, carrots, and beets make them more broadly appealing. Baby greens and baby vegetables are also often milder and sweeter than their fully grown counterparts.

Choose Your Cooking Methods

Use the right cooking method for the vegetable. Avocados are best raw, broccoli is perfect lightly steamed (but gets bitter if over-cooked), sweet potatoes and squash are delicious roasted or baked. Whole grains take differing amounts of time to cook and could be toasted first to enhance flavors.

Find Good Combos

Combining foods in a dish is about bringing together flavors (sweet, savory, sour) and textures (crunchy, soft). Color also plays a role, making a dish more visually appealing. Create interest by bringing together opposites (sweet and sour) or similarities (all green). It's also about personal preference, so try recipes for a point of reference, then play with combinations to see what you enjoy.

Use Salt

A small amount of salt goes a long way in making food delicious. It softens the bitterness of vegetables and their texture. It helps break down the cell walls of plants, so they're easier for us to digest. Salt helps bring all the flavors of your dish together, so that your hummus doesn't taste like each individual ingredient-it tastes like hummus. Use salt while cooking, rub it in to wilt vegetables before roasting, or drizzle a slightly salty dressing on top of your bowl or salad.

Season Your Beans

On their own, grains and beans don't have much flavor. Make them more interesting by doing the following:

- Pair them with fresh, flavorful vegetables or fruit.
- Add spices, herbs, or tea to the water while they cook.
- Use some vegetable broth or juice as some or all of the cooking water.
- Dress them with flavorful seasonings and sauces.

Sauce It Up

Any dish can taste great when paired with the right dressing or sauce. Marinating vegetables in a good sauce will soften the bitterness and texture and help bring the flavors of the vegetable and sauce together. Marinating beans and whole grains in a sauce for an hour (or a day) infuses them, so they're bursting with flavor.

Add Sweetness

Use a bit of natural sweetness in your cooking. Try balsamic vinegar, maple syrup, or applesauce in a dressing; add apples, oranges, dried cranberries, or raisins to a salad or soup.

Use Healthy Fats

Fat makes a dish feel richer and taste more satisfying. Fat carries the flavor of spices and herbs, so be sure to use some in a dish that's heavy on the seasoning. Use more fat when transitioning to a plant-based diet or if you are not used to healthy cooking. For most of your dishes, try to use fats that are naturally part of the foods you're cooking-like nuts, seeds, and avocados-rather than adding oil. Nut and seed butters or blended avocado make a great creamy base to a sauce or dressing.

Camouflage

Get sneaky! Blend vegetables and greens into soups, sauces, or smoothies. Bake vegetables into treats like carrot cake, zucchini loaf, pumpkin muffins, beet-infused chocolate cake, and sweet potato biscuits.

PART TWO

THE PLANT-BASED MEAL PLANS

Are you ready to boost the nutrition, flavor, and energy you get from your food? It can all happen at once, I promise! I put together these meal plans to show you how to make delicious plant-based meals that give you balanced nutrition and nourishment to fuel your day.

The plans laid out over the next three weeks take the guesswork out of cooking for the plant-based diet, giving you three meals a day and snack options that you can pick and choose from throughout the week. There are more recipes in the chapters in part 3 than there are in the meal plans. This leaves room for flexibility, so if something in the meal plan doesn't appeal to you, swap it out for another recipe.

These meal plans use leftovers to make your life easier, because most of us don't have the time to cook three meals a day. Weekday breakfasts and lunches are designed to be grab-and-go. I'll also offer suggestions for how to tackle prep for the week so that you can set yourself up for success.

Desserts aren't included in the plan, but you can try the desserts in chapter 11 if you find yourself having a craving, or if you have a party or potluck where you want to bring something to enjoy and share.

The goal is for you to feel healthy, energized, satisfied, and happy by the end of this plan.

SHOPPING LIST

- KALE
- SPINACH
- PARSLEY
- BASIL
- MINT
- GARLIC
- TURMERIC
- BEETROOT
- SQUASH
- ONIONS
- PLUMS
- PECAN NUTS

SHOPPING

- KALE
- SPINACH
- PARSLE
- BASIL
- MIN
- GAR

chapter 4

WEEK ONE

This first week is about learning how to set up a balanced day of nourishment and fuel for your body. You might be buying and working with foods that are new to you, so cut yourself some slack and don't expect your very first week to go perfectly. Your focus is to stick with whole foods and try the meals I've put together for you in the plan. If you do that, by the end of this week you'll start being more in touch with your body's natural cues and able to gauge when you're hungry and full—not just eating out of boredom or driven by cravings. As you get more balanced nutrition, you should find your energy levels starting to balance out to sustain you throughout the day.

Prep It

If you want to be ready for quick prep throughout the week, here's what you can make ahead and store in the refrigerator.

- Hummus, Five Ways (page 197)
- Quinoa for the full week (1½ cups dry)
- Creamy Balsamic Dressing (page 236)
- Basil Pesto (page 241)

Shopping List

Grocery shopping, and having a good shopping list, is key to sticking to a healthy way of eating. The store and farmers' market is where you choose the foods that are coming into your home. In this section you'll find a detailed shopping list to tell you exactly what you need for the week, so that you don't need to do any of the planning—just head to the store.

You'll need a variety of fruits, vegetables, nuts, seeds, grains, and beans to make the recipes in this week's plan; feel free to swap ingredients for the same quantity of other foods you like better. If you can't find a specific food on the list, or if it's out of season and too expensive, replace it with something similar. I've organized the list into categories that I hope will help you see which foods can easily be substituted for one another.

Leafy Greens and Fresh Herbs

- 1 cup arugula, or use lettuce
- 1 bunch kale and/or chard, or other dark leafy green
- 1 head lettuce
- 1 large bunch fresh basil
- 1 small bunch spinach, or other kind of green
- 1 small bunch fresh cilantro, or parsley
- 1 small bunch fresh mint, or basil
- 1 small bunch scallions, or chives

Vegetables

- 2 avocados
- 1 small head broccoli
- 1 cup snap peas, or snow peas
- 4 ounces mushrooms
- 3 to 4 bell peppers (any color)
- 2 tomatoes
- 2½ cup cherry tomatoes
- 1 zucchini
- 2 beets
- 1 butternut squash

2 sweet potatoes

1 large potato

3 onions (any kind)

1 cup corn kernels or peas
(fresh or frozen)

2 heads garlic

1 small piece fresh ginger
(optional)

1 small jalapeño pepper (optional)

1 carrot (optional)

Fruit

1 apple

4 bananas

2 lemons

2 limes

1 cup cantaloupe, or peach

2 fresh mangos (or about
3 cups frozen)

2½ cups raspberries (fresh
or frozen)

1 cup strawberries (fresh or frozen)

1 cup cranberries (fresh or frozen)

Beans and Legumes

1 cup shelled edamame (soy)
beans, or fava or lima beans

1 (14-ounce) can black beans, or
any other small bean (½ cup dry)

3 (14-ounce) cans chickpeas
(1½ cups dry)

Whole Grains

9 slices whole-grain bread

2½ large whole-grain wraps (corn
or wheat-free for gluten-free)

2½ cups rolled oats (or quinoa or
rice flakes for gluten-free)

2½ cups quinoa, or millet

Nuts, Seeds, and Dried Fruit

- ¼ cup almonds (raw or dry roasted)
- 1 cup ground almonds
- ½ cup pine nuts, or sunflower seeds
- 1 tablespoon walnuts (raw or dry roasted)
- 1 tablespoon flaxseed (ground, or buy whole and grind)
- 3 tablespoons chia seeds, or flax
- 2 tablespoons pumpkin seeds (raw or dry roasted)
- 2 tablespoons sesame seeds (raw or dry roasted)
- ¼ cup natural peanut butter, or sunflower seed butter
- ½ cup tahini, or almond or cashew butter
- ½ tablespoon goji berries (optional)
- 2 tablespoons sun-dried tomatoes (dry, not packed in oil)

Other Items

- 1 small jar black or green olives
- 1 cup non-dairy milk (store-bought or homemade)
- 1 cup coconut milk
- ½ tablespoon miso (soybean paste)
- ½ tablespoon arrowroot powder
- 1 tablespoon unsweetened cocoa powder
- 1 to 2 teaspoons ground sage, or use other dried herbs

Staples

- Pure maple syrup, or brown rice syrup
- Unrefined sugar (sucanat, coconut)
- Balsamic vinegar
- Apple cider vinegar and/or brown rice vinegar
- Coconut oil (unrefined)
- Olive oil (cold-pressed, extra-virgin, unrefined)
- Toasted sesame oil (unrefined)
- Tamari, or soy sauce
- Ketchup (look for natural ingredients and low sugar)

Mustard (look for natural ingredients)

Sea salt

Baking powder (look for aluminum-free)

Baking soda

Pure vanilla extract

Dried basil, or mixed dried herbs

Dried dill, or mixed dried herbs

Dried oregano, or mixed dried herbs

Allspice

Cayenne pepper

Chili powder

Ground cinnamon

Ground cumin

Ground coriander

Ground ginger

Ground nutmeg

Paprika (regular or smoked)

Nutritional yeast (optional)

SNACKS

Pick and choose from these snacks, or similar ideas, if you get hungry between meals. Try to stick to one snack a day; if you're exercising or hungrier than usual one day, have an extra snack.

- Apple with peanut butter
- Almonds and dried cranberries
- Rice cake with hummus and cucumber slices
- Orange slices with ground cinnamon
- Banana with walnuts
- Mini Muesli and Berries Bowl (page 95)
- Handful Savory Roasted Chickpeas (page 195)

WEEK ONE

	Sunday	Monday	Tuesday
Breakfast	Baked Banana French Toast with Raspberry Syrup (page 92)	Max Power Smoothie (page 76)	Overnight Oats On the Go (page 84) with raspberry syrup
Lunch	Black Bean Taco Salad Bowl (page 154)	Roasted Red Pepper and Butternut Squash Soup (page 112) Roasted Beet and Avocado Salad (page 121)	Black Bean Taco Salad Bowl (page 154) 1 large whole-grain wrap ½ cup Fresh Mango Salsa (page 240)
Dinner	Roasted Red Pepper and Butternut Squash Soup (page 112) Roasted Beet and Avocado Salad (page 121) Toast with Classic Hummus (page 197)	Black Bean Taco Salad Bowl (page 154) ½ cup cooked quinoa ½ cup spinach ½ cup Fresh Mango Salsa (page 240)	Sun-dried Tomato and Pesto Quinoa (page 172)

Per day (weekly average):
Calories: 1,504; Total fat: 61g; Carbs: 213g; Fiber: 45g; Protein: 50g

Wednesday	Thursday	Friday	Saturday
Pink Panther Smoothie (page 82)	**PB-Banana Toast** 2 pieces whole-grain bread 1 banana 2 tablespoons natural peanut butter	**Chocolate PB Smoothie (page 81)**	**Chickpea Scramble (page 100)** **Roasted Garlic Pesto Potatoes (page 205)**
Sun-dried Tomato and Pesto Quinoa (page 172) 1 cup lettuce 2 tablespoons Creamy Balsamic Dressing (page 236)	**Simple Sesame Stir-Fry (page 168)**	**Miso-Coconut Dragon Bowl (page 151)**	**Grilled AHLT (page 144)** **Baked Sweet Potato Fries (page 204)**
Simple Sesame Stir-Fry (page 168)	**Miso-Coconut Dragon Bowl (page 151)**	**Mediterranean Hummus Pizza (page 146)**	**Maple Dijon Burgers (page 140)** 2 slices whole-grain bread $\frac{1}{2}$ cup lettuce $\frac{1}{4}$ cup Fresh Mango Salsa (page 240) Baked Sweet Potato Fries (page 204)

chapter 5

WEEK TWO

Hopefully, you enjoyed the flavors of the first week and are feeling pretty good already about the positive steps you're taking. You may notice that your pants are starting to fit better, as you reduce any bloating and maybe even drop a pound or two. Your energy should now be consistent through the day, with no need for afternoon naps and with better sleep at night. You might feel like you're able to start some morning yoga or jogging, or do something fun in the evenings or on weekends, now that you're not dragging through each day. It only gets better from here, so let's keep the momentum going into week two!

Prep It

If you want to be ready for quick prep throughout the week, here's what you can make ahead and store in the refrigerator.

- Greens and Beans Dip (page 202)
- Peanut Sauce (page 239)
- Toasted Sesame Miso Dressing (page 237)
- Ginger Carrot Soup (page 106)

- Bake all of the sweet potatoes whole, and pierce the skin several times with a fork or knife
- Cook ½ cup brown rice in 1 cup of water, bring to a boil then simmer for 45 minutes

Shopping List

This week's list is shorter, since you should have all the staples in your kitchen already, after shopping last week.

Leafy Greens and Fresh Herbs

- 1 bunch kale, chard and/or spinach, or other dark leafy green
- 1 head lettuce (any kind)
- ½ cup any other kind of green
- 1 cup alfalfa sprouts, or other kind of sprout
- 1 bunch fresh cilantro, or parsley
- 1 small bunch fresh basil, or mint
- 1 small bunch scallions, or chives

Vegetables

- 1 avocado
- 1 small head broccoli
- 1 small head cabbage
- 1 small cucumber
- 4½ cups mushrooms
- 2 bell peppers (any color)
- 1 to 2 zucchinis
- 2 beets
- 3 to 4 carrots
- 2 large or 3 medium sweet potatoes
- 3 to 4 onions (any kind)
- 1 (28-ounce) can diced tomatoes (try to find a can with a BPA-free lining)
- 6 garlic cloves
- 1 small piece fresh ginger (optional)

Fruit

- 1 apple
- 5 bananas
- 1 lemon
- ½ lime

1 fresh mango, or 1 cup frozen

1 peach, or cantaloupe

2 pears

1 cup strawberries (fresh or frozen)

Beans and Legumes

3 (14-ounce) cans cannellini beans, or any other white bean, or 1½ cups dry

1 (14-ounce) can kidney beans, or any other soft red bean, or ½ cup dry

1 cup lentils, dry (green or brown are best)

Whole Grains

2½ whole-grain pitas

3 slices whole-grain bread

2 ounces whole-grain pasta, dry (whole-wheat, kamut, spelt)

½ cup brown rice, dry

1½ cups rolled oats (or rice or quinoa flakes for gluten-free)

Nuts, Seeds, and Dried Fruit

2 tablespoons almonds (raw or dry roasted)

2 tablespoons walnuts (raw or dry roasted)

3 tablespoons flaxseed (ground, or buy whole and grind)

1 tablespoon chia seeds, or flaxseed

1 tablespoon sesame seeds (raw or dry roasted)

¼ cup almond butter, or tahini or cashew butter

½ cup natural peanut butter, or sunflower seed butter

2 tablespoons dates (soft, like Medjool), or other dried fruit

¼ cup raisins, or dried cranberries

Other Items

- ½ cup non-dairy milk (store-bought or homemade)
- ½ cup canned coconut milk
- 1 cup unsalted vegetable broth
- 1 tablespoon red wine (cooking or drinking), or balsamic vinegar
- 2 tablespoons red wine vinegar, or balsamic vinegar
- 2 tablespoons miso (soybean paste)
- ¾ cup whole-grain flour
- 1 teaspoon dried rosemary, or other dried herbs

SNACKS

Pick and choose from these snacks, or similar ideas, if you get hungry between meals. Try to stick to one snack a day; if you're exercising or hungrier than usual one day, have an extra snack.

- Grapes and sunflower seeds
- Zucchini slices with pesto
- Applesauce with walnuts
- Ants on a log (celery with peanut butter and raisins or dried cranberries)
- Pita with Avomame Spread (page 201) and cherry tomatoes
- 2 Nori Snack Rolls (page 190)
- 2 Zesty Orange-Cranberry Energy Bites (page 211)

GAS AND THE TROUBLE WITH BEANS

If you haven't noticed, there are quite a lot of beans in the recipes. That's because beans are full of protein, complex carbs, and other essential nutrients that make it a powerhouse ingredient, and it's inexpensive too! But the trouble with beans is that they can cause discomforting gas (they are the musical fruit after all!). If you are not used to eating beans, here are some tips that should help:

- **Buy salt-free.** Buy canned beans that do not have salt listed in the ingredients, because that keeps beans from cooking fully. You could also cook them yourself. If you want to add salt, season after cooking as salt before cooking is trouble.

- **Rinse.** When you drain beans from the can or after cooking, rinse them thoroughly. You may notice the water makes bubbles—that's what you want to rinse away, so it doesn't make bubbles in your tummy.

- **Chew fully.** Your body starts to digest carbohydrates once you start chewing your food due to the enzymes in your saliva, and it's the complex carbohydrates in beans that give them their gas-producing potential. Make sure to chew thoroughly so that your stomach doesn't have to work as hard to break down carbs.

- **Try different types and stick to small sizes.** I do well with split red lentils, chickpeas and edamame beans—but not so much with kidney beans. Try them all to see which are best for you. Generally smaller ones are safer.

- **Swap for quinoa.** Try having a quinoa dish instead of a bean dish every other day, to get the amino acids you need from an easier-to-digest food source.

- **Get moving.** Exercise helps move gas through your digestive tract—try going for a walk after dinner to clear the air.

- **Boost your enzymes.** Digestive enzyme supplements can really help while your body gets used to beans. Take them before a meal if you can, or after if you didn't anticipate issues.

WEEK TWO

	Sunday	Monday	Tuesday
Breakfast	**2 Oatmeal Breakfast Cookies (page 86)** 1 banana	**Chai Chia Smoothie (page 77)** **Oatmeal Breakfast Cookies (page 86)**	**Banana Nut Smoothie (page 83)** **Oatmeal Breakfast Cookies (page 86)**
Lunch	**Maple Dijon Burgers (page 140) Salad** 2 Maple Dijon Burgers 1 cup chopped lettuce ½ cup bell pepper ½ cup sliced cucumber 2 tablespoons Creamy Balsamic Dressing (page 236)	**Maple Dijon Burgers (page 140)** ½ whole-grain pita ¼ cup Greens and Beans Dip (page 202) ½ cup chopped lettuce	**Hearty Chili (page 115) and Salad** ½ cup chopped lettuce ¼ cup chopped bell pepper ½ avocado ½ cup chopped cucumber 2 tablespoons Creamy Balsamic Dressing (page 236)
Dinner	**Hearty Chili (page 115)** 2 slices Garlic Toast (page 207)	1 baked sweet potato ½ serving Hearty Chili (page 115) ½ avocado	**2 Sweet Potato Patties (page 163)** **Wilted Sesame-Miso Kale Salad (page 124)**

Per day (weekly average):
Calories: 1,469; Total fat: 49g; Carbs: 234g; Fiber: 44g; Protein: 49g

Wednesday	Thursday	Friday	Saturday
Oatmeal Breakfast Cookies (page 86) 1 pear	**Mango Madness (page 80)**	**Overnight Oats On the Go (page 84) with pear and walnuts** 1 pear 2 tablespoons walnuts	**Cinnamon Apple Toast (page 94)**
2 Sweet Potato Patties (page 163) **Wilted Sesame-Miso Kale Salad (page 124)**	**Pad Thai Bowl (page 150)**	**Warm Lentil Salad with Red Wine Vinaigrette (page 134)** 1 whole-grain pita $\frac{1}{4}$ cup Greens and Beans Dip (page 202)	**Tuscan White Bean Salad (page 129)** 1 whole-grain pita $\frac{1}{2}$ cup Greens and Beans Dip (page 202)
Pad Thai Bowl (page 150)	**Warm Lentil Salad with Red Wine Vinaigrette (page 134)**	**Olive and White Bean Pasta (page 173)**	**Ginger Carrot Soup (page 106)** 2 slices Garlic Toast (page 207)

chapter 6

WEEK THREE

This is it! Heading into the last week of the plan, you should find that the old cravings hold less power over you, as your taste buds enjoy new flavors and your body breaks out of the vicious cycle created by sugar- and salt-laden foods. You may also find that you've not gotten any new blemishes, and the old ones are starting to fade away, leaving your skin clear and glowing. Pretty soon, people are going to start asking you what your secret is. Let's follow through with another week of amazing food, both healthy and delicious, to cross the finish line of this plan with a smile and arms raised up in the air.

Prep It

If you want to be ready for quick prep throughout the week, here's what you can make ahead and store in the refrigerator.

- Tabbouleh Salad (page 130)
- Weeknight Chickpea Tomato Soup (page 114)
- Blackeye Pea Burritos (page 182)
- Dressing for the Cashew-Ginger Soba Noodle Bowl (page 152)
- Filling for the Curried Mango Chickpea Wrap (page 147)

Shopping List

You should be a grocery store pro by now, skipping whole aisles of the store that are filled with refined foods. If you have foods left over from previous weeks, feel free to swap them for specific foods listed here.

Leafy Greens and Fresh Herbs

1 bunch kale and/or spinach, or other dark leafy green

1 small head lettuce (any kind), or spinach

1 small bunch fresh cilantro

1 large bunch fresh parsley (curly or flat leaf)

1 large bunch fresh basil, or mint

1 bunch scallions, or chives

Vegetables

2 avocados

2 cucumbers

2 cups green beans, or snap or snow peas

1 cup mushrooms

1 large portobello mushroom cap

2 bell peppers (any color)

2 tomatoes

1¼ cups cherry tomatoes

2 zucchini

4 carrots

1 large potato

2 sweet potatoes

2 onions

1 (28-ounce) can diced tomatoes

1 bulb garlic

1 small piece fresh ginger (optional)

Fruit

2 bananas

2 lemons

1 cantaloupe, or 1½ cups peach

2 fresh mangos, or 3 cups frozen

3 oranges

2 pears

1 cup pineapple (fresh, frozen, or canned)

4 cups strawberries (fresh or frozen)

1 cup cranberries (fresh or frozen)

Beans and Legumes

1 (14-ounce) can blackeye peas, or any other small bean, or ½ cup dry

3 (14-ounce) cans chickpeas, or 2 cups dry

Whole Grains

2 whole-grain pita

8 large whole-grain wraps (corn or wheat-free for gluten-free)

4 ounces soba noodles (about 1 cup)

1¼ cups dry couscous (or dry quinoa for gluten-free)

1¾ cups rolled oats (or rice or quinoa flakes for gluten-free)

Nuts, Seeds, and Dried Fruit

¼ cup cashews (raw or dry roasted)

1 tablespoon shredded coconut (unsweetened)

3 tablespoons flaxseed (ground, or buy whole and grind)

1 tablespoon chia seeds (or 1 additional tablespoon flaxseed)

⅓ cup sunflower seeds (raw or dry roasted)

¼ cup almond and/or cashew butter

½ cup tahini

2 tablespoons dried apricots, or other dried fruit

1 tablespoon goji berries (optional)

2 tablespoons raisins, or dried cranberries

Other Items

- 1¼ cups non-dairy milk
- 1 cup canned coconut milk
- ½ cup salsa (make your own Fresh Mango Salsa [page 240], or look for whole-food ingredients and not much sugar)
- 3 tablespoons molasses
- 1¼ cups whole-grain flour

SNACKS

Pick and choose from these snacks, or similar ideas, if you get hungry between meals.

- Pear with almonds
- Dates with walnuts
- Dried figs with cashews
- Sliced tomatoes drizzled with balsamic vinegar
- ½ cup applesauce or non-dairy yogurt with ¼ cup Fruity Granola (page 98)
- 1 cup Baked Kale Chips, Five Ways (page 192)
- 1 Almond-Date Energy Bite (page 210) and 1 banana

We all love making the most of our time in the kitchen by cooking extra to have leftovers. The easiest way to use leftovers is to have it the same way again, but you can get creative and make totally new meals. One of my favorite things to do is take leftover steamed or roasted vegetables that I had with rice, and have it on salad greens with a drizzle of dressing. I also like putting leftover vegetables together into a soup and using salad dressing as the flavoring for the broth. And another favorite option is to put make a wrap using leftover whole grains with just a leafy green like napa cabbage or swiss chard).

Grains are perfect for repurposing meals as it gives you a ton of options to play with. If you cook a big batch of brown rice, quinoa, or other whole grains and leave it plain, you can use it in a whole variety of ways:

· toss it into a salad

· stir it into a soup

· make it into veggie burgers

· have it with nondairy milk as cereal/porridge

· put it in a smoothie

· make it into a pizza crust

· top it with some tomato sauce (use instead of pasta)

· make it into cookies or muffins

· puree it with seasonings into a sauce

WEEK THREE

	Sunday	Monday	Tuesday
Breakfast	2 Sunshine Muffins (page 88)	Hydration Station (page 79) 1 Sunshine Muffin (page 88)	Mango Madness (page 80) 1 Sunshine Muffin (page 88)
Lunch	Ginger Carrot Soup (page 106) Tuscan White Bean Salad (page 129)	2 falafel patties (page 148; see Leftovers note on page 149) 1 pita ½ cup lettuce ½ cup cherry tomatoes 2 tablespoons Green Goddess Dressing (page 235)	Falafel Wrap (page 148)
Dinner	2 falafel patties (page 148; see Leftovers note on page 149) Falafel 1 whole-grain pita ½ cup chopped lettuce ½ cup cherry tomatoes 2 tablespoons Green Goddess Dressing (page 235)	Ginger Carrot Soup (page 106) Tabbouleh Salad (page 130)	Weeknight Chickpea Tomato Soup (page 114)

Per day (weekly average):
Calories: 1,460; Total fat: 49g; Carbs: 234g; Fiber: 42g; Protein: 45g

Wednesday	Thursday	Friday	Saturday
Overnight Oats On the Go (page 84) with pear and cashews 1 pear 2 tablespoons cashews	**Tropi-Kale Breeze (page 78)**	**Pink Panther Smoothie (page 82)**	**Fruit Salad with Zesty Citrus Couscous (page 97)**
Weeknight Chickpea Tomato Soup (page 114) **Tabbouleh Salad (page 130)**	**1½ servings Blackeye Pea Burritos (page 182)**	**1½ servings Blackeye Pea Burritos (page 182)**	**Cashew-Ginger Soba Noodle Bowl (page 152)** 1 pear
Blackeye Pea Burritos (page 182)	**Curried Mango Chickpea Wrap (page 147)**	**Cashew-Ginger Soba Noodle Bowl (page 152)**	**Grilled Portobello with Mashed Potatoes and Green Beans (page 183)** **2 Sweet Potato Biscuits (page 206)**

Beyond Three Weeks

Congratulations! You've had an amazingly nourishing and healthy three weeks of food. Even if you didn't stick to everything exactly, had something off the plan here or there, or only dabbled with one or two recipes, if you ate more vegetables than you did this time last month, that's a step in the right direction. And if you had fun making some healthy food, and enjoyed eating it, that's a success.

You should have noticed at least a slight change in your sleep, digestion, energy level, and mood. Seeing and feeling those connections between what you eat and how you feel are great ways to stay motivated to keep eating healthy when faced with temptations.

After following a plan like this, a lot of people start saying to themselves, "I've been so good! I deserve a treat." You definitely do, you've done well. But keep the big picture in mind, and try to think about healthy options to indulge your cravings, like those in chapters 10 and 11.

The recipes in this book offer countless possibilities to continue eating to support your overall health, even after you've completed the meal plan. So, don't stop at three weeks. Let's go for a long-term lifestyle change, not a short-term diet.

Get yourself set for next week using the plan all over again, but swap in some other recipes from this book. Or make your own meal plans with the principles and guidelines you have here for balanced nutrition and incredible flavor. Plan the full week, or just stock your kitchen with enough healthy stuff to make meals as you go. When you get the hang of it, you can even start improvising with your own recipes. Try doing the plan over again a few times a year, as a cleanse or to easily reset after a vacation or the holidays.

Note which recipes you liked, what prep you found easy to work into your daily routine, and anything else you found useful. Pick out a few meals that you really enjoy, and those can become your new go-tos: those meals you can whip up any day of the week in no time flat. Make them again and again, changing up the vegetables and seasonings to keep it interesting.

When making food for an average weeknight, stick with the basics—steamed veggies and rice with tahini dressing, baked sweet potato with avocado dip, or just a super simple soup with a bunch of veggies and lentils in a pot with whatever seasonings you like. Don't make this hard on yourself; it doesn't need to be complicated.

And most importantly, share a meal or a recipe with a friend or loved one, so you can show them how delicious it can be to eat in a healthy, sustainable, and compassionate way. Just don't tell them it's plant-based until after they finish eating and tell you how delicious it tastes.

In addition to diet, here are some lifestyle changes that can help you maintain your weight loss and feel great.

Get Enough Sleep

There's some research showing that sleep affects the part of your brain that controls willpower. So if you're short on sleep, you'll likely find it harder to resist temptation. Your ability to make clear decisions is reduced, which makes you more liable to turn to foods that don't really serve you.

You're also less able to handle stress in a constructive way, which makes you more susceptible to overeating or other negative coping mechanisms to compensate. Getting quality sleep regularly will not only make you a lot healthier and more energetic, but it will also help you keep your cravings in check. Here are some ways to cultivate healthy sleep habits.

- Try to have roughly the same wake time and bedtime every day.
- No TV, computer, tablet, or phone use 30 minutes before bed.
- No exercise after dinner.
- No caffeine after 2 p.m.
- No sugar after dinner.
- Try meditation, restorative yoga, or something relaxing in the evening.

Get Active Three Times a Week

Exercise is critical to maintain bone mass, cardiovascular health, lymphatic and immune system function, and can help prevent diabetes. Exercise also releases hormones into your bloodstream that make you feel happy, reduce hunger, and generally keep your body functioning properly. Try doing a quick workout after work and you may find that you don't need as big a meal for dinner.

Regular exercise helps reduce fatigue, depression, tension, worry, and feeling inadequate; it improves mood and the ability to handle stressful situations. As you get stronger and have more endurance, your body functions more effectively. Start with something you enjoy—walking, Rollerblading, Hula-Hooping. If you enjoy it, you're much more likely to stick with it for the long term. Aim for something you can do for 20 to 30 minutes, three times a week. It doesn't have to be the same activity every time. Mix it up to keep things interesting. As you get in the habit, you can add more days, go longer, or try something more intense.

Don't Stress About Being Perfect

Stress takes a toll on your health, and stressing too much about eating is self-defeating. While it would be great if you could always eat a perfect diet and maintain a perfect exercise plan, I don't know anyone who can do that every single day of their life. Don't feel guilty if you have a day that's less than perfect, because that will only bring negative energy into your life. Some people tend to eat more when they feel bad about themselves. I don't like using the words "slip," "cheat," or "mistake" because I think everything we do is just part of life and makes us the person we will be tomorrow.

Don't punish yourself with less food or more exercise. Instead, take each day at face value and move on, reinvigorated to maintain or possibly adjust your plan going forward so that it works for you in real life.

Listen to Your Body and Have Fun!

Staying in balance doesn't mean following strict rules or meal plans forever—it means finding your own balance for what your body needs. Now that you've gotten yourself on the path to better health, you can get back in touch with and trust your own instincts to continue learning what works for you. Eat consciously by chewing your food thoroughly, enjoying the flavors, and recognizing when you've eaten enough.

When your body is in balance and you follow the basics of healthy eating in the long term, you should be able to listen to the messages your body is giving you about what it needs to be healthy. Everyone is different and will have different ways of being healthy. But your body's messages can get twisted or muted when out of balance, so it's hard at first to tell whether what you feel is craving or actual hunger.

Positive energy can make such a huge difference in achieving your goals. It's unfortunate that many diet plans focus on avoiding unhealthy foods when transitioning to a healthy diet, because it is so much more fun and effective to focus your attention on nourishing yourself with good foods. Find some good foods that you really enjoy, like certain fruits, nuts, or a special dinner, and eat them often to keep yourself feeling happy and excited about your healthy lifestyle.

HOW TO ORDER PLANT BASED AT RESTAURANTS

Telling your friends that you're eating healthy up front will make you accountable for your choices and avoid embarrassment over not wanting to share nachos. If you can't go to a fully vegan restaurant, check the menu online before you go. Vietnamese, Greek, Italian, Mexican, Indian, and sushi restaurants generally have some healthy options to choose from and offer both vegan and non-vegan dishes. For example, an avocado roll, a cucumber roll, and some steamed edamame beans is a fantastic balanced meal. Don't be afraid to ask for something on the menu with a salad instead of fries, or with salsa instead of mayonnaise. These kinds of changes are usually no problem and can make a huge difference for your healthy life.

PART THREE

THE RECIPES

Recipes are where we put knowledge into practice—and have some fun. In the chapters that follow, I'll give you more than 100 recipes to explore the flavors of plant foods and, hopefully, help you fall in love with this lifestyle.

These recipes have zero cholesterol, are low in saturated fat, are sodium-potassium balanced, heart healthy, and high in antioxidants. While they all have immune-boosting and anti-inflammatory properties, I'll call out some recipes that are turbocharged in this area due to some specific ingredients. I'll indicate which recipes are especially kid-friendly, nut-free, gluten-free, or quick prep (15 minutes or less).

There are lots of meals here beyond the ones in the meal plans, along with some delicious and nutritious desserts, so you can enjoy eating healthy for the long term.

Baked Banana French
Toast with Raspberry
Syrup page 92

chapter 7

SMOOTHIES AND BREAKFASTS

Max Power Smoothie 76

Chai Chia Smoothie 77

Tropi-Kale Breeze 78

Hydration Station 79

Mango Madness 80

Chocolate PB Smoothie 81

Pink Panther Smoothie 82

Banana Nut Smoothie 83

Overnight Oats On the Go 84

Oatmeal Breakfast Cookies 86

Sunshine Muffins 88

Applesauce Crumble Muffins 90

Baked Banana French Toast with Raspberry Syrup 92

Cinnamon Apple Toast 94

Muesli and Berries Bowl 95

Chocolate Quinoa Breakfast Bowl 96

Fruit Salad with Zesty Citrus Couscous 97

Fruity Granola 98

Chickpea Scramble 100

Roasted Veg with Creamy Avocado Dip 102

Max Power Smoothie

Makes 3 to 4 cups
Prep time: 5 minutes

This is a delicious breakfast smoothie base to start your day, with some optional booster additions to max out the nutrient density. The stems of kale and chard can be tough, so it's best to tear the leaves off the stem and work only with the leaves. The greens and carrot do best if you have a high-powered blender, like a Blendtec or Vitamix. If you have a regular blender, omit the fresh greens and use a greens powder, such as greens+ brand, to get the nutrient boost without the chunkiness.

1 banana

¼ cup rolled oats, or 1 scoop plant protein powder

1 tablespoon flaxseed, or chia seeds

1 cup raspberries, or other berries

1 cup chopped mango (frozen or fresh)

½ cup non-dairy milk (optional)

1 cup water

BONUS BOOSTERS (OPTIONAL)

2 tablespoons fresh parsley, or basil, chopped

1 cup chopped fresh kale, spinach, collards, or other green

1 carrot, peeled

1 tablespoon grated fresh ginger

1. Purée everything in a blender until smooth, adding more water (or non-dairy milk) if needed.

2. Add none, some, or all of the bonus boosters, as desired. Purée until blended.

Make ahead: Buy extra bananas, so that when they ripen you can peel them and put them in the freezer. Frozen bananas make for max creaminess in your smoothie.

Per Serving (3 to 4 cups)

Calories: 550; Total fat: 9g; Carbs: 116g; Fiber: 29g; Protein: 13g

Chai Chia Smoothie

Makes 3 cups
Prep time: 5 minutes

GLUTEN-FREE NUT-FREE QUICK PREP ANTI-INFLAMMATORY

Chai spices can aid digestion, improve blood sugar balance, and boost metabolism. Chia seeds are a fantastic source of omega-3 fatty acids, as well as calcium, phosphorus, and manganese. Whip up this delicious smoothie to sip on your commute as a super nourishing alternative to a chai latte.

1 banana

½ cup coconut milk

1 cup water

1 cup alfalfa sprouts (optional)

1 to 2 soft Medjool dates, pitted

1 tablespoon chia seeds, or ground flax or hemp hearts

¼ teaspoon ground cinnamon

Pinch ground cardamom

1 tablespoon grated fresh ginger, or ¼ teaspoon ground ginger

Purée everything in a blender until smooth, adding more water (or coconut milk) if needed.

Did you know? Although dates are super sweet, they don't cause a large blood sugar spike. They're great to boost sweetness while also boosting your intake of fiber and potassium.

Per Serving (3 cups)

Calories: 477; Total fat: 29g; Carbs: 57g; Fiber: 14g; Protein: 8g

Tropi-Kale Breeze

Makes 3 to 4 cups
Prep time: 5 minutes

**GLUTEN-FREE NUT-FREE QUICK PREP KID-FRIENDLY ANTI-INFLAMMATORY
IMMUNE BOOSTER**

Pineapple is a natural metabolism booster, has an enzyme that helps with digestion, and helps cut through the bitterness of kale. If you haven't tried greens in a smoothie before, this is the one to try first. You could swap the kale for spinach if you want a milder flavor to start. We're also using avocado for creaminess instead of a banana, so this is a lower-carb option than other smoothies. Add a teaspoon of matcha green tea powder for an extra boost, if you'd like.

1 cup chopped pineapple
   (frozen or fresh)

1 cup chopped mango
   (frozen or fresh)

½ to 1 cup chopped kale

½ avocado

½ cup coconut milk

1 cup water, or coconut water

1 teaspoon matcha green tea
   powder (optional)

Purée everything in a blender until smooth, adding more water (or coconut milk) if needed.

Did you know? Matcha green tea powder contains catechins, which minimize inflammation and maximize fat-burning potential.

Per Serving (3 to 4 cups)

Calories: 566; Total fat: 36g; Carbs: 66g; Fiber: 12g; Protein: 8g

Hydration Station

Makes 3 to 4 cups
Prep time: 5 minutes

GLUTEN-FREE NUT-FREE QUICK PREP KID-FRIENDLY IMMUNE BOOSTER

If you tend to get morning headaches, this is the smoothie for you. Headaches are often a sign of dehydration, so boost your water and electrolyte intake with this powerful and delicious smoothie. This is also perfect after a workout or a run to replenish and cool down.

1 banana

1 orange, peeled and sectioned,
   or 1 cup pure orange juice

1 cup strawberries (frozen or fresh)

1 cup chopped cucumber

½ cup coconut water

1 cup water

½ cup ice

BONUS BOOSTERS (OPTIONAL)

1 cup chopped spinach

¼ cup fresh mint, chopped

1. Purée everything in a blender until smooth, adding more water if needed.
2. Add bonus boosters, as desired. Purée until blended.

Make ahead: Pour your smoothie in an insulated travel mug or thermos to keep it chilled if you're on the go.

Per Serving (3 to 4 cups)

Calories: 320; Total fat: 3g; Carbs: 76g; Fiber: 13g; Protein: 6g

Mango Madness

Makes 3 to 4 cups
Prep time: 5 minutes

Charge up your immune system with this vitamin C–rich smoothie. This one's also rich in beta-carotene for sharp eyes and clear skin. If you don't have a high-powered blender, or don't want carrot in your smoothie, you can leave it out.

1 banana

1 cup chopped mango
(frozen or fresh)

1 cup chopped peach
(frozen or fresh)

1 cup strawberries

1 carrot, peeled and chopped
(optional)

1 cup water

Purée everything in a blender until smooth, adding more water if needed.

Options: If you can't find frozen peaches and fresh ones aren't in season, just use extra mango or strawberries, or try cantaloupe.

Per Serving (3 to 4 cups)

Calories: 376; Total fat: 2g; Carbs: 95g; Fiber: 14g; Protein: 5g

Chocolate PB Smoothie

Makes 3 to 4 cups
Prep time: 5 minutes

QUICK PREP KID-FRIENDLY

This smoothie is so delicious, you might not believe it's healthy. But it's 100 percent goodness. It covers all your nutritional bases to start the day off right, keeps you fueled until lunch, and is an excellent offset to the Monday morning blues.

1 banana

¼ cup rolled oats, or 1 scoop plant protein powder

1 tablespoon flaxseed, or chia seeds

1 tablespoon unsweetened cocoa powder

1 tablespoon peanut butter, or almond or sunflower seed butter

1 tablespoon maple syrup (optional)

1 cup alfalfa sprouts, or spinach, chopped (optional)

½ cup non-dairy milk (optional)

1 cup water

BONUS BOOSTERS (OPTIONAL)

1 teaspoon maca powder

1 teaspoon cocoa nibs

1. Purée everything in a blender until smooth, adding more water (or non-dairy milk) if needed.
2. Add bonus boosters, as desired. Purée until blended.

Did you know? Flavonols found in cocoa appear to help protect our blood vessel linings, and postmenopausal women seem to reap the most cardio-vascular benefits from consuming cocoa.

Per Serving (3 to 4 cups)

Calories: 474; Total fat: 16g; Carbs: 79g; Fiber: 18g; Protein: 13g

Pink Panther Smoothie

Makes 3 cups
Prep time: 5 minutes

This smoothie is silky smooth with a little pizzazz. Cranberries are a rich source of vitamin C and have several unique phytonutrients that give them cardioprotective, antioxidant, anti-inflammatory, and liver-cleansing benefits and offer preventive effects against cancer (particularly breast, colon, lung, and prostate) and urinary tract infections.

1 cup strawberries

1 cup chopped melon (any kind)

1 cup cranberries, or raspberries

1 tablespoon chia seeds

½ cup coconut milk, or other non-dairy milk

1 cup water

BONUS BOOSTERS (OPTIONAL)

1 teaspoon goji berries

2 tablespoons fresh mint, chopped

1. Purée everything in a blender until smooth, adding more water (or coconut milk) if needed.
2. Add bonus boosters, as desired. Purée until blended.

Options: If you don't have (or don't like) coconut, try using sunflower seeds for an immune boost of zinc and selenium.

Per Serving (3 cups)

Calories: 459; Total fat: 30g; Carbs: 52g; Fiber: 19g; Protein: 8g

Banana Nut Smoothie

Makes 2 to 3 cups
Prep time: 5 minutes

GLUTEN-FREE QUICK PREP KID-FRIENDLY

This is like banana bread in a glass. Whip it up for a quick breakfast or dessert. Almond butter is already creamy, but if you have a powerful blender this is also really tasty with 2 tablespoons walnuts instead of the almond butter. Make it super thick for a smoothie bowl, topped with Fruity Granola (page 98) or Muesli (page 95) and fresh fruit slices.

1 banana

1 tablespoon almond butter, or
    sunflower seed butter

¼ teaspoon ground cinnamon

Pinch ground nutmeg

1 to 2 tablespoons dates, or
    maple syrup

1 tablespoon ground flaxseed, or
    chia, or hemp hearts

½ cup non-dairy milk (optional)

1 cup water

Purée everything in a blender until smooth, adding more water (or non-dairy milk) if needed.

Options: You could make this a pumpkin spice smoothie by adding 1 cup cooked pumpkin and a pinch allspice.

Per Serving (2 to 3 cups)

Calories: 343; Total fat: 14g; Carbs: 55g; Fiber: 8g; Protein: 6g

Overnight Oats On the Go

Makes 1 serving
Prep time: 5 minutes / Cook time: 5 minutes or overnight

GLUTEN-FREE NUT-FREE QUICK PREP KID-FRIENDLY

Oats are well known for their cardioprotective benefits. From their cholesterol-lowering beta-glucan fiber, to their unique antioxidant avenanthramides that can help keep your arterial walls clean, to their lignans that are thought to protect against heart disease, they are a compelling package. Your basic bowl of porridge is pretty much a superhero.

BASIC OVERNIGHT OATS

½ cup rolled oats, or quinoa flakes for gluten-free

1 tablespoon ground flaxseed, or chia seeds, or hemp hearts

1 tablespoon maple syrup, or coconut sugar (optional)

¼ teaspoon ground cinnamon (optional)

TOPPING OPTIONS

1 apple, chopped, and 1 tablespoon walnuts

2 tablespoons dried cranberries and 1 tablespoon pumpkin seeds

1 pear, chopped, and 1 tablespoon cashews

1 cup sliced grapes and 1 tablespoon sunflower seeds

1 banana, sliced, and 1 tablespoon peanut butter

2 tablespoons raisins and 1 tablespoon hazelnuts

1 cup berries and 1 tablespoon unsweetened coconut flakes

1. Mix the oats, flax, maple syrup, and cinnamon (if using) together in a bowl or to-go container (a travel mug or short thermos works beautifully).

2. Pour enough cool water over the oats to submerge them, and stir to combine. Leave to soak for a minimum of half an hour, or overnight.

3. Add your choice of toppings.

Quick morning option: Boil about ½ cup water and pour over the oats. Let them soak about 5 minutes before eating.

Did you know? Cinnamon has been shown to help control blood sugar levels, improve insulin response, and reduce triglycerides, LDL (bad) cholesterol, and total cholesterol.

Per Serving (Basic)

Calories: 244; Total fat: 6g; Carbs: 30g; Fiber: 6g; Protein: 7g

Per Serving (Apple and Walnut version)

Calories: 401; Total fat: 15g; Carbs: 63g; Fiber: 10g; Protein: 10g

Oatmeal Breakfast Cookies

Makes 5 big cookies
Prep time: 15 minutes / Cook time: 12 minutes

QUICK PREP KID-FRIENDLY

Breakfast can still be super healthy, even when you bake it into a cookie. Think of these as a wholesome bowl of porridge—just more fun. Oats, flaxseed, nuts, and whole grains are known to be beneficial for cardio-vascular health, so these cookies are the perfect start to fuel your morning. Make them gluten-free by simply using sorghum flour and gluten-free rolled oats or rolled quinoa flakes instead of regular rolled oats.

1 tablespoon ground flaxseed

2 tablespoons almond butter, or sunflower seed butter

2 tablespoons maple syrup

1 banana, mashed

1 teaspoon ground cinnamon

¼ teaspoon ground nutmeg (optional)

Pinch sea salt

½ cup rolled oats

¼ cup raisins, or dark chocolate chips

1. Preheat the oven to 350°F. Line a large baking sheet with parchment paper.
2. Mix the ground flax with just enough water to cover it in a small dish, and leave it to sit.
3. In a large bowl, mix together the almond butter and maple syrup until creamy, then add the banana. Add the flax-water mixture.
4. Sift the cinnamon, nutmeg, and salt into a separate medium bowl, then stir into the wet mixture.
5. Add the oats and raisins, and fold in.
6. Form 3 to 4 tablespoons batter into a ball and press lightly to flatten onto the baking sheet. Repeat, spacing the cookies 2 to 3 inches apart.

7. Bake for 12 minutes, or until golden brown.
8. Store the cookies in an airtight container in the fridge, or freeze them for later.

Make ahead: The quantity here is for one person, so you don't have too many cookies lying around to tempt you. But they're great to double for a full batch of snacks.

Per Serving (1 cookie)

Calories: 192; Total fat: 6g; Carbs: 34g; Fiber: 4g; Protein: 4g

Sunshine Muffins

Makes 6 muffins
Prep time: 15 minutes / Cook time: 30 minutes

QUICK PREP KID-FRIENDLY ANTI-INFLAMMATORY IMMUNE BOOSTER

These muffins are a perfect start to your day, bursting with flavor and nutrients. They're very low in fat and added sugar, relying instead on the wholesome sweetness of fruit. If you want to make them a bit sweeter, add a couple of tablespoons of maple syrup along with the molasses. Try pairing a muffin with half a smoothie for a balanced breakfast.

1 teaspoon coconut oil, for greasing muffin tins (optional)

2 tablespoons almond butter, or sunflower seed butter

¼ cup non-dairy milk

1 orange, peeled

1 carrot, coarsely chopped

2 tablespoons chopped dried apricots, or other dried fruit

3 tablespoons molasses

2 tablespoons ground flaxseed

1 teaspoon apple cider vinegar

1 teaspoon pure vanilla extract

½ teaspoon ground cinnamon

½ teaspoon ground ginger (optional)

¼ teaspoon ground nutmeg (optional)

¼ teaspoon allspice (optional)

¾ cup rolled oats, or whole-grain flour

1 teaspoon baking powder

½ teaspoon baking soda

MIX-INS (OPTIONAL)

½ cup rolled oats

2 tablespoons raisins, or other chopped dried fruit

2 tablespoons sunflower seeds

1. Preheat the oven to 350°F. Prepare a 6-cup muffin tin by rubbing the insides of the cups with coconut oil or using silicone or paper muffin cups.

2. Purée the nut butter, milk, orange, carrot, apricots, molasses, flaxseed, vinegar, vanilla, cinnamon, ginger, nutmeg, and allspice in a food processor or blender until somewhat smooth.

3. Grind the oats in a clean coffee grinder until they're the consistency of flour (or use whole-grain flour). In a large bowl, mix the oats with the baking powder and baking soda.

4. Mix the wet ingredients into the dry ingredients until just combined. Fold in the mix-ins (if using).

5. Spoon about ¼ cup batter into each muffin cup and bake for 30 minutes, or until a toothpick inserted into the center comes out clean. The orange creates a very moist base, so the muffins may take longer than 30 minutes, depending on how heavy your muffin tin is.

Leftovers: Store the muffins in the fridge or freezer, because they are so moist. If you plan to keep them frozen, you can easily double the batch for a full dozen.

Per Serving (1 muffin)

Calories: 287; Total fat: 12g; Carbs: 41g; Fiber: 6g; Protein: 8g

Applesauce Crumble Muffins

Makes 12 muffins
Prep time: 15 minutes / Cook time: 15 to 20 minutes

QUICK PREP KID-FRIENDLY

These are adapted from my favorite childhood muffins to be fully plant based and lower in fat and sugar. Coconut sugar is a great option for a low-glycemic sweetener, but if you can't find it, go for a whole, unprocessed cane sugar such as sucanat, date sugar, or some other unrefined granular sugar. Don't use brown sugar, which is just refined white sugar with some molasses added. Muscovado, demerara, or turbinado sugars are only partially refined, and so would be okay too.

1 teaspoon coconut oil, for greasing muffin tins (optional)

2 tablespoons nut butter, or seed butter

1½ cups unsweetened applesauce

⅓ cup coconut sugar

½ cup non-dairy milk

2 tablespoons ground flaxseed

1 teaspoon apple cider vinegar

1 teaspoon pure vanilla extract

2 cups whole-grain flour

1 teaspoon baking soda

½ teaspoon baking powder

1 teaspoon ground cinnamon

Pinch sea salt

½ cup walnuts, chopped

TOPPINGS (OPTIONAL)

¼ cup walnuts

¼ cup coconut sugar

½ teaspoon ground cinnamon

1. Preheat the oven to 350°F. Prepare two 6-cup muffin tins by rubbing the insides of the cups with coconut oil, or using silicone or paper muffin cups.
2. In a large bowl, mix the nut butter, applesauce, coconut sugar, milk, flaxseed, vinegar, and vanilla until thoroughly combined, or purée in a food processor or blender.
3. In another large bowl, sift together the flour, baking soda, baking powder, cinnamon, salt, and chopped walnuts.
4. Mix the dry ingredients into the wet ingredients until just combined.
5. Spoon about ¼ cup batter into each muffin cup and sprinkle with the topping of your choice (if using). Bake for 15 to 20 minutes, or until a toothpick inserted into the center comes out clean. The applesauce creates a very moist base, so the muffins may take longer, depending on how heavy your muffin tins are.

Options: To make this nut-free, swap the walnuts for sunflower seeds and use sunflower seed butter.

Per Serving (1 muffin)

Calories: 287; Total fat: 12g; Carbs: 41g; Fiber: 6g; Protein: 8g

Baked Banana French Toast with Raspberry Syrup

Makes 8 slices

Prep time: 10 minutes / Cook time: 30 minutes

NUT-FREE QUICK PREP KID-FRIENDLY

Making French toast with bananas instead of eggs gives it a natural sweetness and a new flavor—plus you don't have to worry about under-cooking it. The beauty of this raspberry syrup is that the sweetness of the berries means you only need a very small amount of maple syrup, so you reduce the amount of sugar you're adding.

FOR THE FRENCH TOAST

1 banana

1 cup coconut milk

1 teaspoon pure vanilla extract

¼ teaspoon ground nutmeg

½ teaspoon ground cinnamon

1½ teaspoons arrowroot powder, or flour

Pinch sea salt

8 slices whole-grain bread

FOR THE RASPBERRY SYRUP

1 cup fresh or frozen raspberries, or other berries

2 tablespoons water, or pure fruit juice

1 to 2 tablespoons maple syrup, or coconut sugar (optional)

TO MAKE THE FRENCH TOAST

1. Preheat the oven to 350°F.

2. In a shallow bowl, purée or mash the banana well. Mix in the coconut milk, vanilla, nutmeg, cinnamon, arrowroot, and salt.

3. Dip the slices of bread in the banana mixture, and then lay them out in a 13-by-9-inch baking dish. They should cover the bottom of the dish and can overlap a bit but shouldn't be stacked on top of each other. Pour any leftover banana mixture over the bread, and put the dish in the oven. Bake about 30 minutes, or until the tops are lightly browned.

4. Serve topped with raspberry syrup.

TO MAKE THE RASPBERRY SYRUP

1. Heat the raspberries in a small pot with the water and the maple syrup (if using) on medium heat.
2. Leave to simmer, stirring occasionally and breaking up the berries, for 15 to 20 minutes, until the liquid has reduced.

Leftovers: Leftover raspberry syrup makes a great topping for simple oatmeal as a quick and delicious breakfast, or as a drizzle on top of whole-grain toast smeared with natural peanut butter.

Per Serving (1 slice with syrup)

Calories: 166; Total fat: 7g; Carbs: 23g; Fiber: 4g; Protein: 5g

Cinnamon Apple Toast

Makes 2 slices
Prep time: 5 minutes / Cook time: 10 to 20 minutes

NUT-FREE QUICK PREP KID-FRIENDLY

This is a very simple way to make a decadent brunch. Apples help regulate blood sugar, lower fat and cholesterol, and may even help keep our gut flora in balance. There's a phytonutrient in apples called quercetin, which is an anti-inflammatory and antihistamine, and it's much more concentrated in the skin than the flesh. In fact, there are several phytonutrients in apples that are all concentrated in the skin, so be sure to eat it.

1 to 2 teaspoons coconut oil

½ teaspoon ground cinnamon

1 tablespoon maple syrup, or coconut sugar

1 apple, cored and thinly sliced

2 slices whole-grain bread

Options: For a more everyday version, toast the bread, spread with nut butter, top with apple slices, and sprinkle with a pinch cinnamon and coconut sugar.

Per Serving (1 slice)

Calories: 187; Total fat: 8g; Carbs: 27g; Fiber: 4g; Protein: 4g

1. In a large bowl, mix the coconut oil, cinnamon, and maple syrup together. Add the apple slices and toss with your hands to coat them.

2. To panfry the toast, place the apple slices in a medium skillet on medium-high and cook for about 5 minutes, or until slightly soft, then transfer to a plate. Cook the bread in the same skillet for 2 to 3 minutes on each side. Top the toast with the apples. Alternately, you can bake the toast. Use your hands to rub each slice of bread with some of the coconut oil mixture on both sides. Lay them on a small baking sheet, top with the coated apples, and put in the oven or toaster oven at 350°F for 15 to 20 minutes, or until the apples have softened.

Muesli and Berries Bowl

Makes about 5 cups
Prep time: 10 minutes

QUICK PREP KID-FRIENDLY

Muesli is a great alternative to granola; it's lower in fat and there's no cooking. You'll find whole-grain puffed cereals in health food stores—look for the fewest number of ingredients and no added sugar. This is a really tasty and energizing weekday breakfast alternative to oatmeal or smoothies. Have fun experimenting with all the different nuts, seeds, fruits, and spices that could go in it.

FOR THE MUESLI

1 cup rolled oats

1 cup spelt flakes, or quinoa flakes, or more rolled oats

2 cups puffed cereal

¼ cup sunflower seeds

¼ cup almonds

¼ cup raisins

¼ cup dried cranberries

¼ cup chopped dried figs

¼ cup unsweetened shredded coconut

¼ cup non-dairy chocolate chips

1 to 3 teaspoons ground cinnamon

FOR THE BOWL

½ cup non-dairy milk, or unsweetened applesauce

¾ cup muesli

½ cup berries

1. Put the muesli ingredients in a container or bag and shake.
2. Combine the muesli and bowl ingredients in a bowl or to-go container.

Substitutions: Try chopped Brazil nuts, peanuts, dried cranberries, dried blueberries, dried mango, or whatever inspires you. Ginger and cardamom are interesting flavors if you want to branch out on spices.

Per Serving (1 bowl)

Calories: 441; Total fat: 20g; Carbs: 63g; Fiber: 13g; Protein: 10g

Chocolate Quinoa Breakfast Bowl

Makes 2 servings
Prep time: 5 minutes / Cook time: 30 minutes

GLUTEN-FREE GRAIN-FREE QUICK PREP KID-FRIENDLY

You can have dessert for breakfast in a totally healthy way. Quinoa is great for adding a protein boost to your morning, but you could use any cooked whole grain, from oatmeal to brown rice. The pudding is also great on its own as a snack or dessert to get your chocolate fix.

1 cup quinoa

1 teaspoon ground cinnamon

1 cup non-dairy milk

1 cup water

1 large banana

2 to 3 tablespoons unsweetened cocoa powder, or carob

1 to 2 tablespoons almond butter, or other nut or seed butter

1 tablespoon ground flaxseed, or chia or hemp seeds

2 tablespoons walnuts

¼ cup raspberries

1. Put the quinoa, cinnamon, milk, and water in a medium pot. Bring to a boil over high heat, then turn down low and simmer, covered, for 25 to 30 minutes.

2. While the quinoa is simmering, purée or mash the banana in a medium bowl and stir in the cocoa powder, almond butter, and flaxseed.

3. To serve, spoon 1 cup cooked quinoa into a bowl, top with half the pudding and half the walnuts and raspberries.

Make ahead: This is a great way to use leftover quinoa, or plan ahead and make extra quinoa for dinner, so you can whip this together on a weekday morning as quickly as you would a smoothie.

Per Serving (1 bowl)

Calories: 392; Total fat: 19g; Carbs: 49g; Fiber: 10g; Protein: 12g

Fruit Salad with Zesty Citrus Couscous

Makes 1 serving
Prep time: 5 minutes / Cook time: 5 minutes

NUT-FREE QUICK PREP KID-FRIENDLY **ANTI-INFLAMMATORY** IMMUNE BOOSTER

This is a fresh and flavorful breakfast that comes together quickly. Zesting an orange is not tricky; you want to take just the very outer bits of peel off—that's where the intensely flavorful (and antioxidant-rich) citrus oils are—and leave the bitter white pith behind. You can use a zester, Microplane, or even just a fine grater. If you haven't used citrus zest before, trust me, it's worth a little effort.

1 orange, zested and juiced

¼ cup whole-wheat couscous, or corn couscous

1 cup assorted berries (strawberries, blackberries, blueberries)

½ cup cubed or balled melon (cantaloupe or honeydew)

1 tablespoon maple syrup, or coconut sugar (optional)

1 tablespoon fresh mint, minced (optional)

1 tablespoon unsweetened coconut flakes

Options: This would also be fantastic with cooked quinoa instead of the couscous. Just leave it to marinate with the orange juice while you prepare the fruit.

1. Put the orange juice in a small pot, add half the zest, and bring to a boil.
2. Put the dry couscous in a small bowl and pour the boiling orange juice over it. If there isn't enough juice to fully submerge the couscous, add just enough boiling water to do so. Cover the bowl with a plate or seal with wrap, and let steep for 5 minutes.
3. In a medium bowl, toss the berries and melon with the maple syrup (if using) and the rest of the zest. You can either keep the fruit cool, or heat it lightly in the small pot you used for the orange juice.
4. When the couscous is soft, remove the cover and fluff it with a fork. Top with the fruit, fresh mint, and coconut.

Per Serving

Calories: 496; Total fat: 10g; Carbs: 97g; Fiber: 14g; Protein: 11g

Fruity Granola

Makes 5 cups
Prep time: 15 minutes / Cook time: 45 minutes

QUICK PREP KID-FRIENDLY ANTI-INFLAMMATORY

It can be difficult to find store-bought granolas that aren't loaded with sugar and oil. This granola is sweetened only with pure fruit juice. If you want something a bit sweeter, you can replace a quarter of the juice with maple syrup or add some unrefined sugar. I like it with this light sweetness, though, and the flavor of the juice will add character.

2 cups rolled oats

¾ cup whole-grain flour

1 tablespoon ground cinnamon

1 teaspoon ground ginger (optional)

½ cup sunflower seeds, or walnuts, chopped

½ cup almonds, chopped

½ cup pumpkin seeds

½ cup unsweetened shredded coconut

1¼ cups pure fruit juice (cranberry, apple, or something similar)

½ cup raisins, or dried cranberries

½ cup goji berries (optional)

1. Preheat the oven to 350°F.
2. Mix together the oats, flour, cinnamon, ginger, sunflower seeds, almonds, pumpkin seeds, and coconut in a large bowl.
3. Sprinkle the juice over the mixture, and stir until it's just moistened. You might need a bit more or a bit less liquid, depending on how much your oats and flour absorb.
4. Spread the granola on a large baking sheet (the more spread out it is the better), and put it in the oven. After about 15 minutes, use a spatula to turn the granola so that the middle gets dried out. Let the granola bake until it's as crunchy as you want it, about 30 minutes more.
5. Take the granola out of the oven and stir in the raisins and goji berries (if using).
6. Store leftovers in an airtight container for up to 2 weeks.

Leftovers: Serve with non-dairy milk and fresh fruit, use as a topper for morning porridge or a smoothie bowl to add a bit of crunch, or make a granola parfait by layering with non-dairy yogurt or puréed banana.

Per Serving ($\frac{1}{2}$ cup)

Calories: 398; Total fat: 25g; Carbs: 39g; Fiber: 8g; Protein: 11g

Chickpea Scramble

Makes 1 serving
Prep time: 5 minutes / Cook time: 15 minutes

GLUTEN-FREE NUT-FREE GRAIN-FREE QUICK PREP KID-FRIENDLY
ANTI-INFLAMMATORY IMMUNE BOOSTER

A tofu scramble is one of the most common vegan brunch options. For those who are allergic to soy or just aren't too fond of tofu, here's a soy-free chickpea scramble. Make this for yourself, your family, or have a weekend brunch potluck party with your friends. You can switch up the vegetables and seasonings as you like—the dish is incredibly versatile. Serve it over chopped spinach, with some whole-grain toast, or just on its own. It would also be lovely topped with chopped fresh avocado.

1 teaspoon olive oil, or 1 tablespoon vegetable broth or water

½ cup mushrooms, sliced

Pinch sea salt

½ cup chopped zucchini

½ cup chickpeas (cooked or canned)

1 teaspoon smoked paprika, or regular paprika

1 teaspoon turmeric

1 tablespoon nutritional yeast (optional)

Freshly ground black pepper

½ cup cherry tomatoes, chopped

¼ cup fresh parsley, chopped

1. Heat a large skillet to medium-high. Once the skillet is hot, add the olive oil and mushrooms, along with the sea salt to help them soften, and sauté, stirring occasionally, 7 to 8 minutes.

2. Add the zucchini to the skillet.

3. If you're using canned chickpeas, rinse and drain them. Mash the chickpeas with a potato masher, fork, or your fingers. Add them to the skillet and cook until they are heated through.

4. Sprinkle the paprika, turmeric, and nutritional yeast over the chickpeas, and stir to combine.

5. Toss in the black pepper, cherry tomatoes and fresh parsley at the end, just to warm, reserving a small bit of parsley to use as garnish.

Did You Know? Nutritional yeast is a yellow flaky seasoning with a savory and salty flavor. Most regular grocery stores carry it these days. Vegans often use it to add a cheesy or deeply savory taste to foods like popcorn.

Per Serving

Calories: 265; Total fat: 8g; Carbs: 37g; Fiber: 12g; Protein: 16g

Roasted Veg with Creamy Avocado Dip

Makes 2 servings
Prep time: 10 minutes / Cook time: 30 minutes

GLUTEN-FREE NUT-FREE QUICK PREP ANTI-INFLAMMATORY IMMUNE BOOSTER

These subtly spiced roasted root vegetables are paired with a creamy and savory avocado dip. With a variety of root vegetables, you get a variety of nutrients, flavors, and textures. You could also try parsnips or celery root. This would make a great brunch plate, served as a side dish with the Chickpea Scramble (page 100).

FOR THE AVOCADO DIP

1 avocado

1 tablespoon apple cider vinegar

¼ to ½ cup water

2 tablespoons nutritional yeast

1 teaspoon dried dill, or 1 tablespoon fresh dill

Pinch sea salt

FOR THE ROASTED VEG

1 small sweet potato, peeled and cubed

2 small beets, peeled and cubed

2 small carrots, peeled and cubed

1 teaspoon sea salt

1 teaspoon dried oregano

¼ teaspoon cayenne pepper

Pinch freshly ground black pepper

TO MAKE THE AVOCADO DIP

In a blender, purée the avocado with the other dip ingredients, using just enough water to get a smooth, creamy texture. Alternately, you can mash the avocado thoroughly in a large bowl, then stir in the rest of the dip ingredients.

TO MAKE THE ROASTED VEG

1. Preheat the oven to 350°F.

2. Put the sweet potato, beets, and carrots in a large pot with a small amount of water, and bring to a boil over high heat. Boil for 15 minutes, until they're just barely soft, then drain. Sprinkle the salt, oregano, cayenne, and pepper over them and stir gently to combine. (Use more or less cayenne depending on your taste.)

3. Spread the vegetables on a large baking sheet and roast them in the oven 10 to 15 minutes, until they've browned around the edges.

4. Serve the veg with the avocado dip on the side.

Make ahead: Make the roasted veg in large batches, so that you have them on hand through the week to add to salads, bowls, and wraps.

Per Serving

Calories: 335; Total fat: 12g; Carbs: 51g; Fiber: 16g; Protein: 11g

Hearty Chili *page 115*

chapter 8

SOUPS AND SALADS

Ginger Carrot Soup 106

Coconut Watercress Soup 107

Minty Beet and Sweet Potato Soup 108

Miso Noodle Soup 110

Creamy Pumpkin and Toasted Walnut Soup 111

Roasted Red Pepper and Butternut Squash Soup 112

Weeknight Chickpea Tomato Soup 114

Hearty Chili 115

Indian Red Split Lentil Soup 116

Savory Split Pea Soup 118

Basil Mango Jicama Salad 120

Roasted Beet and Avocado Salad 121

Creamy Avocado-Dressed Kale Salad 122

Wilted Sesame-Miso Kale Salad 124

Moroccan Aubergine Salad 126

Dill Potato Salad 128

Tuscan White Bean Salad 129

Tabbouleh Salad 130

Forbidden Black Rice and Edamame Salad 132

Warm Lentil Salad with Red Wine Vinaigrette 134

Ginger Carrot Soup

Makes 3 to 4 large bowls
Prep time: 10 minutes / Cook time: 20 minutes

GLUTEN-FREE QUICK PREP

This ginger carrot soup is quick and easy to make on weeknights—plus, of course, it's nourishing and really tasty. Carrots are always associated with good eyesight, due to their high beta-carotene content, but the antioxidants and other nutrients in carrots have also been shown to be protective against cardiovascular disease, cancer, and liver problems. The addition of some white beans (I've listed cannellini here, which are white kidney beans, but any kind of white bean will work) makes the soup filling, thick, creamy, and rich in protein.

1 teaspoon olive oil

1 cup chopped onion

1 tablespoon minced fresh ginger

4 large carrots, peeled, or scrubbed and chopped (about 2 cups)

1 cup cooked, or canned and rinsed cannellini beans, or other soft white beans

½ cup vegetable broth, or water and a bit extra salt

2 cups water

¼ teaspoon sea salt

1. In a large pot, warm the olive oil, then sauté the onion and ginger for 2 or 3 minutes. Add the carrots and cook to soften, about 3 minutes.
2. Add the beans, vegetable broth, water, and salt, and simmer for 20 minutes.
3. Transfer the soup to a blender or use an immersion blender to purée. Serve warm.

Leftovers: Save leftovers in an airtight container in the fridge for up to a week or in the freezer for a month or two.

Per Serving (1 bowl)

Calories: 141; Total fat: 2g; Carbs: 26g; Fiber: 7g; Protein: 7g

Coconut Watercress Soup

Makes 4 bowls

Prep time: 10 minutes / Cook time: 20 minutes

GLUTEN-FREE NUT-FREE QUICK PREP ANTI-INFLAMMATORY IMMUNE BOOSTER

Blended soups like this are the perfect way to put a lot of vegetables together incognito. This soup is so delicious that no one will complain about eating their greens, and the creamy, sweet coconut milk offsets any bitterness in the watercress. To make this recipe raw use 2 to 3 scallions instead of sautéing a regular onion, and blend the soup while it's cold.

1 teaspoon coconut oil

1 onion, diced

2 cups fresh or frozen peas

4 cups water, or vegetable stock

1 cup fresh watercress, chopped

1 tablespoon fresh mint, chopped

Pinch sea salt

Pinch freshly ground black pepper

¾ cup coconut milk

1. Melt the coconut oil in a large pot over medium-high heat. Add the onion and cook until soft, about 5 minutes, then add the peas and the water.

2. Bring to a boil, then lower the heat and add the watercress, mint, salt, and pepper. Cover and simmer for 5 minutes.

3. Stir in the coconut milk, and purée the soup until smooth in a blender or with an immersion blender.

Options: Try this soup with any other fresh, leafy green—anything from spinach to collard greens to arugula to Swiss chard.

Per Serving (1 bowl)

Calories: 178; Total fat: 10g; Carbs: 18g; Fiber: 5g; Protein: 6g

Minty Beet and Sweet Potato Soup

Makes 6 bowls
Prep time: 10 minutes / Cook time: 30 minutes

GLUTEN-FREE NUT-FREE QUICK PREP KID-FRIENDLY ANTI-INFLAMMATORY
IMMUNE BOOSTER

This sweet potato and beet soup recipe is easy to make and tastes amazing. The combo of beets and sweet potato supply a rich flavor and a thick, creamy texture. The soup has a gorgeous color from the beets and is so satisfyingly warm on a chilly evening.

5 cups water, or salt-free vegetable broth (if salted, omit the sea salt below)

1 to 2 teaspoons olive oil, or vegetable broth

1 cup chopped onion

3 garlic cloves, minced

1 tablespoon thyme, fresh or dried

1 to 2 teaspoons paprika

2 cups peeled and chopped beets

2 cups peeled and chopped sweet potato

2 cups peeled and chopped parsnips

½ teaspoon sea salt

1 cup fresh mint, chopped

½ avocado, or 2 tablespoons nut or seed butter (optional)

2 tablespoons balsamic vinegar (optional)

2 tablespoons pumpkin seeds

1. In large pot, boil the water.
2. In another large pot, warm the olive oil and sauté the onion and garlic until softened, about 5 minutes.
3. Add the thyme, paprika, beets, sweet potato, and parsnips, along with the boiling water and salt. Cover and leave to gently boil for about 30 minutes, or until the vegetables are soft.
4. Set aside a little mint for a garnish and add the rest, along with the avocado (if using). Stir until well combined.

5. Transfer the soup to a blender or use an immersion blender to purée, adding the balsamic vinegar (if using).

6. Serve topped with fresh mint and pumpkin seeds—and maybe chunks of the other half of the avocado, if you used it.

Leftovers: This soup is perfect to make in big batches and keep in single-serving containers in the freezer for quick weeknight meals.

Per Serving (1 bowl)

Calories: 156; Total fat: 4g; Carbs: 31g; Fiber: 7g; Protein: 4g

Miso Noodle Soup

Makes 4 bowls

Prep time: 10 minutes / Cook time: 15 minutes

GLUTEN-FREE NUT-FREE QUICK PREP ANTI-INFLAMMATORY

Miso soup is Japanese and is traditionally served as simply as possible: broth, miso, hijiki seaweed, cubes of tofu, and scallions. Many Japanese miso soups will also have sardine and tuna steeped into the stock, but we're going to keep it plant-based. We're also taking a fusion approach, tying the concept of North American chicken noodle soup to Japanese ingredients, using cleansing adzuki beans and earthy soba noodles. (Soba usually comes in little bundles inside the package, and 7 ounces is about two bundles in a typical package.)

7 ounces soba noodles
   (use 100% buckwheat for
   gluten-free)

4 cups water

4 tablespoons miso

1 cup adzuki beans (cooked or
   canned), drained and rinsed

2 tablespoons fresh cilantro, or
   basil, finely chopped

2 scallions, thinly sliced

Technique: Miso is a fermented product, and the good brands have live microbial cultures, like yogurt, so it should be added to the stock when it is warm, not hot. Adding miso to boiling water changes the flavor.

1. Bring a large pot of water to a boil, then add the soba noodles. Stir them occasionally; they'll take about 5 minutes to cook.

2. Meanwhile, prepare the rest of the soup by warming the water in a separate pot to just below boiling, then remove it from heat. Stir the miso into the water until it has dissolved.

3. Once the soba noodles are cooked, drain them and rinse with hot water.

4. Add the cooked noodles, adzuki beans, cilantro, and scallions to the miso broth and serve.

Per Serving (1 bowl)

Calories: 102; Total fat: 1g; Carbs: 18g; Fiber: 5g; Protein: 6g

Creamy Pumpkin and Toasted Walnut Soup

Makes 4 bowls
Prep time: 15 minutes / Cook time: 30 minutes

GLUTEN-FREE GRAIN-FREE QUICK PREP **ANTI-INFLAMMATORY** IMMUNE BOOSTER

This is a perfect soup to warm and satisfy you while also helping your body cleanse. It's so flavorful and feels really rich but doesn't leave you feeling heavy. This makes a great post-holiday meal, when you've eaten too much the day before.

1 small pie pumpkin, peeled, seeded, and chopped (about 6 cups)

1 teaspoon olive oil

¼ teaspoon sea salt

1 onion, diced

4 cups water, or vegetable stock

2 to 3 teaspoons ground sage

2 to 3 tablespoons nutritional yeast

1 cup non-dairy milk, or 1 tablespoon nut or seed butter plus 1 cup water or stock

¼ cup toasted walnuts

Freshly ground black pepper

Substitution: Winter squash or sweet potato would be an excellent alternative to pumpkin, in terms of texture, flavor, and nutrients.

1. Place a large saucepan on medium and sauté the pumpkin in the oil, seasoning with the salt, until slightly softened, about 10 minutes. Add the onion to the pot and sauté until slightly softened, about 5 minutes.

2. Add the water and bring to a boil. Then turn down to a simmer, cover, and cook 15 to 20 minutes, until the pumpkin is tender when pierced with a fork.

3. Stir in the sage, nutritional yeast, and non-dairy milk. Then purée the soup with an immersion blender or in a regular blender until smooth.

4. Garnish with toasted walnuts and pepper.

Per Serving (1 bowl)

Calories: 236; Total fat: 12g; Carbs: 29g; Fiber: 8g; Protein: 10g

Roasted Red Pepper and Butternut Squash Soup

Makes 6 bowls
Prep time: 10 minutes / Cook time: 40 to 50 minutes

GLUTEN-FREE NUT-FREE QUICK PREP KID-FRIENDLY ANTI-INFLAMMATORY
IMMUNE BOOSTER

Roasting vegetables brings out sugars and gives a full flavor to this soup. The beautiful thing about roasting vegetables is that even though they take a while to cook, you just put them in the oven and can then do other things. It's so wonderful to have a dairy-free soup that's this thick, creamy, and flavorful.

1 small butternut squash

1 tablespoon olive oil

1 teaspoon sea salt

2 red bell peppers

1 yellow onion

1 head garlic

2 cups water, or vegetable broth

Zest and juice of 1 lime

1 to 2 tablespoons tahini

Pinch cayenne pepper

½ teaspoon ground coriander

½ teaspoon ground cumin

Toasted squash seeds (optional)

1. Preheat the oven to 350°F.

2. Prepare the squash for roasting by cutting it in half lengthwise, scooping out the seeds, and poking some holes in the flesh with a fork. Reserve the seeds if desired. Rub a small amount of oil over the flesh and skin, then rub with a bit of sea salt and put the halves skin-side down in a large baking dish. Put it in the oven while you prepare the rest of the vegetables.

3. Prepare the peppers the exact same way, except they do not need to be poked. Slice the onion in half and rub oil on the exposed faces. Slice the top off the head of garlic and rub oil on the exposed flesh.

4. After the squash has cooked for 20 minutes, add the peppers, onion, and garlic, and roast for another 20 minutes. Optionally, you can toast the squash seeds by putting them in the oven in a separate baking

dish 10 to 15 minutes before the vegetables are finished. Keep a close eye on them.

5. When the vegetables are cooked, take them out and let them cool before handling them. The squash will be very soft when poked with a fork.

6. Scoop the flesh out of the squash skin into a large pot (if you have an immersion blender) or into a blender. Chop the pepper roughly, remove the onion skin and chop the onion roughly, and squeeze the garlic cloves out of the head, all into the pot or blender. Add the water, the lime zest and juice, and the tahini. Purée the soup, adding more water if you like, to your desired consistency.

7. Season with the salt, cayenne, coriander, and cumin. Serve garnished with toasted squash seeds (if using).

Did you know? Winter squash has plenty of vitamin A, which is good for eye health and the repair and maintenance of skin; it also boosts the immune system. According to Chinese medicine, winter squash improves the circulation of qi energy, which is your life force.

Per Serving (1 bowl)

Calories: 156; Total fat: 7g; Carbs: 22g; Fiber: 5g; Protein: 4g

Weeknight Chickpea Tomato Soup

Makes 2 servings
Prep time: 10 minutes / Cook time: 20 minutes

GLUTEN-FREE NUT-FREE GRAIN-FREE QUICK PREP KID-FRIENDLY IMMUNE BOOSTER

This soup is easy and quick to put together, as well as super tasty, with some wonderful rich flavors. It's perfect for a quick weeknight dinner and will make enough to take for lunch the next day. If you're cooking for two or more, the recipe will double or triple easily.

1 to 2 teaspoons olive oil, or vegetable broth

½ cup chopped onion

3 garlic cloves, minced

1 cup mushrooms, chopped

⅛ to ¼ teaspoon sea salt, divided

1 tablespoon dried basil

½ tablespoon dried oregano

1 to 2 tablespoons balsamic vinegar, or red wine

1 (19-ounce) can diced tomatoes

1 (14-ounce) can chickpeas, drained and rinsed, or 1½ cups cooked

2 cups water

1 to 2 cups chopped kale

1. In a large pot, warm the olive oil and sauté the onion, garlic, and mushrooms with a pinch salt until softened, 7 to 8 minutes.
2. Add the basil and oregano and stir to mix. Then add the vinegar to deglaze the pan, using a wooden spoon to scrape all the browned, savory bits up from the bottom.
3. Add the tomatoes and chickpeas. Stir to combine, adding enough water to get the consistency you want.
4. Add the kale and the remaining salt. Cover and simmer for 5 to 15 minutes, until the kale is as soft as you like it.

Per Serving (1 bowl)

Calories: 343; Total fat: 9g; Carbs: 61g; Fiber: 15g; Protein: 17g

Topping: This is delicious topped with a tablespoon of toasted walnuts and a sprinkle of nutritional yeast, or the Cheesy Sprinkle (page 229).

Hearty Chili

Makes 4 bowls

Prep time: 10 minutes / Cook time: 10 to 20 minutes

GLUTEN-FREE NUT-FREE QUICK PREP IMMUNE BOOSTER

Kidney beans are a wonderful source of protein, with cholesterol-lowering and blood sugar–stabilizing fiber, folate, iron, and manganese—without the saturated fat or cholesterol of ground meat. Pairing iron-rich kidney beans with vitamin C–rich tomatoes and cilantro means you'll be absorbing more energy-boosting iron.

1 onion, diced

2 to 3 garlic cloves, minced

1 teaspoon olive oil, or 1 to 2 tablespoons water, vegetable broth, or red wine

1 (28-ounce) can tomatoes

¼ cup tomato paste, or crushed tomatoes

1 (14-ounce) can kidney beans, rinsed and drained, or 1½ cups cooked

2 to 3 teaspoons chili powder

¼ teaspoon sea salt

¼ cup fresh cilantro, or parsley leaves

1. In a large pot, sauté the onion and garlic in the oil, about 5 minutes. Once they're soft, add the tomatoes, tomato paste, beans, and chili powder. Season with the salt.
2. Let simmer for at least 10 minutes, or as long as you like. The flavors will get better the longer it simmers, and it's even better as leftovers.
3. Garnish with cilantro and serve.

Options: Other beans have similar nutrients, so feel free to change up the kidney beans, if you prefer. Try black or adzuki beans or any dark bean. Spice it up with some hot sauce, if you like.

Per Serving (1 bowl)

Calories: 160; Total fat: 3g; Carbs: 29g; Fiber: 7g; Protein: 8g

Indian Red Split Lentil Soup

Makes 4 bowls
Prep time: 5 minutes / Cook time: 50 minutes

GLUTEN-FREE NUT-FREE QUICK PREP ANTI-INFLAMMATORY IMMUNE BOOSTER

This is a rich and hearty soup, with the bold and warming flavor of fresh ginger, plus Indian spices like coriander, cumin, and turmeric. Sweet potatoes are high in vitamin A, they add a soft sweetness to counter the spice, and as a root vegetable they help ground and concentrate the mind.

1 cup red split lentils

2 cups water

**1 teaspoon curry powder plus
   1 tablespoon, divided, or
   5 coriander seeds (optional)**

**1 teaspoon coconut oil, or
   1 tablespoon water or
   vegetable broth**

1 red onion, diced

1 tablespoon minced fresh ginger

**2 cups peeled and cubed
   sweet potato**

1 cup sliced zucchini

Freshly ground black pepper

Sea salt

**3 to 4 cups vegetable stock,
   or water**

1 to 2 teaspoons toasted sesame oil

1 bunch spinach, chopped

Toasted sesame seeds

1. Put the lentils in a large pot with 2 cups water, and 1 teaspoon of the curry powder. Bring the lentils to a boil, then reduce the heat and simmer, covered, for about 10 minutes, until the lentils are soft.

2. Meanwhile, heat a large pot over medium heat. Add the coconut oil and sauté the onion and ginger until soft, about 5 minutes. Add the sweet potato and leave it on the heat about 10 minutes to soften slightly, then add the zucchini and cook until it starts to look shiny, about 5 minutes. Add the remaining 1 tablespoon curry powder, pepper, and salt, and stir the vegetables to coat.

3. Add the vegetable stock, bring to a boil, then turn down to simmer and cover. Let the vegetables slowly cook for 20 to 30 minutes, or until the sweet potato is tender.

4. Add the fully cooked lentils to the soup. Add another pinch salt, the toasted sesame oil, and the spinach. Stir, allowing the spinach to wilt before removing the pot from the heat.

5. Serve garnished with toasted sesame seeds.

Did you know? Orange-fleshed sweet potatoes are the tastiest and are often called yams, although both the white and orange varieties are both technically sweet potatoes. True yams are a tropical tuber and are not usually sold in North America.

Per Serving (1 bowl)

Calories: 319; Total fat: 8g; Carbs: 50g; Fiber: 10g; Protein: 16g

Savory Split Pea Soup

Makes 6 bowls
Prep time: 15 minutes / Cook time: 60 to 75 minutes

GLUTEN-FREE NUT-FREE QUICK PREP ANTI-INFLAMMATORY

Pea soup is perfect for those cold winter days. It's great along with a fresh green salad. Peas have quite a bit of protein, along with iron and selenium. Including a carrot or zucchini in this rich soup brings extra nutrients and lightens up the flavor. Split pea soups traditionally include small pieces of bacon, but small pieces of sun-dried tomatoes or olives are a healthier way to get that pop of savory flavor. Stir in a little red wine at the end, if you have it, for a more full-bodied soup.

¼ cup white wine, or vegetable stock, or water

1 onion, chopped

1 to 2 garlic cloves, minced

1 cup split peas

2 bay leaves

1 tablespoon dried thyme

1 tablespoon dried oregano

3 to 4 cups water, or salt-free vegetable stock

1 large carrot, or zucchini, chopped (optional)

1 tablespoon miso, or tamari, or ¼ teaspoon sea salt

Pinch freshly ground black pepper

2 tablespoons nutritional yeast (optional)

¼ cup sun-dried tomatoes, or olives, chopped

¼ cup cherry tomatoes, chopped

2 tablespoons chopped scallions

1. In a large pot over medium-high heat add the wine, onion, and garlic. Stir them every so often until they're lightly cooked, about 5 minutes. Add the peas and the bay leaves, thyme, and oregano. Pour in the water and bring to a boil. (If you want a thick soup, use 3 cups liquid and add more if needed when you purée the soup.)

2. Cover and turn down to simmer. The peas will take about an hour to cook, but if you leave them to cook longer they'll get even softer.

3. Add the carrot (if using), about 20 minutes before you finish cooking the soup. This will allow it to soften but not overcook.

4. Once the peas are soft, take the bay leaves out and purée the soup in the blender or with an immersion blender. Return to the pot.

5. Stir in the miso, pepper, and nutritional yeast (if using), and then add the sun-dried tomatoes. They can be soaked before you add them to the soup, or let them soften in the soup for a few minutes.

6. Serve topped with cherry tomatoes and some scallions.

Make ahead: This recipe has one of the longest cooking times in the book. That's to let the peas cook properly, and to get the best flavor for the soup. This is a great one to make in a slow cooker, and you could leave it on low for the day.

Per Serving (1 bowl)

Calories: 183; Total fat: 1g; Carbs: 32g; Fiber: 12g; Protein: 12g

Basil Mango Jicama Salad

Makes 6 servings
Prep time: 15 minutes / Chill time: 1 hour

GLUTEN-FREE NUT-FREE QUICK PREP KID-FRIENDLY ANTI-INFLAMMATORY
IMMUNE BOOSTER

If you've never tried jicama, you're in for a treat. It's a root vegetable native to Central and South America, also called Mexican yam or Mexican turnip. It's not used in Asian dishes, but you can often find jicama being sold at markets in the "Chinatown" areas of North American cities. If you can't find jicama, this salad is fantastic with grated zucchini or parsnips. Dressed with mango and basil, this summer salad is full of flavor.

1 jicama, peeled and grated

1 mango, peeled and sliced

¼ cup non-dairy milk

2 tablespoons fresh basil, chopped

1 large scallion, chopped

⅛ teaspoon sea salt

1½ tablespoons tahini (optional)

Fresh greens (for serving)

Chopped cashews (optional,
 for serving)

Cheesy Sprinkle (page 229; optional,
 for serving)

1. Put the jicama in a large bowl.
2. Purée the mango in a food processor or blender, with just enough non-dairy milk to make a thick sauce. Add the basil, scallions, and salt. Stir in the tahini if you want to make a thicker, creamier, and more filling sauce.
3. Pour the dressing over the jicama and marinate, covered in the fridge, for 1 hour or more to break down some of the starch.
4. Serve over a bed of greens, topped with chopped cashews and/or Cheesy Sprinkle (if using).

Make ahead: This dish is best made ahead and kept in the fridge for a few hours. Make this in advance of a dinner party, as a starter or side salad, or keep it ready for yourself as a tasty side to meals throughout the week.

Per Serving

Calories: 76; Total fat: 2g; Carbs: 14g; Fiber: 5g; Protein: 1g

Roasted Beet and Avocado Salad

Makes 2 servings
Prep time: 10 minutes / Cook time: 30 minutes

GLUTEN-FREE GRAIN-FREE QUICK PREP

This is a gorgeous and delicious salad that my brother calls "restaurant level." It would be perfect paired with a bowl of Ginger Carrot Soup (page 106). Although they may stain your hands, beets are full of powerful nutrients that help protect against heart disease, birth defects, and certain cancers, especially colon cancer.

2 beets, peeled and thinly sliced

1 teaspoon olive oil

Pinch sea salt

1 avocado

2 cups mixed greens

3 to 4 tablespoons Creamy Balsamic Dressing (page 236)

2 tablespoons chopped almonds, pumpkin seeds, or sunflower seeds (raw or toasted)

Make ahead: Roast the beets in large batches and keep them in the refrigerator for various salads and wraps and to use on top of hummus toast. As a shortcut, you could also boil the beets whole, with their skin on, for 10 minutes and then let cool before peeling and slicing; finish cooking by roasting.

1. Preheat the oven to 400°F.

2. Put the beets, oil, and salt in a large bowl, and toss the beets with your hands to coat. Lay them in a single layer in a large baking dish, and roast them in the oven 20 to 30 minutes, or until they're softened and slightly browned around the edges.

3. While the beets are roasting, cut the avocado in half and take the pit out. Scoop the flesh out, as intact as possible, and slice it into crescents.

4. Once the beets are cooked, lay slices out on two plates and top each beet slice with a similar-size avocado slice. Top with a handful of mixed greens. Drizzle the dressing over everything, and sprinkle on a few chopped almonds.

Per Serving

Calories: 167; Total fat: 13g; Carbs: 15g; Fiber: 5g; Protein: 4g

Creamy Avocado-Dressed Kale Salad

Makes 4 servings
Prep time: 10 minutes / Cook time: 20 minutes

GLUTEN-FREE NUT-FREE QUICK PREP ANTI-INFLAMMATORY IMMUNE BOOSTER

Making a creamy dressing out of avocado is simple, quick, and so healthy. It will make any salad spectacular, coating the greens in creaminess. It's also one of those things you can flavor in an endless variety of ways. So, keep this dressing recipe in the back of your mind and explore the possibilities.

FOR THE DRESSING

1 avocado, peeled and pitted

1 tablespoon fresh lemon juice, or
   1 teaspoon lemon juice
   concentrate and
   2 teaspoons water

1 tablespoon fresh or dried dill

1 small garlic clove, pressed

1 scallion, chopped

Pinch sea salt

¼ cup water

FOR THE SALAD

8 large kale leaves

½ cup chopped green beans,
   raw or lightly steamed

1 cup cherry tomatoes, halved

1 bell pepper, chopped

2 scallions, chopped

2 cups cooked millet, or other
   cooked whole grain, such as
   quinoa or brown rice

Hummus (optional)

TO MAKE THE DRESSING

1. Put all the ingredients in a blender or food processor. Purée until smooth, then add water as necessary to get the consistency you're looking for in your dressing.

2. Taste for seasoning, and add more salt if you need to.

TO MAKE THE SALAD

1. Chop the kale, removing the stems if you want your salad less bitter, and then massage the leaves with your fingers until it wilts and gets a bit moist, about 2 minutes. You can use a pinch salt if you like to help it soften.

2. Toss the kale with the green beans, cherry tomatoes, bell pepper, scallions, millet, and the dressing.

3. Pile the salad onto plates, and top them off with a spoonful of hummus (if using).

Options: Try lime juice and fresh mint, or rice vinegar and fresh cilantro, instead of lemon and dill.

Per Serving

Calories: 225; Total fat: 7g; Carbs: 37g; Fiber: 7g; Protein: 7g

Wilted Sesame-Miso Kale Salad

Makes 2 servings
Prep time: 20 minutes / Cook time: 20 minutes

GLUTEN-FREE GRAIN-FREE ANTI-INFLAMMATORY IMMUNE BOOSTER

If you want to eat kale but don't like it raw, try this wilting technique. Massaging kale before putting it in a salad or steaming or stir-frying it softens it enough to make it both delicious and much more easily digested. Kale is full of antioxidants, calcium, and other nutrients, so it is a good thing to get more of in your diet. Pairing it with a salty dressing neutralizes its bitterness, so you can enjoy a tasty and super nutritious salad.

1 beet

3 large mushrooms, sliced

1 tablespoon tamari, or soy sauce

3 to 4 large kale leaves

Sea salt

½ head broccoli, chopped

3 to 4 tablespoons Toasted Sesame Miso Dressing (page 237)

2 tablespoons chopped toasted almonds, or pumpkin seeds

1. Boil the beet whole, with the skin on, for 20 minutes. Leave it to cool, then remove the skin and chop.

2. Marinate the mushrooms by putting the slices in a container, sprinkling the tamari on them, putting a lid on the container, and shaking it vigorously. This will draw moisture out of the mushrooms and they will wilt and soften. Marinate for a few minutes, or up to 5 hours if you want them really soft.

3. Prepare the kale by chopping it up, sprinkling some sea salt over it, and massaging with your fingers until it releases some moisture and starts to wilt, about 2 minutes. You can do the same thing to the broccoli if you want to soften it a bit.

4. Toss the beets, mushrooms, and kale together in a large bowl. Toss with the dressing, and top with almonds.

Make ahead: Boil a bunch of beets at once and keep them in the refrigerator, so you have them on hand to add to various meals. If you only half-boil them (about 10 minutes), you could finish them off by roasting.

Per Serving

Calories: 265; Total fat: 12g; Carbs: 30g; Fiber: 9g; Protein: 14g

Moroccan Aubergine Salad

Makes 2 servings

Prep time: 30 minutes / Cook time: 15 minutes

GLUTEN-FREE NUT-FREE KID-FRIENDLY ANTI-INFLAMMATORY IMMUNE BOOSTER

This salad uses lightly sautéed and spiced eggplant (called by its French name, aubergine, in Europe and many other parts of the world) with lemon and capers for some zesty Moroccan flavors. Eggplant is rich in phytonutrients, like nasunin, which is a free radical scavenger that protects the fats in brain cell membranes, and chlorogenic acid, which has anticancer, antimicrobial, anti-LDL (bad cholesterol), and antiviral benefits. It's a nightshade vegetable, related to the tomato, bell pepper, and potato. If you're sensitive to nightshades or have arthritis, try this dish with mushrooms instead.

1 teaspoon olive oil

1 eggplant, diced

½ teaspoon ground cumin

½ teaspoon ground ginger

¼ teaspoon turmeric

¼ teaspoon ground nutmeg

Pinch sea salt

1 lemon, half zested and juiced, half cut into wedges

2 tablespoons capers

1 tablespoon chopped green olives

1 garlic clove, pressed

Handful fresh mint, finely chopped

2 cups spinach, chopped

1. Heat the oil in a large skillet on medium heat, then sauté the eggplant. Once it has softened slightly, about 5 minutes, stir in the cumin, ginger, turmeric, nutmeg, and salt. Cook until the eggplant is very soft, about 10 minutes.

2. Add the lemon zest and juice, capers, olives, garlic, and mint. Sauté for another minute or two, to blend the flavors.

3. Put a handful of spinach on each plate, and spoon the eggplant mixture on top. Serve with a wedge of lemon, to squeeze the fresh juice over the greens.

Technique: To tenderize the eggplant and reduce some of its naturally occurring bitter taste, you can sweat the eggplant by salting it. After dicing the eggplant, sprinkle it with salt and let it sit in a colander for about 30 minutes. Rinse the eggplant to remove the salt, then continue with the recipe as written.

Options: Instead of the cumin, ginger, turmeric, and nutmeg, you can use 1½ teaspoons mild curry powder or ras el hanout, a North African spice blend.

Per Serving

Calories: 97; Total fat: 4g; Carbs: 16g; Fiber: 8g; Protein: 4g

Dill Potato Salad

Makes 4 servings
Prep time: 15 minutes / Cook time: 20 minutes

GLUTEN-FREE NUT-FREE QUICK PREP KID-FRIENDLY

Potato salad is the quintessential North American summer picnic or barbecue dish. We can make it healthier by making a creamy dressing that doesn't rely on mayonnaise and pairing those potatoes with zucchini for a nutritional boost.

6 medium potatoes, scrubbed and chopped into bite-size pieces

1 zucchini, chopped (same size pieces as the potatoes)

¼ cup chopped fresh dill, or about 2 tablespoons dried

1 to 2 teaspoons Dijon mustard

⅛ teaspoon sea salt

Freshly ground black pepper

1 tablespoon nutritional yeast (optional)

Non-dairy milk or water (optional)

3 celery stalks, chopped

1 green or red bell pepper, seeded and chopped

1 tablespoon chopped chives, or scallions

Options: Make it a meal served over a bed of fresh or steamed greens, or enjoy this as a side dish with the Maple Dijon Burgers (page 140) or the Grilled Porto-bello (page 183).

1. Fill a large pot about a quarter of the way with water and bring to a boil. Add the potatoes and boil 10 minutes. Add the zucchini to the pot after 10 minutes, and boil an additional 10 minutes. Remove the pot from the heat and drain the water, reserving about 1 cup liquid. Set the cooked vegetables aside in a large bowl to cool.

2. Take about ½ cup potatoes and transfer them to a blender or food processor, along with the reserved cooking liquid and the dill, mustard, salt, pepper, and nutritional yeast (if using). Purée until smooth. If you need to, add a little non-dairy milk or water for the consistency you want.

3. Toss the celery, bell pepper, and chives in with the cooked potatoes and zucchini. Pour the dressing over them and toss to coat.

Per Serving

Calories: 246; Total fat: 1g; Carbs: 55g; Fiber: 7g; Protein: 8g

Tuscan White Bean Salad

Makes 2 servings
Prep time: 10 minutes / Marinating time: 30 minutes

GLUTEN-FREE NUT-FREE QUICK PREP ANTI-INFLAMMATORY IMMUNE BOOSTER

Imagine yourself in Florence, sitting by the side of the Arno river and enjoying a bite of fresh local flavors. This salad is made from produce that could be found at a local market in Florence, inviting the soft, warm flavors of Tuscany into your kitchen.

FOR THE DRESSING

1 tablespoon olive oil

2 tablespoons balsamic vinegar

1 teaspoon minced fresh chives, or scallions

1 garlic clove, pressed or minced

1 tablespoon fresh rosemary, chopped, or 1 teaspoon dried

1 tablespoon fresh oregano, chopped, or 1 teaspoon dried

Pinch sea salt

FOR THE SALAD

1 (14-ounce) can cannellini beans, drained and rinsed, or 1½ cups cooked

6 mushrooms, thinly sliced

1 zucchini, diced

2 carrots, diced

2 tablespoons fresh basil, chopped

1. Make the dressing by whisking all the dressing ingredients together in a large bowl.

2. Toss all the salad ingredients with the dressing. For the best flavor, put the salad in a sealed container, shake it vigorously, and leave to marinate 15 to 30 minutes.

Options: The cannellini bean is local to the Tuscany region of Italy and is the white version of the kidney bean. Feel free to swap another white bean, like navy or flageolet, if you can't find or don't like cannellini.

Per Serving

Calories: 360; Total fat: 8g; Carbs: 68g; Fiber: 15g; Protein: 18g

Tabbouleh Salad

Makes 4 servings
Prep time: 15 minutes / Cook time: 10 minutes

NUT-FREE QUICK PREP ANTI-INFLAMMATORY IMMUNE BOOSTER

Tabbouleh is a lovely and fresh summer salad and makes a perfect side dish with baked falafel patties (in the recipe for Falafel Wrap, page 148). Tabbouleh relies heavily on parsley, a nutrient-dense superstar that too often is relegated to garnish status. With the ¼ cup in each serving of this salad, it adds just 10 calories, and gives you 47 percent of your daily vitamin A intake (for healthy eyes and skin), 10 percent iron intake (for energy), 62 percent vitamin C intake (for immunity and iron absorption), 11 percent folate intake (for healthy blood and brain function), 4 percent calcium intake (for bones, heart, muscles, and nerves), and 574 percent vitamin K intake (for bone mineralization).

1 cup whole-wheat couscous

1 cup boiling water

Zest and juice of 1 lemon

1 garlic clove, pressed

Pinch sea salt

1 tablespoon olive oil, or flaxseed oil (optional)

½ cucumber, diced small

1 tomato, diced small

1 cup fresh parsley, chopped

¼ cup fresh mint, finely chopped

2 scallions, finely chopped

4 tablespoons sunflower seeds (optional)

1. Put the couscous in a medium bowl, and cover with boiling water until all the grains are submerged. Cover the bowl with a plate or wrap. Set aside.

2. Put the lemon zest and juice in a large salad bowl, then stir in the garlic, salt, and the olive oil (if using). Put the cucumber, tomato, parsley, mint, and scallions in the bowl, and toss them to coat with the dressing.

3. Take the plate off the couscous and fluff with a fork. Add the cooked couscous to the vegetables, and toss to combine.

4. Serve topped with the sunflower seeds (if using).

Options: If you want to go more authentic, tabbouleh is made traditionally with cracked bulgur wheat. Or branch into new flavors and textures and try quinoa (which will make this dish gluten-free). You can make the grain in a large batch ahead of time, and toss it in chilled.

Per Serving

Calories: 304; Total fat: 11g; Carbs: 44g; Fiber: 6g; Protein: 10g

Forbidden Black Rice and Edamame Salad

Makes 4 servings
Prep time: 10 minutes / Cook time: 30 minutes

GLUTEN-FREE NUT-FREE QUICK PREP ANTI-INFLAMMATORY IMMUNE BOOSTER

Edamame are the young green pods of soybeans and are packed with protein, vitamin K, and folate. Red bell pepper is rich in immune-boosting vitamins A and C and adds a sweet crunch to this salad, complemented perfectly by the soft sweetness of roasted sweet potato. Black rice adds antioxidants, iron, and fiber, though you can use brown rice if you can't find black. This is lovely with Toasted Sesame Miso Dressing (page 237), but the sweet-salty orange dressing here is divine.

FOR THE SALAD

1 cup black rice

2 cups water

Pinch sea salt

1 large sweet potato

1 teaspoon olive oil

1 cup shelled frozen
    edamame, thawed

1 red bell pepper, seeded
    and chopped

½ head broccoli, chopped

4 scallions, chopped

Fresh cilantro, chopped

Sesame seeds

FOR THE DRESSING

Juice of ½ orange, or ½ cup pure
    orange juice

1 tablespoon soy sauce

1 tablespoon rice vinegar, or apple
    cider vinegar

2 teaspoons maple syrup

2 teaspoons sesame oil

1. Preheat the oven to 400°F.
2. Put the rice in a medium pot with the water and salt. Bring to a boil over high heat, then cover and simmer for 30 minutes, or until it's soft.
3. While the rice is cooking, peel and dice the sweet potato into small cubes and toss with the olive oil. Spread the cubes in a 9-inch square baking dish and roast 15 to 20 minutes, or until the cubes are tender.
4. While the rice and sweet potato cubes are cooling, combine all the ingredients for the dressing in a jar and shake well.
5. In a large bowl, combine the rice, sweet potato, edamame, bell pepper, broccoli, and scallions. Pour on the dressing and toss. Top with a sprinkle of chopped fresh cilantro and sesame seeds.

Did you know? Black rice is lower in carbs but higher in fiber and a better source of protein than brown rice. Plus, it has more antioxidants. The pigment that makes it black is anthocyanin—the same pigment in blueberries and eggplant skin.

Per Serving

Calories: 445; Total fat: 11g; Carbs: 75g; Fiber: 11g; Protein: 15g

Warm Lentil Salad with Red Wine Vinaigrette

Makes 4 servings
Prep time: 10 minutes / Cook time: 50 minutes

GLUTEN-FREE NUT-FREE QUICK PREP ANTI-INFLAMMATORY IMMUNE BOOSTER

Adding lentils to a green salad gives it more substance, so it's more of a meal than a side dish. Pairing greens with lentils is great way to make the lentils easier to digest and help your body absorb the protein and calcium they offer. The tangy-savory Cheesy Sprinkle (page 229) is a perfect contrast to the earthy lentils.

1 teaspoon olive oil plus ¼ cup, divided, or 1 tablespoon vegetable broth or water

1 small onion, diced

1 garlic clove, minced

1 carrot, diced

1 cup lentils

1 tablespoon dried basil

1 tablespoon dried oregano

1 tablespoon red wine or balsamic vinegar (optional)

2 cups water

¼ cup red wine vinegar or balsamic vinegar

1 teaspoon sea salt

2 cups chopped Swiss chard

2 cups torn red leaf lettuce

4 tablespoons Cheesy Sprinkle (page 229)

1. Heat 1 teaspoon of the oil in a large pot on medium heat, then sauté the onion and garlic until they are translucent, about 5 minutes.

2. Add the carrot and sauté until it is slightly cooked, about 3 minutes.

3. Stir in the lentils, basil, and oregano, then add the wine or balsamic vinegar (if using). Pour the water into the pot and turn the heat up to high to bring to a boil. Turn the heat down to a simmer and let the lentils cook, uncovered, 20 to 30 minutes, until they are soft but not falling apart.

4. While the lentils are cooking, whisk together the red wine vinegar, olive oil, and salt in a small bowl and set aside.

5. Once the lentils have cooked, drain any excess liquid and stir in most of the red wine vinegar dressing. Set a little bit of dressing aside. Add the Swiss chard to the pot and stir it into the lentils. Leave the heat on low and cook, stirring, for at least 10 minutes.

6. Toss the lettuce with the remaining dressing. Place some lettuce on a plate, and top with the lentil mixture. Finish the plate off with a little Cheesy Sprinkle and enjoy!

Did you know? Swiss chard is a relative of the beet plant, and the kind that has red stems shares the powerful phytonutrients that are in beets.

Per Serving

Calories: 387; Total fat: 17g; Carbs: 42g; Fiber: 19g; Protein: 18g

Cashew-Ginger Soba Noodle Bowl page 152

chapter 9

MAIN DISHES

Curry Spiced Lentil Burgers 138

Maple Dijon Burgers 140

Cajun Burgers 142

Grilled AHLT 144

Loaded Black Bean Pizza 145

Mediterranean Hummus
Pizza 146

Curried Mango Chickpea
Wrap 147

Falafel Wrap 148

Pad Thai Bowl 150

Miso-Coconut Dragon Bowl 151

Cashew-Ginger Soba Noodle
Bowl 152

Black Bean Taco Salad Bowl 154

Bibimbap Bowl 156

Avocado Red Pepper Sushi
Rolls 158

Spicy Chickpea Sushi Rolls 160

Sushi Bowl 162

Sweet Potato Patties 163

Vietnamese Summer Rolls 164

Potato Skin Samosas 166

Simple Sesame Stir-Fry 168

Creamy Mint-Lime Spaghetti
Squash 170

Sun-dried Tomato and Pesto
Quinoa 172

Olive and White Bean Pasta 173

Spaghetti and Buckwheat
Meatballs 174

Orange Walnut Pasta 176

Roasted Cauliflower Tacos 178

Build Your Own Mushroom
Fajitas 180

Blackeye Pea Burritos 182

Grilled Portobello with
Mashed Potatoes and Green
Beans 183

Shepherd's Pie 186

Curry Spiced Lentil Burgers

Makes 12 burgers
Prep time: 40 minutes / Cook time: 30 to 40 minutes

GLUTEN-FREE NUT-FREE ANTI-INFLAMMATORY IMMUNE BOOSTER

When I first started making veggie burgers, I struggled to get a good texture that stuck together but wasn't too bean-heavy. I tried a lot of recipes before merging aspects of a few into my own version, using carrots and lots of spices to lighten up the lentils. These burgers come out thick and hearty, with tons of flavor and nutrition.

1 cup lentils

2½ to 3 cups water

3 carrots, grated

1 small onion, diced

**¾ cup whole-grain flour
(see Options for gluten-free
on next page)**

1½ to 2 teaspoons curry powder

½ teaspoon sea salt

Pinch freshly ground black pepper

1. Put the lentils in a medium pot with the water. Bring to a boil and then simmer for about 30 minutes, until soft.

2. While the lentils are cooking, put the carrots and onion in a large bowl. Toss them with the flour, curry powder, salt, and pepper.

3. When the lentils are cooked, drain off any excess water, then add them to the bowl with the veggies. Use a potato masher or a large spoon to mash them slightly, and add more flour if you need to get the mixture to stick together. The amount of flour depends on how much water the lentils absorbed, and on the texture of the flour, so use more or less until the mixture sticks when you form it into a ball. Scoop up ¼-cup portions and form into 12 patties.

4. You can either panfry or bake the burgers. To panfry, heat a large skillet to medium, add a tiny bit of oil, and cook the burgers about 10 minutes on the first side. Flip, and cook another 5 to 7 minutes. To bake them, put them on a baking sheet lined with parchment paper and bake at 350°F for 30 to 40 minutes.

Options: For the whole-grain flour, use whatever flour you like. Sorghum, rice, oat, buckwheat, and even almond meal would work and make these gluten-free. The flour in this recipe is just a binding agent, so it can be any type.

Per Serving (1 burger)

Calories: 114; Total fat: 1g; Carbs: 22g; Fiber: 7g; Protein: 6g

Maple Dijon Burgers

Makes 12 burgers

Prep time: 20 minutes / Cook time: 30 minutes

KID-FRIENDLY ANTI-INFLAMMATORY IMMUNE BOOSTER

A lot of the fun in veggie burgers comes from what you decide to top them with. You can mix 'n' match the burger with the topping, based on the flavors in the burger. These go nicely with some pickle slices, Avo-nnaise (page 238), cherry tomatoes, and lettuce.

1 red bell pepper

1 (19-ounce) can chickpeas, rinsed and drained, or 2 cups cooked

1 cup ground almonds

2 teaspoons Dijon mustard

2 teaspoons maple syrup

1 garlic clove, pressed

Juice of ½ lemon

1 teaspoon dried oregano

½ teaspoon dried sage

1 cup spinach

1 to 1½ cups rolled oats

1. Preheat the oven to 350°F. Line a large baking sheet with parchment paper.

2. Cut the red pepper in half, remove the stem and seeds, and put on the baking sheet cut side up in the oven. Roast in the oven while you prep the other ingredients.

3. Put the chickpeas in the food processor, along with the almonds, mustard, maple syrup, garlic, lemon juice, oregano, sage, and spinach. Pulse until things are thoroughly combined but not puréed. When the red pepper is softened a bit, about 10 minutes, add it to the processor along with the oats and pulse until they are chopped just enough to form patties.

4. If you don't have a food processor, mash the chickpeas with a potato masher or fork, and make sure everything else is chopped up as finely as possible, then stir together.

5. Scoop up ¼-cup portions and form into 12 patties, and lay them out on the baking sheet.

6. Put the burgers in the oven and bake until the outside is lightly browned, about 30 minutes.

Technique: It's important not to purée the ingredients, because you want texture to your burgers, not mush. Use short pulses in the processor, until the ingredients are just chopped.

Per Serving (1 burger)

Calories: 200; Total fat: 11g; Carbs: 21g; Fiber: 6g; Protein: 8g

Cajun Burgers

Makes 5 to 6 burgers

Prep time: 25 minutes / Cook time: 10 to 30 minutes

GLUTEN-FREE NUT-FREE ANTI-INFLAMMATORY

These burgers are made with a base of toasted buckwheat (also known as kasha), which has a flavonoid called rutin, contains plant lignans, and is a good source of magnesium—all of which are cardio-protective. The nutrients in buckwheat may also help with blood sugar control. Pair that nutrition with some amazing flavors, form it into a burger, and you have one of the best meals ever.

FOR THE DRESSING

1 tablespoon tahini

1 tablespoon apple cider vinegar

2 teaspoons Dijon mustard

1 to 2 tablespoons water

1 to 2 garlic cloves, pressed

1 teaspoon dried basil

1 teaspoon dried thyme

½ teaspoon dried oregano

½ teaspoon dried sage

½ teaspoon smoked paprika

¼ teaspoon cayenne pepper

¼ teaspoon sea salt

Pinch freshly ground black pepper

FOR THE BURGERS

2 cups water

1 cup kasha (toasted buckwheat)

Pinch sea salt

2 carrots, grated

Handful fresh parsley, chopped

1 teaspoon olive oil (optional)

TO MAKE THE DRESSING

1. In a medium bowl, whisk together the tahini, vinegar, and mustard until the mixture is very thick. Add 1 to 2 tablespoons water to thin it out, and whisk again until smooth.

2. Stir in the rest of the ingredients. Set aside for the flavors to blend.

TO MAKE THE BURGERS

1. Put the water, buckwheat, and sea salt in a medium pot. Bring to a boil and let boil for 2 to 3 minutes, then turn down to low, cover, and simmer for 15 minutes. Buckwheat is fully cooked when it is soft and no liquid is left at the bottom of the pot. Do not stir the buckwheat while it is cooking.

2. Once the buckwheat is cooked, transfer it to a large bowl. Stir the grated carrot, fresh parsley, and all the dressing into the buckwheat. Scoop up ¼-cup portions and form into patties.

3. You can either panfry or bake the burgers. To panfry, heat a large skillet to medium, add 1 teaspoon olive oil, and cook the burgers about 5 minutes on the first side. Flip, and cook another 5 minutes. To bake them, put them on a baking sheet lined with parchment paper and bake at 350°F for about 30 minutes.

Did you know? Buckwheat is not related to wheat. It's actually a seed, and is gluten-free. It has a different nutrient profile than whole grains, too. Buckwheat is high in the amino acid lysine, which helps balance a plant-based diet, since many plant foods are high in the other amino acids but low in lysine. Other lysine-rich foods include beans and legumes, quinoa, and pistachios.

Per Serving (1 burger)

Calories: 124; Total fat: 2g; Carbs: 24g; Fiber: 4g; Protein: 4g

Grilled AHLT

Makes 1 sandwich

Prep time: 5 minutes / Cook time: 10 minutes

NUT-FREE QUICK PREP KID-FRIENDLY ANTI-INFLAMMATORY

Make a healthy and delicious twist on a BLT, substituting avocado and hummus for the bacon. Since it's grilled, I've also swapped spinach for the lettuce. You could also use massaged kale if you like, massaging it with your fingers until it wilts and gets a bit moist. This is perfect as a quick dinner, along with some Baked Sweet Potato Fries (page 204).

¼ cup Classic Hummus (page 197)

2 slices whole-grain bread

¼ avocado, sliced

½ cup lettuce, chopped

½ tomato, sliced

Pinch sea salt

Pinch freshly ground black pepper

1 teaspoon olive oil, divided

Technique: You can also toast the bread and assemble as a simple sandwich, or brush the bread with olive oil, assemble the sandwich, and put in the toaster oven for 10 to 15 minutes at 350°F.

1. Spread some hummus on each slice of bread. Then layer the avocado, lettuce, and tomato on one slice, sprinkle with salt and pepper, and top with the other slice.

2. Heat a skillet to medium heat, and drizzle ½ teaspoon of the olive oil just before putting the sandwich in the skillet. Cook for 3 to 5 minutes, then lift the sandwich with a spatula, drizzle the remaining ½ teaspoon olive oil into the skillet, and flip the sandwich to grill the other side for 3 to 5 minutes. Press it down with the spatula to seal the vegetables inside.

3. Once done, remove from the skillet and slice in half to serve.

Per Serving

Calories: 322; Total fat: 14g; Carbs: 40g; Fiber: 11g; Protein: 12g

Loaded Black Bean Pizza

Makes 2 small pizzas
Prep time: 10 minutes / Cook time: 10 to 20 minutes

GLUTEN-FREE NUT-FREE QUICK PREP KID-FRIENDLY IMMUNE BOOSTER

This pizza is not only super tasty but is loaded with delicious fresh vegetables. You can bake it, or try it with raw toppings for a summer twist. Using a bean dip as the sauce on your pizza gives you a protein boost. You have a lot of crust options here. Go store-bought with two whole-grain pitas or wraps, or make it yourself with one Easy DIY Pizza Crust (page 234) or Herbed Millet Pizza Crust (page 232), divided to make two pizzas.

2 prebaked pizza crusts

½ cup Spicy Black Bean Dip (page 200)

1 tomato, thinly sliced

Pinch freshly ground black pepper

1 carrot, grated

Pinch sea salt

1 red onion, thinly sliced

1 avocado, sliced

Options: Try having this as a fresh unbaked pizza. Just toast a pita or bake the crust before loading it up, and perhaps use scallions instead of red. Bonus points—and flavor—if you top it with fresh alfalfa sprouts.

1. Preheat the oven to 400°F.

2. Lay the two crusts out on a large baking sheet. Spread half the Spicy Black Bean Dip on each pizza crust. Then layer on the tomato slices with a pinch pepper if you like.

3. Sprinkle the grated carrot with the sea salt and lightly massage it in with your hands. Spread the carrot on top of the tomato, then add the onion.

4. Pop the pizzas in the oven for 10 to 20 minutes, or until they're done to your taste.

5. Top the cooked pizzas with sliced avocado and another sprinkle of pepper.

Per Serving (1 pizza)

Calories: 379; Total fat: 13g; Carbs: 59g; Fiber: 15g; Protein: 13g

Mediterranean Hummus Pizza

Makes 2 small pizzas
Prep time: 10 minutes / Cook time: 20 to 30 minutes

GLUTEN-FREE NUT-FREE QUICK PREP KID-FRIENDLY ANTI-INFLAMMATORY
IMMUNE BOOSTER

This is a favorite go-to weeknight meal in my house, since everything is usually on hand and it comes together quickly for a satisfying meal. Pile these pizzas high with vegetables—make as much or as little of a mountain as you like. The olives give a nice savory pop to the pizza, but if you don't want them, try some chopped sun-dried tomatoes instead. You can use two whole-grain pitas or wraps for the crust, or make it yourself with one Easy DIY Pizza Crust (page 234) or Herbed Millet Pizza Crust (page 232), divided to make two pizzas.

½ **zucchini, thinly sliced**

½ **red onion, thinly sliced**

1 cup **cherry tomatoes, halved**

2 to 4 tablespoons **pitted and chopped black olives**

Pinch sea salt

Drizzle olive oil (optional)

2 **prebaked pizza crusts**

½ cup **Classic Hummus (page 197), or Roasted Red Pepper Hummus (page 197)**

2 to 4 tablespoons **Cheesy Sprinkle (page 229)**

1. Preheat the oven to 400°F.

2. Place the zucchini, onion, cherry tomatoes, and olives in a large bowl, sprinkle them with the sea salt, and toss them a bit. Drizzle with a bit of olive oil (if using), to seal in the flavor and keep them from drying out in the oven.

3. Lay the two crusts out on a large baking sheet. Spread half the hummus on each crust, and top with the veggie mixture and some Cheesy Sprinkle.

4. Pop the pizzas in the oven for 20 to 30 minutes, or until the veggies are soft.

Make Ahead: For a shortcut, lightly sauté the veggies before putting them on the pizza, so you only have to bake it for a few minutes until warmed through. You could even use some leftover sautéed vegetables.

Per Serving (1 pizza)

Calories: 500; Total fat: 25g; Carbs: 58g; Fiber: 12g; Protein: 19g

Curried Mango Chickpea Wrap

Makes 3 wraps
Prep time: 15 minutes

NUT-FREE QUICK PREP KID-FRIENDLY ANTI-INFLAMMATORY

Sweet mango paired with curry and flavored by calcium-rich tahini is perfection. Have it for dinner; you could heat the vegetables and chickpeas before putting them in the wrap, and then pack leftovers for lunch on the go. Just be sure to bring napkins, because these get a bit messy.

3 tablespoons tahini

Zest and juice of 1 lime

1 tablespoon curry powder

¼ teaspoon sea salt

3 to 4 tablespoons water

1 (14-ounce) can chickpeas, rinsed and drained, or 1½ cups cooked

1 cup diced mango

1 red bell pepper, seeded and diced small

½ cup fresh cilantro, chopped

3 large whole-grain wraps

1 to 2 cups shredded green leaf lettuce

1. In a medium bowl, whisk together the tahini, lime zest and juice, curry powder, and salt until the mixture is creamy and thick. Add 3 to 4 tablespoons water to thin it out a bit. Or you can process this all in a blender. The taste should be strong and salty, to flavor the whole salad.

2. Toss the chickpeas, mango, bell pepper, and cilantro with the tahini dressing.

3. Spoon the salad down the center of the wraps, top with shredded lettuce, and then roll up and enjoy.

Options: Substitute lettuce leaves for whole-grain wraps. Use a sturdy type of lettuce, like Boston, Bibb, or butter lettuce, or spoon the filling into endive leaves if you're okay with their slightly bitter flavor.

Per Serving (1 wrap)

Calories: 437; Total fat: 8g; Carbs: 79g; Fiber: 12g; Protein: 15g

Falafel Wrap

Makes 6 patties, 1 wrap
Prep time: 30 minutes / Cook time: 30 to 40 minutes

NUT-FREE KID-FRIENDLY IMMUNE BOOSTER

Falafel and hummus are probably the two most popular chickpea dishes in global cuisine—so put them together in a wrap. Infuse your falafel with nutrient-dense additions like parsley and bake or panfry, rather than deep-frying, for plant-powered goodness. This recipe is for one wrap, but because making falafel takes a little time, the recipe makes six patties— enough for six wraps. Just make more wraps for the whole gang, or I'll give you some tips below about what to do with the leftover falafel.

FOR THE FALAFEL PATTIES

1 (14-ounce) can chickpeas, drained and rinsed, or 1½ cups cooked

1 zucchini, grated

2 scallions, minced

¼ cup fresh parsley, chopped

2 tablespoons black olives, pitted and chopped (optional)

1 tablespoon tahini, or almond, cashew, or sunflower seed butter

1 tablespoon lemon juice, or apple cider vinegar

½ teaspoon ground cumin

¼ teaspoon paprika

¼ teaspoon sea salt

1 teaspoon olive oil (optional, if frying)

FOR THE WRAP

1 whole-grain wrap or pita

¼ cup Classic Hummus (page 197)

½ cup fresh greens

1 baked falafel patty

¼ cup cherry tomatoes, halved

¼ cup diced cucumber

¼ cup chopped avocado, or Guacamole (page 203)

¼ cup cooked quinoa, or Tabbouleh Salad (page 130; optional)

TO MAKE THE FALAFEL

1. Use a food processor to pulse the chickpeas, zucchini, scallions, parsley, and olives (if using) until roughly chopped. Just pulse—don't purée. Or use a potato masher to mash the chickpeas in a large bowl and stir in the grated and chopped veggies.

2. In a small bowl, whisk together the tahini and lemon juice, and stir in the cumin, paprika, and salt. Pour this into the chickpea mixture, and stir well (or pulse the food processor) to combine. Taste and add more salt, if needed. Using your hands, form the mix into 6 patties.

3. You can either panfry or bake the patties. To panfry, heat a large skillet to medium, add 1 teaspoon of olive oil, and cook the patties about 10 minutes on the first side. Flip, and cook another 5 to 7 minutes. To bake them, put them on a baking sheet lined with parchment paper and bake at 350°F for 30 to 40 minutes.

TO MAKE THE WRAP

1. Lay the wrap on a plate and spread the hummus down the center. Then lay on the greens and crumble the falafel patty on top. Add the tomatoes, cucumber, avocado, and quinoa.

2. Fold in both ends, and wrap up as tightly as you can. If you have a sandwich press, you can press the wraps for about 5 minutes. This will travel best in a reusable lunch box, or reusable plastic lunch wrap.

Leftovers: Store the rest of the patties in an airtight container in the fridge for up to one week, or in the freezer for up to two months. Have them as burgers, topped with your favorite condiments (the Greens and Beans Dip on page 202 pairs nicely), crumbled atop a salad, or as stand-alone patties with a side of Creamy Avocado-Dressed Kale Salad (page 122).

Per Serving (1 wrap)

Calories: 546; Total fat: 19g; Carbs: 81g; Fiber: 14g; Protein: 18g

Pad Thai Bowl

Makes 2 bowls
Prep time: 10 minutes / Cook time: 10 minutes

GLUTEN-FREE QUICK PREP IMMUNE BOOSTER

Pad thai is usually made with eggs and fish sauce, so it's hard for plant-based eaters to get their fix. Not to worry, though, because you can make your own—and infuse so much flavor that you'll prefer this to the restaurant version. Plus, you can pack it full of fresh and flavorful vegetables to boost the nutrient density. Rather than just peanuts on top, you can infuse that peanutty goodness right into the sauce, and slurp it up.

7 ounces brown rice noodles

1 teaspoon olive oil, or 1 tablespoon vegetable broth or water

2 carrots, peeled or scrubbed, and julienned

1 cup thinly sliced napa cabbage, or red cabbage

1 red bell pepper, seeded and thinly sliced

2 scallions, finely chopped

2 to 3 tablespoons fresh mint, finely chopped

1 cup bean sprouts

¼ cup Peanut Sauce (page 239)

¼ cup fresh cilantro, finely chopped

2 tablespoons roasted peanuts, chopped

Fresh lime wedges

1. Put the rice noodles in a large bowl or pot, and cover with boiling water. Let sit until they soften, about 10 minutes. Rinse, drain, and set aside to cool.

2. Heat the oil in a large skillet to medium-high, and sauté the carrots, cabbage, and bell pepper until softened, 7 to 8 minutes. Toss in the scallions, mint, and bean sprouts and cook for just a minute or two, then remove from the heat.

3. Toss the noodles with the vegetables, and mix in the Peanut Sauce.

4. Transfer to bowls, and sprinkle with cilantro and peanuts. Serve with a lime wedge to squeeze onto the dish for a flavor boost.

Options: To enjoy an even more nutrient-dense version of this bowl, leave out the rice noodles and peel or spiralize a zucchini or carrot into long "noodles."

Per Serving

Calories: 660; Total fat: 19g;
Carbs: 110g; Fiber: 10g; Protein: 15g

Miso-Coconut Dragon Bowl

Makes 1 bowl

Prep time: 10 minutes / Cook time: 20 minutes

GLUTEN-FREE QUICK PREP **ANTI-INFLAMMATORY** IMMUNE BOOSTER

This salty, creamy bowl is simple to make, and yet tasty and nutritious. It is oil-free, but the fat content of the coconut milk makes it satisfying. When choosing a coconut milk, the low-fat varieties are okay if you look for a can that lists only coconut, water, and guar gum as ingredients. Guar gum is a plant-derived soluble fiber that helps thicken the coconut milk when some of the fat is filtered out.

FOR THE BOWL

1 teaspoon coconut oil, or vegetable
  broth or water

½ red onion, thinly sliced

Pinch sea salt

½ cup brown mushrooms, sliced

½ cup cherry tomatoes, halved

FOR THE DRESSING

2 tablespoons fresh mint,
  finely chopped

¼ cup canned coconut milk

1 to 2 teaspoons miso paste

1 teaspoon coconut sugar, or maple
  syrup (optional)

FOR SERVING

¾ cup cooked quinoa, or millet,
  brown rice, or any other
  whole grain

1 cup baby arugula, or spinach
  (if mature leaves, chopped)

1 tablespoon slivered almonds

1. Heat the oil in a medium skillet over medium heat and lightly sauté the onion with the salt, about 5 minutes. Add the mushrooms, cooking until they're fully softened. Then add the cherry tomatoes and cook until just softened, about 10 minutes total.

2. Make the dressing by whisking or puréeing the mint, coconut milk, miso paste, and coconut sugar or maple syrup (if using) together in a medium bowl. Stir this into the cooked vegetables, then remove them from the heat.

3. Serve the cooked vegetables over the quinoa, with the arugula on top and the almonds to garnish.

Options: You could use green or red curry paste instead of miso for a delicious curry bowl.

Per Serving

Calories: 495; Total fat: 27g; Carbs: 54g; Fiber: 10g; Protein: 14g

Cashew-Ginger Soba Noodle Bowl

Makes 2 bowls
Prep time: 5 minutes / Cook time: 20 minutes

GLUTEN-FREE QUICK PREP IMMUNE BOOSTER

This is a lovely dish served cold in summer or warm in winter. Soba are
thin Japanese noodles made of buckwheat flour, so they are generally
gluten-free. But check the ingredients, as some soba noodles may use
wheat flour as well. If you can't find or don't like soba noodles, try udon
or brown rice noodles instead. It's socially acceptable in Japan to slurp
these noodles, especially if they're eaten hot. Slurp away, friends.

FOR THE BOWLS

7 ounces soba noodles

1 carrot, peeled or scrubbed, and
   julienned

1 bell pepper, any color, seeded and
   thinly sliced

1 cup snow peas, or snap peas,
   trimmed and sliced in half

2 tablespoons chopped scallions

1 cup chopped kale, spinach,
   or lettuce

1 avocado, thinly sliced

2 tablespoons cashews, chopped

FOR THE DRESSING

1 tablespoon grated fresh ginger

2 tablespoons cashew butter, or
   almond or sunflower seed butter

2 tablespoons rice vinegar, or apple
   cider vinegar

2 tablespoons tamari, or soy sauce

1 teaspoon toasted sesame oil

2 to 3 tablespoons water (optional)

1. Boil a medium pot of water and add the noodles. Keep it at a low boil, turning down the heat and adding cool water if necessary to keep it just below a rolling boil. The soba will take 6 to 7 minutes to cook, and you can stir occasionally to make sure they don't stick to each other or the bottom of the pot. Once they're cooked, drain them in a colander and rinse with hot or cold water, depending on whether you want a hot or cold bowl.

2. You can have the vegetables raw, in which case you just need to cut them up. If you'd like to cook them, heat a skillet to medium-high, and sauté the carrot with a little water, broth, olive oil, or sesame oil. Once the carrot has softened slightly, add the bell pepper. Then add the peas and scallions, to warm for a minute, before turning off the heat.

3. Make the dressing by squeezing the grated ginger for its juice, then whisking together all the ingredients, or puréeing in a small blender, adding 2 to 3 tablespoons of water as needed to make a creamy consistency. Set aside.

4. Arrange your bowl, starting with a layer of chopped kale or spinach (for hot noodles) or lettuce (for cold noodles), then the noodles drizzled with some extra tamari, then the vegetables.

5. Top with the dressing, sliced avocado, and a sprinkle of chopped cashews.

Make ahead: Cooked and rinsed soba noodles keep well in the fridge, so make a whole package and keep them on hand for quick weeknight bowls or lunches to go.

Per Serving

Calories: 392; Total fat: 28g; Carbs: 31g; Fiber: 10g; Protein: 12g

Black Bean Taco Salad Bowl

Makes 3 servings
Prep time: 15 minutes / Cook time: 5 minutes

GLUTEN-FREE NUT-FREE QUICK PREP IMMUNE BOOSTER

Get all the flavor of tacos in a fresh and simple bean salad. I've given you enough black bean taco mixture for three servings here. Try one serving as a salad bowl, then have another serving tucked into a lightly heated whole-grain wrap. Or enjoy a small bowl of the black beans as a snack with tortilla chips. The tortilla chip and bowl recipes here use just one serving of the black bean mixture.

FOR THE BLACK BEAN SALAD

1 (14-ounce) can black beans, drained and rinsed, or 1½ cups cooked

1 cup corn kernels, fresh and blanched, or frozen and thawed

¼ cup fresh cilantro, or parsley, chopped

Zest and juice of 1 lime

1 to 2 teaspoons chili powder

Pinch sea salt

1½ cups cherry tomatoes, halved

1 red bell pepper, seeded and chopped

2 scallions, chopped

FOR 1 SERVING OF TORTILLA CHIPS

1 large whole-grain tortilla or wrap

1 teaspoon olive oil

Pinch sea salt

Pinch freshly ground black pepper

Pinch dried oregano

Pinch chili powder

FOR 1 BOWL

1 cup fresh greens (lettuce, spinach, or whatever you like)

¾ cup cooked quinoa, or brown rice, millet, or other whole grain

¼ cup chopped avocado, or Guacamole (page 203)

¼ cup Fresh Mango Salsa (page 240)

TO MAKE THE BLACK BEAN SALAD

Toss all the ingredients together in a large bowl.

TO MAKE THE TORTILLA CHIPS

Brush the tortilla with olive oil, then sprinkle with salt, pepper, oregano, chili powder, and any other seasonings you like. Slice it into eighths like a pizza. Transfer the tortilla pieces to a small baking sheet lined with parchment paper and put in the oven or toaster oven to toast or broil for 3 to 5 minutes, until browned. Keep an eye on them, as they can go from just barely done to burned very quickly.

TO MAKE THE BOWL

Lay the greens in the bowl, top with the cooked quinoa, ⅓ of the black bean salad, the avocado, and salsa.

Make ahead: The black bean mixture tastes better if you make it in advance, so the flavors have time to mix and mingle. Keep leftovers in the fridge in an airtight container.

Per Serving

Calories: 589; Total fat: 14g; Carbs: 101g; Fiber: 20g; Protein: 21g

Bibimbap Bowl

Makes 1 bowl
Prep time: 10 minutes / Cook time: 20 minutes

GLUTEN-FREE NUT-FREE QUICK PREP ANTI-INFLAMMATORY IMMUNE BOOSTER

Bibimbap is such a fun word to say—and bibimbap is fun to eat, too. This is basically a bowl full of brown rice and veggies, dressed with a spicy sauce. Traditionally, Korean bibimbap is made by cooking each vegetable individually, arranging them separately around the bowl, and then stirring it all together. But if you don't have the patience you can just sauté them all in one go. I won't tell.

½ cup cooked chickpeas

2 tablespoons tamari or
   soy sauce, divided

1 tablespoon plus 2 teaspoons
   toasted sesame oil, divided

¾ cup cooked brown rice, or quinoa,
   millet, or any other whole grain

1 teaspoon olive oil, or 1 tablespoon
   vegetable broth or water

1 carrot, scrubbed or peeled, and
   julienned

2 garlic cloves, minced, divided

Pinch sea salt

½ cup asparagus, cut into
   2-inch pieces

½ cup chopped spinach

½ cup bean sprouts

3 tablespoons hot pepper paste
   (the Korean version is gochujang)

1 tablespoon toasted sesame seeds

1 scallion, chopped

1. In a small bowl, toss the chickpeas with 1 tablespoon tamari and 1 teaspoon toasted sesame oil. Set aside to marinate.

2. Put the cooked brown rice in a large serving bowl, so that you'll be ready to add the vegetables as they cook.

3. Heat the olive oil a large skillet over medium heat, and start by sautéing the carrot and 1 garlic clove with the salt. Once they've softened, about 5 minutes, remove them from the skillet and put them on top of the rice in one area of the bowl.

4. Next, sauté the asparagus, adding a bit more oil if necessary, and when soft, about 5 minutes, place next to the carrots in the bowl.

5. Add a bit of water to the skillet and quick steam the spinach with the other garlic clove, just until the spinach wilts. Drizzle with the remaining 1 tablespoon tamari and 1 teaspoon toasted sesame oil. Lay the spinach on the other side of the carrots in the bowl.

6. You could lightly sauté the bean sprouts if you wish, but they're nice raw. However you prefer them, add them to the bowl.

7. Place the marinated chickpeas in the final area of the bowl.

8. In a small bowl, mix together the hot pepper paste with 1 tablespoon sesame oil. Scoop that into the middle of the bowl. Sprinkle with sesame seeds and scallions, then mix it all together and enjoy!

Make ahead: Have some brown rice, quinoa, or other whole grain cooked and ready in the fridge, so you can throw this (and other bowls) together quickly on a weeknight.

Per Serving

Calories: 665; Total fat: 33g; Carbs: 76g; Fiber: 16g; Protein: 22g

Avocado Red Pepper Sushi Rolls

Makes 4 rolls
Prep time: 30 minutes / Cook time: 45 minutes

GLUTEN-FREE NUT-FREE KID-FRIENDLY ANTI-INFLAMMATORY IMMUNE BOOSTER

Rolling sushi takes some practice, but it's completely worth the effort. You'll need a sushi mat for this, which is a small, flexible mat, usually made of strips of bamboo. Many stores that sell cooking supplies have it. Short-grain brown rice is sticky enough to use instead of white sushi rice; long-grain brown rice will not be sticky enough. Leave plenty of time to cook the rice in advance, and let it thoroughly cool. A great way to do that is to spread it out on a large baking sheet. If it hasn't fully cooled, it will soften the nori too much, which makes it tough and chewy.

FOR THE SUSHI RICE

1 cup short-grain brown rice

2 cups water

Pinch sea salt

1 to 2 tablespoons brown
    rice vinegar

FOR THE SUSHI ROLLS

4 standard nori sheets (typically
    7 by 8 inches)

1 avocado, thinly sliced

¼ red bell pepper, thinly sliced

¼ cup alfalfa sprouts, or clover
    sprouts (optional)

TO SERVE

Tamari or soy sauce

1 tablespoon pickled ginger

1 teaspoon wasabi

TO MAKE THE SUSHI RICE

1. Put the rice and water in a large pot. Add the sea salt, bring to a boil for a couple of minutes, then turn to low and simmer, covered, for 45 minutes. The rice is fully cooked when it is dry and fluffy. Do not stir the rice while it is cooking. This will yield about 3 to 3½ cups sushi rice, which is the perfect amount for 4 rolls.

2. Transfer the rice to a large bowl so that it can cool completely. Stir in the vinegar, just enough to make the rice stick to itself, along with another sprinkle of salt. Stir the rice occasionally to speed up the cooling. You can also put it in the fridge to cool it more quickly.

TO MAKE THE SUSHI ROLLS

1. Set out a small dish of water, then lay out a nori sheet on your rolling mat. It has a smooth side and a rough side; lay it rough side up, with the long side parallel to you.

2. Lightly wet your hands and put a small handful of rice onto the nori. Gently spread the rice out to cover the sheet. Leave about 1 inch along the top edge free of rice.

3. Lay a row of avocado slices along the bottom edge, side to side, then bell pepper slices, then sprouts (if using). You can pile them up on top of each other; all the veggies should only cover about one-third of the nori sheet.

4. Dry your hands, and pick up the bottom of the rolling mat. Roll it over the row of vegetables. Press tightly back toward you as you roll, and press down on the roll a bit. Do not squish, but make sure you are getting a tight roll.

5. Pick up the back end of the rolling mat. Dip a finger in the water, and run it along the top edge of the nori, where there is no rice. Then finish rolling, so the bare edge seals against the outside of the roll. Cover it back over with the mat and gently compress the roll, just to help it seal.

6. Let your sushi roll sit for a few minutes for the nori to be softened by the rice, then cut it into 6 to 8 slices. Repeat to make 4 rolls total.

7. Serve with a dipping bowl of tamari, some pickled ginger, and some wasabi, and practice your skills with chopsticks.

Did you know? Nori is dried seaweed. Sea vegetables, like nori, are rich in minerals and contain sulfated polysaccharides, which have anti-inflammatory, anticancer, anticoagulant, antithrombotic, and antiviral properties. They have cholesterol-lowering effects, which is good not only for cardiovascular protection but also protection against estrogen-related cancers because estrogen production relies on cholesterol as a building block.

Per Serving (1 roll, 8 pieces)

Calories: 248; Total fat: 7g; Carbs: 41g; Fiber: 6g; Protein: 6g

Spicy Chickpea Sushi Rolls

Makes 4 rolls

Prep time: 30 minutes / Cook time: 45 minutes

GLUTEN-FREE NUT-FREE KID-FRIENDLY ANTI-INFLAMMATORY IMMUNE BOOSTER

Take a plant-based spin on spicy tuna, with mineral-rich and mercury-free chickpeas. Sushi rolls travel easily, and people who have never made sushi will be impressed with your skills. Experiment with different fillings and have fun sharing them with friends and family.

FOR THE SUSHI RICE

1 cup short-grain brown rice

2 cups water

Pinch sea salt

1 to 2 tablespoons brown
   rice vinegar

FOR THE SPICY CHICKPEA FILLING

½ cup cooked chickpeas

2 to 3 scallions, finely chopped

⅛ teaspoon cayenne pepper (more
   or less, to your taste)

1 to 2 tablespoons Avo-nnaise
   (page 238)

FOR THE SUSHI ROLLS

3 cups cooked sushi rice

4 nori sheets

¼ cucumber, julienned

TO SERVE

Tamari or soy sauce

1 tablespoon pickled ginger

1 teaspoon wasabi

TO MAKE THE SUSHI RICE

1. Put the rice and water in a large pot. Add a bit of sea salt, bring to a boil for a couple of minutes, then turn to low and simmer, covered, for 45 minutes. The rice is fully cooked when it is dry and fluffy. Do not stir the rice while it is cooking. This will yield about 3 to 3½ cups sushi rice, which is the perfect amount for 4 rolls.

2. Transfer the rice to a large bowl so that it can fully cool. Stir in the vinegar, just enough to make the rice stick to itself, along with another sprinkle of salt. Stir the rice occasionally to speed up the cooling. You can also put it in the fridge to cool it more quickly.

TO MAKE THE SPICY CHICKPEA FILLING

Mash the chickpeas with a potato masher, fork, or your hands. Mix in the scallions, cayenne, and just enough Avo-nnaise to make it stick together. You don't want this to be too creamy, or it will make your sushi soggy.

TO MAKE THE SUSHI ROLLS

1. Set out a small dish of water, then lay out a sheet of nori on your rolling mat. It has a smooth side and a rough side; lay it rough side up, with the long side parallel to you.

2. Lightly wet your hands and put a small handful of rice onto the nori. Gently spread the rice out to cover the sheet. Leave about 1 inch along the top edge free of rice.

3. Spoon about 2 tablespoons spicy chickpea filling along the bottom edge, side to side, along with a few cucumber sticks. All the veggies should only cover about one-third of the nori sheet.

4. Dry your hands, and pick up the bottom of the rolling mat. Roll it over the row of vegetables. Press tightly back toward you as you roll, and press down on the roll a bit. Do not squish, but make sure you are getting a tight roll.

5. Pick up the back end of the rolling mat. Dip a finger in the water, and run it along the top edge of the nori, where there is no rice. Then finish rolling, so the bare edge seals against the outside of the roll. Cover it back over with the mat, and gently compress the roll, just to help it seal.

6. Let your sushi roll sit for a few minutes for the nori to be softened by the rice, then cut into 6 to 8 slices and serve. Repeat to make 4 rolls.

7. Serve with a dipping bowl of tamari, some pickled ginger, and some wasabi.

Make ahead: Make double the rice if you want to make 4 of both this roll and the Avocado Red Pepper Sushi Rolls (page 158) for a sushi party, or make one batch of rice and then 2 of each roll. Enjoy a piece of pickled ginger between as a palate cleanser.

Per Serving (1 roll, 8 pieces)

Calories: 221; Total fat: 3g; Carbs: 42g; Fiber: 6g; Protein: 7g

Sushi Bowl

Makes 1 bowl
Prep time: 20 minutes / Cook time: 20 minutes

GLUTEN-FREE NUT-FREE

Make a quick sushi night by putting all the fixings in a bowl, rather than making hand rolls. Vegetables from the sea, like nori (dried seaweed), are a rich source of minerals, including iron, manganese, and iodine. Edamame beans are the young green pods of the soybean, and are the best way to get that heart-healthy soy protein in a whole and unprocessed form. Making your quinoa or rice in big batches for the week allows you to throw a meal like this together in about 15 minutes on a weeknight.

½ cup shelled edamame beans (fresh or frozen)

¾ cup cooked brown rice, or quinoa, millet, or other whole grain

½ cup chopped spinach

¼ cup sliced avocado

¼ cup sliced bell pepper

¼ cup fresh cilantro, chopped

1 scallion, chopped

¼ nori sheet

1 to 2 tablespoons tamari, or soy sauce

1 tablespoon sesame seeds (toasted if you like)

1. Thaw or steam the edamame beans, then assemble the edamame, rice, spinach, avocado, bell pepper, cilantro, and scallions in a bowl.

2. Cut the nori with scissors into small ribbons and sprinkle on top.

3. Drizzle the bowl with tamari and top with sesame seeds.

Toppings: If you like pickled ginger and/or wasabi, feel free to add those to your sushi bowl. You could top with the Toasted Sesame Miso Dressing (page 237) instead of plain tamari.

Per Serving

Calories: 467; Total fat: 20g; Carbs: 56g; Fiber: 13g; Protein: 22g

Sweet Potato Patties

Makes 5 to 6 patties
Prep time: 15 minutes / Cook time: 20 minutes

GLUTEN-FREE NUT-FREE QUICK PREP KID-FRIENDLY

This is a delicious and easy dish to make with leftover brown rice. Paired with sweet potatoes for wonderful flavor and lots of nutrients, it makes for a much lighter patty than a bean-based veggie burger. This recipe is also versatile and allows for a lot of variation in seasonings, such as dried basil or curry powder instead of the dill. It can easily be made with potato rather than sweet potato for a more neutral flavor, too. Serve these patties garnished with Avo-nnaise (page 238) along with a lemon wedge and a side of steamed kale or on a bun as a burger.

1 cup cooked short-grain brown rice, fully cooled

1 cup grated sweet potato

½ cup diced onion

Pinch sea salt

¼ cup fresh parsley, finely chopped

1 tablespoon dried dill, or 2 tablespoons fresh

1 to 2 tablespoons nutritional yeast (optional)

½ cup whole-grain flour, or bread crumbs, or gluten-free flour

1 teaspoon olive oil

Make ahead: Be sure your rice is thoroughly cooled before you begin, or it will not be sticky enough to make into a patty. This is a great way to use up leftover rice.

1. Stir together the rice, sweet potato, onion, and salt in a large bowl. Allow it to sit for a few minutes, so that the salt can draw the moisture out of the potato and onion. Stir in the parsley, dill, and nutritional yeast (if using), then add enough flour to make the batter sticky, adding a spoonful or two of water if necessary.

2. Form the mixture into tight balls, and squish slightly into patties.

3. Heat a large skillet on medium, then add the oil. Cook for 7 to 10 minutes, then flip. Cook another 5 to 7 minutes, and serve.

Per Serving (1 patty)

Calories: 146; Total fat: 2g; Carbs: 29g; Fiber: 5g; Protein: 6g

Vietnamese Summer Rolls

Makes 10 rolls
Prep time: 50 minutes

GLUTEN-FREE NUT-FREE KID-FRIENDLY IMMUNE BOOSTER

Don't be intimidated by rolling your own spring rolls. It's easy once you give it a try. These are loaded up with lots of fresh vegetables and enjoyed with a delicious peanut dipping sauce. Rice roll wraps are thin sheets made from rice and water. They're brittle when dry and are soaked in water rather than cooked to use for wrapping. They're often found in the Asian-foods aisle of a regular grocery store, in a flat, round package. I recommend the larger ones, so that you have more room for the veggies.

10 round rice roll wraps

¼ cup fresh basil, mint, cilantro, or parsley leaves (or a combination)

10 palm-size lettuce leaves (either small leaves, or tear larger leaves into smaller pieces)

2 carrots, grated or julienned

½ cucumber, julienned

1 mango, peeled and sliced into long, thin pieces

3 scallions, sliced lengthwise into quarters

1 cup bean sprouts

½ cup Peanut Sauce (page 239)

1. Fill a deep plate with room-temperature water, and put a rice roll wrap in to soften. It will take a couple of minutes to get very soft. Pull it out of the water and allow it to drip for a few seconds, then place it on a dry plate.

2. Down the center of the wrap, lay 2 fresh basil leaves and a lettuce leaf, then cover with the carrots, cucumber, mango, scallions, and bean sprouts. Don't overfill, or it will be difficult to roll.

3. Fold over the top and bottom of the rice wrap, then fold one side over the filling and tuck it under the filling a bit. Squeeze slightly with your hands and then roll to the end of the other side. Allow the wraps to sit and stick together before serving.
4. Slice each wrap in half, and serve with Peanut Sauce for dipping.

Technique: Put the next wrap in the water to soften while you roll the current one, so that you don't have to wait for them to soften each time.

Per Serving (1 roll + 2 tablespoons sauce)

Calories: 77; Total fat: 5g; Carbs: 8g; Fiber: 1g; Protein: 3g

Potato Skin Samosas

Makes 8 samosas
Prep time: 20 minutes / Cook time: 30 minutes

GLUTEN-FREE NUT-FREE KID-FRIENDLY IMMUNE BOOSTER

This recipe was inspired by the *Veganomicon* cookbook and a suggestion it made to make a samosa filling but stuff it into the skins of baked potatoes instead of a pastry. Much healthier and easier. The skin of a potato has more fiber, as well as most of the iron content of the potato and lots of other minerals and vitamins.

4 small baking potatoes

1 teaspoon coconut oil

1 small onion, finely chopped

2 garlic cloves, minced

1 small piece ginger, minced or grated

2 to 3 teaspoons curry powder

Pinch sea salt

Pinch freshly ground black pepper

2 carrots, grated

¼ cup frozen peas, thawed

¼ cup fresh cilantro, or parsley, chopped

1. Preheat the oven to 350°F.

2. Pierce the potatoes with a fork, wrap them in aluminum foil, and bake 30 minutes, or until soft.

3. While the potatoes are cooking, heat the oil in a medium skillet and sauté the onion until it's soft, about 5 minutes. Add the garlic and ginger and sauté until they're soft as well, about 3 minutes. Add the curry powder, salt, and pepper, and stir to fully coat the onion. Turn off the heat.

4. When the potatoes are cooked, take them out of the foil and slice them in half.

5. Scoop out the flesh of the potatoes into the skillet with the onion. Add the carrots, peas, and cilantro. Stir to combine, then spoon the mixture back into the potato skins.

6. If you like, you can prepare these in advance and then heat them up in the oven at 350°F for 10 minutes when you're ready to serve.

Toppings: Cashew Sour Cream (page 230) is lovely with these, as is a drizzle of Peanut Sauce (page 239). Or you could try Fresh Mango Salsa (page 240).

Per Serving (1 samosa)

Calories: 130; Total fat: 1g; Carbs: 29g; Fiber: 3g; Protein: 3g

Simple Sesame Stir-Fry

Makes 4 servings
Prep time: 10 minutes / Cook time: 20 minutes

GLUTEN-FREE NUT-FREE QUICK PREP ANTI-INFLAMMATORY

The flavor of broccoli can be a little harsh, but lightly cooking softens it. Broccoli helps regulate insulin and blood sugar, and as a dark green vegetable has a decent amount of calcium, so it's a great addition to your diet. Pair this all-green stir-fry with calcium-rich sesame seeds for even more nutrition, flavor, and a beautiful color contrast.

1 cup quinoa

2 cups water

Pinch sea salt

1 head broccoli

1 to 2 teaspoons untoasted sesame oil, or olive oil

1 cup snow peas, or snap peas, ends trimmed and cut in half

1 cup frozen shelled edamame beans, or peas

2 cups chopped Swiss chard, or other large-leafed green

2 scallions, chopped

2 tablespoons water

1 teaspoon toasted sesame oil

1 tablespoon tamari, or soy sauce

2 tablespoons sesame seeds

1. Put the quinoa, water, and sea salt in a medium pot, bring it to a boil for a minute, then turn to low and simmer, covered, for 20 minutes. The quinoa is fully cooked when you see the swirl of the grains with a translucent center, and it is fluffy. Do not stir the quinoa while it is cooking.

2. Meanwhile, cut the broccoli into bite-size florets, cutting and pulling apart from the stem. Also chop the stem into bite-size pieces.

3. Heat a large skillet to high, and sauté the broccoli in the untoasted sesame oil, with a pinch of salt to help it soften. Keep this moving continuously, so that it doesn't burn, and add an extra drizzle of oil if needed as you add the rest of the vegetables. Add the snow peas next, continuing to stir. Add the edamame until they thaw. Add the Swiss chard and scallions at the same time, tossing for only a minute to wilt.

Then add 2 tablespoons of water to the hot skillet so that it sizzles and finishes the vegetables with a quick steam.

4. Dress with the toasted sesame oil and tamari, and toss one last time. Remove from the heat immediately.

5. Serve a scoop of cooked quinoa, topped with stir-fry and sprinkled with some sesame seeds, and an extra drizzle of tamari and/or toasted sesame oil if you like.

Options: I went for a green theme here, but make this with pretty much any vegetables you like (or have left in the fridge): bell peppers, carrots, mushrooms, eggplant, zucchini, cherry tomatoes. Just think through which take the longest to cook, and add them first, finishing with whatever takes the least time to cook.

Per Serving

Calories: 334; Total fat: 13g; Carbs: 42g; Fiber: 9g; Protein: 17g

Creamy Mint-Lime Spaghetti Squash

Makes 3 servings

Prep time: 10 minutes / Cook time: 30 minutes

GLUTEN-FREE NUT-FREE QUICK PREP IMMUNE BOOSTER

Spaghetti squash is a delicious, nutrient-dense, and low-carb alternative to pasta. It cooks differently from other winter squash. It doesn't get soft, and it makes strands that look like spaghetti noodles. But it's super simple to cook once you know how, and it's full of immune-boosting vitamins and antioxidants. Paired here with a creamy mint-lime dressing, and topped with sweet and crunchy fresh vegetables, your taste buds will be fully satisfied and your body fully nourished. This squash is also wonderful with Basil Pesto (page 241). And it pairs perfectly with a toasted whole-wheat pita spread with Greens and Beans Dip (page 202).

FOR THE DRESSING

3 tablespoons tahini

Zest and juice of 1 small lime

2 tablespoons fresh mint, minced

1 small garlic clove, pressed

1 tablespoon nutritional yeast

Pinch sea salt

FOR THE SPAGHETTI SQUASH

1 spaghetti squash

Pinch sea salt

1 cup cherry tomatoes, chopped

1 cup chopped bell pepper, any color

Freshly ground black pepper

TO MAKE THE DRESSING

Make the dressing by whisking together the tahini and lime juice until thick, stirring in water if you need it, until smooth, then add the rest of the ingredients. Or you can purée all the ingredients in a blender.

TO MAKE THE SPAGHETTI SQUASH

1. Put a large pot of water on high and bring to a boil.

2. Cut the squash in half and scoop out the seeds. Put the squash halves in the pot with the salt, and boil for about 30 minutes. Carefully remove the squash from the pot and let it cool until you can safely handle it. Set half the squash aside for another meal.

3. Scoop out the squash from the skin, which stays hard like a shell, and break the strands apart. The flesh absorbs water while boiling, so set the "noodles" in a strainer for 10 minutes, tossing occasionally to drain.

4. Transfer the cooked spaghetti squash to a large bowl and toss with the mint-lime dressing. Then top with the cherry tomatoes and bell pepper. Add an extra sprinkle of nutritional yeast and black pepper, if you wish.

Options: If you can't find fresh mint, don't use dried mint. Go for fresh cilantro or parsley or whatever fresh leafy herb you can find. Arugula would also be lovely.

Per Serving

Calories: 199; Total fat: 10g; Carbs: 27g; Fiber: 5g; Protein: 7g

Sun-dried Tomato and Pesto Quinoa

Makes 1 serving

Prep time: 10 minutes / Cook time: 15 minutes

GLUTEN-FREE QUICK PREP IMMUNE BOOSTER

Sun-dried tomatoes add a strong savory flavor to this meal, and paired with fresh basil pesto, this dish will give your taste buds a full experience. Eating foods with big, savory flavors can be helpful when transitioning to plant foods, to fill that flavor category normally occupied by animal foods.

1 teaspoon olive oil, or 1 tablespoon vegetable broth or water

1 cup chopped onion

1 garlic clove, minced

1 cup chopped zucchini

Pinch sea salt

1 tomato, chopped

2 tablespoons chopped sun-dried tomatoes

2 to 3 tablespoons Basil Pesto (page 241)

1 cup chopped spinach

2 cups cooked quinoa

1 tablespoon Cheesy Sprinkle (page 229), optional

1. Heat the oil in a large skillet on medium-high, then sauté the onion, about 5 minutes. Add the garlic when the onion has softened, then add the zucchini and salt.

2. Once the zucchini is somewhat soft, about 5 minutes, turn off the heat and add the fresh and sun-dried tomatoes. Mix to combine, then toss in the pesto. Toss the vegetables to coat them.

3. Layer the spinach, then quinoa, then the zucchini mixture on a plate, topped with a bit of Cheesy Sprinkle (if using).

Options: This is a great way to use leftover cooked quinoa, but this dish is also nice with whole-grain pasta.

Per Serving

Calories: 535; Total fat: 23g; Carbs: 69g; Fiber: 14g; Protein: 20

Olive and White Bean Pasta

Makes 1 serving
Prep time: 10 minutes / Cook time: 20 minutes

NUT-FREE QUICK PREP

Branch out from typical pasta with tomato sauce and try this flavorful dish. Adding beans to a pasta dish boosts the protein content, and these cannellini (white kidney) beans will soak up the rich flavors. Using kitchen staples, this meal is a breeze to put together on a weeknight.

½ cup whole-grain pasta

Pinch sea salt

1 teaspoon olive oil, or 1 tablespoon
   vegetable broth

¼ cup thinly sliced red bell pepper

¼ cup thinly sliced zucchini

½ cup cooked cannellini beans

½ cup spinach

1 tablespoon balsamic vinegar

2 or 3 black olives, pitted
   and chopped

1 tablespoon nutritional yeast

1. Bring a pot of water to a boil, then add the pasta with the salt to cook until just tender (per the package directions).

2. Meanwhile, in a large skillet, heat the oil and lightly sauté the bell pepper and zucchini, 7 to 8 minutes. Add the beans to warm for 2 minutes, then add the spinach last, just until it wilts. Drizzle with the vinegar at the end.

3. Serve the pasta topped or tossed with the bean mixture, and sprinkled with the olives and nutritional yeast.

Options: Use brown rice, quinoa, or corn pasta to easily make this dish gluten-free. It would also be nice with cooked basmati rice instead of pasta.

Per Serving

Calories: 387; Total fat: 17g; Carbs: 42g; Fiber: 19g; Protein: 18g

Spaghetti and Buckwheat Meatballs

Makes 20 to 24 meatballs, 2 servings pasta
Prep time: 20 minutes / Cook time: 45 minutes

NUT-FREE KID-FRIENDLY ANTI-INFLAMMATORY

These meatballs are made with toasted buckwheat (a.k.a. kasha), and seasonings to create a rich, savory flavor. Buckwheat has lots of fiber, minerals, B vitamins, and antioxidants, along with a compound called D-chiro-inositol, which seems to have some effect in improving blood sugar balance. You can find kasha in the section of the supermarket with the whole grains, or maybe in the bulk bins in specialty stores. It's reddish-brown and each grain is shaped like a little pyramid. It cooks incredibly quickly, so keep an eye on it, and you can get these meatballs made in a snap.

FOR THE BUCKWHEAT MEATBALLS

½ cup toasted buckwheat

2¼ cups water, divided

Pinch sea salt

2 tablespoons ground flaxseed, or chia seeds

2 tablespoons tomato paste, or ketchup

1 tablespoon stone-ground mustard

2 tablespoons tamari, or soy sauce

1 tablespoon mixed dried herbs (basil, oregano, marjoram)

1 teaspoon onion powder

1 teaspoon garlic powder

½ teaspoon ground cumin

½ teaspoon smoked paprika, or regular paprika

FOR THE SPAGHETTI

7 ounces whole-grain spaghetti, or ½ spaghetti squash

2 cups Marinara Sauce (page 242)

2 to 3 tablespoons Cheesy Sprinkle (page 229)

1. Preheat the oven to 350°F. Lightly grease a large rectangular baking sheet with olive oil, or line it with parchment paper.

2. Put the buckwheat in a small pot with 2 cups of the water and the salt, and bring to a boil. Turn the heat down and simmer, covered, for about 5 minutes. (If you use untoasted buckwheat, it will take closer to 20 minutes to cook after boiling.)

3. In a small bowl, mix the ground flaxseed with the remaining ¼ cup water and set aside.

4. In a large bowl, mix the tomato paste, mustard, tamari, herbs, onion powder, garlic powder, cumin, and paprika. Add the cooked buckwheat and soaked flax and stir to combine.

5. Shape spoonfuls of the mix into 20 to 24 small balls. Transfer to the baking sheet and put in the oven for 30 minutes.

6. Cook the spaghetti (or spaghetti squash) by putting it in a pot of boiling water and boiling until soft, about 10 minutes (15 to 20 for the squash). Drain the pasta, or scoop the flesh out of the squash's skin.

7. Once the meatballs are done, take them out of the oven and let cool for a few minutes.

8. Serve a plate of spaghetti (or squash) topped with Marinara Sauce, a few buckwheat meatballs, and Cheesy Sprinkle.

Leftovers: Six meatballs are a serving, so this recipe makes more meatballs than you will need for two servings of pasta. Leftover meatballs keep in the refrigerator for a few days, and are perfect to top a salad, put in a wrap, or even add to a vegetable soup.

Per Serving

Calories: 651; Total fat: 15g; Carbs: 115g; Fiber: 18g; Protein: 26g

Orange Walnut Pasta

Makes 3 servings
Prep time: 20 minutes / Cook time: 20 minutes

GLUTEN-FREE KID-FRIENDLY IMMUNE BOOSTER

This simple dish features a light orange dressing paired with the Mediterranean flavors of olives and parsley and topped with heart-healthy walnuts. I've given you a lot of noodle options here. Make this with the other half of the spaghetti squash from the Spaghetti and Buckwheat Meatballs (page 174), or use whole-grain pasta, or try spiralizing a mixture of vegetables. You can turn firm vegetables (such as zucchini, carrot, or even rutabaga) into noodles.

½ **spaghetti squash, or 7 ounces whole-grain pasta, or 14 ounces mixed vegetables**

Zest and juice of 1 orange

2 tablespoons olive oil

1 garlic clove, pressed

Pinch sea salt

2 to 3 tablespoons fresh parsley, finely chopped

10 olives, pitted and chopped

¼ cup walnuts, chopped

2 to 3 tablespoons nutritional yeast (optional)

1. Cook your noodle of choice:

   - Spaghetti squash: Boil until soft, about 15 to 20 minutes. Scoop the flesh out of the skin. Drain for a few minutes.
   - Whole-grain pasta: Put it in a pot of boiling water with a pinch salt and cook until just soft, about 10 to 15 minutes. Drain.
   - Mixed vegetables: Peel, and cut the ends flat to each other. Run through a spiralizer, or use a vegetable peeler to make long noodles. Either have them raw (in which case, you can toss with a sprinkle of salt and leave to soften and drain for 20 to 30 minutes), or cook lightly by steaming or boiling for just a few minutes.

2. In a large bowl, add the orange zest and juice. Whisk in an amount of olive oil that's about half the volume of the orange juice, along with the pressed garlic, and the salt; stir to blend. Add the noodles to the dressing, and toss.

3. Serve topped with a sprinkling of fresh parsley, chopped olives, walnuts, and a dusting of nutritional yeast (if using).

Did you know? Garlic has powerful antioxidant compounds, which are released and made more available when the clove is pressed, crushed, or chopped.

Per Serving

Calories: 402; Total fat: 30g; Carbs: 32g; Fiber: 6g; Protein: 10g

Roasted Cauliflower Tacos

Makes 8 tacos
Prep time: 10 minutes / Cook time: 20 to 30 minutes

NUT-FREE QUICK PREP KID-FRIENDLY ANTI-INFLAMMATORY IMMUNE BOOSTER

Tacos in Mexico are always made with a soft shell and finished with a squirt from a fresh lime wedge. You can turn cauliflower into a smoky, spicy, savory centerpiece for these plant-based tacos, topped with all the fixings, including grated carrot as a stand-in for cheese. Cauliflower is a cruciferous vegetable, related to broccoli and cabbage, so it's packed with anti-inflammatory and cancer-fighting compounds, but it has a much milder flavor than its green cousins.

FOR THE ROASTED CAULIFLOWER

1 head cauliflower, cut into
   bite-size pieces

1 tablespoon olive oil (optional)

2 tablespoons whole-grain flour

2 tablespoons nutritional yeast

1 to 2 teaspoons smoked paprika

½ to 1 teaspoon chili powder

Pinch sea salt

FOR THE TACOS

2 cups shredded lettuce

2 cups cherry tomatoes, quartered

2 carrots, scrubbed or peeled,
   and grated

½ cup Fresh Mango Salsa (page 240)

½ cup Guacamole (page 203)

8 small whole-grain or corn tortillas

1 lime, cut into 8 wedges

TO MAKE THE ROASTED CAULIFLOWER

1. Preheat the oven to 350°F. Lightly grease a large rectangular baking sheet with olive oil, or line it with parchment paper.

2. In a large bowl, toss the cauliflower pieces with oil (if using), or just rinse them so they're wet. The idea is to get the seasonings to stick.

3. In a smaller bowl, mix together the flour, nutritional yeast, paprika, chili powder, and salt. Add the seasonings to the cauliflower, and mix it around with your hands to thoroughly coat.

4. Spread the cauliflower on the baking sheet, and roast for 20 to 30 minutes, or until softened.

TO MAKE THE TACOS

1. Prep the veggies, salsa, and guacamole while the cauliflower is roasting.

2. Once the cauliflower is cooked, heat the tortillas for just a few minutes in the oven or in a small skillet.

3. Set everything out on the table, and assemble your tacos as you go. Give a squeeze of fresh lime just before eating.

Leftovers: Double the batch of roasted cauliflower and add it to salads, bowls, and wraps, or serve as a side dish with Avo-nnaise (page 238).

Per Serving (1 taco)

Calories: 198; Total fat: 6g; Carbs: 32g; Fiber: 6g; Protein: 7g

Build Your Own Mushroom Fajitas

Makes 6 fajitas
Prep time: 20 minutes / Cook time: 20 minutes

GLUTEN-FREE NUT-FREE KID-FRIENDLY

Use this recipe to have fun on a Friday evening with a table full of delicious fajita fillings. We'll center these fajitas on some spicy glazed mushrooms, and then you can load them up with all the fixings to your preference. This is a great way to use up vegetables at the end of the week.

FOR THE SPICY GLAZED MUSHROOMS

1 (10- to 12-ounce) package cremini mushrooms

1 teaspoon olive oil

½ to 1 teaspoon chili powder

Pinch freshly ground black pepper

Pinch sea salt

1 teaspoon maple syrup

FOR THE FAJITAS

1 onion

1 to 2 teaspoons olive oil, or 1 tablespoon vegetable broth or water

Pinch sea salt

1 zucchini, cut into large matchsticks

1 bell pepper, any color, seeded and sliced into long strips

½ cup fresh cilantro, finely chopped

3 to 4 scallions, sliced

2 carrots, grated

6 whole-grain or corn tortilla wraps

Guacamole (page 203)

Fresh Mango Salsa (page 240)

Cashew Sour Cream (page 230)

Your favorite hot sauce (optional)

TO MAKE THE SPICY GLAZED MUSHROOMS

1. To glaze the mushrooms, wipe them clean with a paper towel, then cut them into thin slices.

2. Heat the oil in a large skillet over medium heat, then sauté the mushrooms until soft, about 10 minutes. Add the chili powder, pepper, and salt and stir to coat the mushrooms. Add the maple syrup to the skillet, stir to coat, and allow to cook for a few minutes to create a glaze.

3. Transfer the mushrooms to a heatproof dish, and keep them warm in the oven on very low, or allow them to cool if you aren't particular.

TO MAKE THE FAJITAS

1. Cut the onion in half from stem to tip. Then slice the strips perpendicular to that cut, so they make half moons. Separate the layers into arc-like shapes.

2. Rinse the mushroom skillet if you want to clear the flavors, or leave it as is, and put the skillet back on the heat. Sauté the onion in the olive oil and salt. Once the onion is translucent, about 5 minutes, add the zucchini and bell pepper, and sauté until they're soft, 7 to 8 minutes.

3. While the zucchini is cooking, prepare the cilantro, scallions, and carrots.

4. Heat your tortilla wraps for a few minutes in a toaster oven, oven, or dry skillet. Place everything on the table so each person can assemble their own fajita.

Did you know? Flour tortillas will stay soft and flexible longer than corn tortillas. Use whichever you prefer, but if you notice the corn tortillas breaking in half, it's because of the different proteins in corn and wheat.

Per Serving

Calories: 404; Total fat: 15g; Carbs: 59g; Fiber: 7g; Protein: 11g

Blackeye Pea Burritos

Makes 6 burritos
Prep time: 10 minutes / Cook time: 30 to 40 minutes

GLUTEN-FREE NUT-FREE QUICK PREP KID-FRIENDLY ANTI-INFLAMMATORY
IMMUNE BOOSTER

These come together quickly for a weeknight meal, and are a much healthier (and cheaper) option than frozen burritos. You can make these in a big batch, and then put them in individual containers to take for lunches. Serve along with Baked Sweet Potato Fries (page 204) and a green salad, like Creamy Avocado-Dressed Kale Salad (page 122).

1 teaspoon olive oil, or water or vegetable broth

1 red onion, diced

2 garlic cloves, minced

1 zucchini, chopped

1 bell pepper, any color, seeded and diced

1 tomato, diced

2 teaspoons chili powder

Pinch sea salt

1 (14-ounce) can blackeye peas, rinsed and drained, or 1½ cups cooked

6 whole-grain tortillas, or corn tortillas

1. Preheat the oven to 325°F.
2. In a large skillet over medium heat, add the olive oil and sauté the onion until softened, about 5 minutes. Add the garlic, and sauté briefly. Add the zucchini to the skillet and sauté until soft, about 5 minutes. The bell pepper goes in next, then the tomato. Cook a minute or two.
3. As soon as the tomato is warmed through, add the chili powder, salt, and blackeye peas. Stir to combine.
4. Place some of the blackeye pea mix in the center of each tortilla, fold in the ends, and roll into a burrito.
5. Place the burritos seam side down in a baking dish. Pour any vegetable juice from the pan on top. Bake in the oven for 20 to 30 minutes.

Toppings: Spoon a bit of salsa on top of each burrito before putting it in the oven for a burst of flavor and a softer burrito. You can buy a healthy salsa, or make your own Fresh Mango Salsa (page 240), but just leave out the mango, which does not pair well with this dish. To counter the spiciness, top the cooked burritos with a scoop of cooling Guacamole (page 203) or Cashew Sour Cream (page 230).

Per Serving

Calories: 334; Total fat: 6g; Carbs: 58g; Fiber: 8g; Protein: 12g

Grilled Portobello with Mashed Potatoes and Green Beans

Makes 4 servings
Prep time: 20 minutes / Cook time: 40 minutes

GLUTEN-FREE NUT-FREE KID-FRIENDLY IMMUNE BOOSTER

Portobellos are those giant brown mushroom caps and are perfect for grilling. Here, you'll see the simple techniques to make them soft, juicy, and delicious, cooked either on the grill or in the oven. Try them at your next cookout and watch plant-eaters and meat-eaters alike gobble them up. We have them in my family as entrées with side dishes, but you could put them on a whole-grain bun, like a burger. Add any other seasonings you like to the mushrooms before you cook them; try paprika, Cajun seasoning, celery salt, or whatever your taste buds desire.

FOR THE GRILLED PORTOBELLOS

4 large portobello mushrooms

1 teaspoon olive oil

Pinch sea salt

FOR THE MASHED POTATOES

6 large potatoes, scrubbed or peeled, and chopped

3 to 4 garlic cloves, minced

½ teaspoon olive oil

½ cup non-dairy milk

2 tablespoons coconut oil (optional)

2 tablespoons nutritional yeast (optional)

Pinch sea salt

FOR THE GREEN BEANS

2 cups green beans, cut into 1-inch pieces

2 to 3 teaspoons coconut oil

Pinch sea salt

1 to 2 tablespoons nutritional yeast (optional)

continued

TO MAKE THE GRILLED PORTOBELLOS

1. Preheat the grill to medium, or the oven to 350°F.

2. Take the stems out of the mushrooms. Wipe the caps clean with a damp paper towel, then dry them.

3. Spray the caps with a bit of olive oil, or put some oil in your hand and rub it over the mushrooms. Rub the oil onto the top and bottom of each mushroom, then sprinkle them with a bit of salt on top and bottom.

4. Put them bottom side facing up on a baking sheet in the oven, or straight on the grill. They'll take about 30 minutes in the oven, or 20 minutes on the grill. Wait until they're soft and wrinkling around the edges. If you keep them bottom up, all the delicious mushroom juice will pool in the cap. Then at the very end, you can flip them over to drain the juice. If you like it, you can drizzle it over the mashed potatoes.

TO MAKE THE MASHED POTATOES

1. Boil the chopped potatoes in lightly salted water for about 20 minutes, until soft.

2. While they're cooking, sauté the garlic in the olive oil, or bake them whole in a 350°F oven for 10 minutes, then squeeze out the flesh.

3. Drain the potatoes, reserving about ½ cup water to mash them.

4. In a large bowl, mash the potatoes with a little bit of the reserved water, the cooked garlic, milk, coconut oil (if using), nutritional yeast (if using), and salt to taste. Add more water, a little at a time, if needed, to get the texture you want. If you use an immersion blender or beater to purée them, you'll have some extra-creamy potatoes.

TO MAKE THE GREEN BEANS

1. Heat a medium pot with a small amount of water to boil, then steam the green beans by either putting them directly in the pot or in a steaming basket.

2. Once they're slightly soft and vibrantly green, 7 to 8 minutes, take them off the heat and toss them with the oil, salt, and nutritional yeast (if using).

Make ahead: Roast whole garlic bulbs in advance, squeeze out the cloves into a baking dish and freeze, then keep in airtight bags or containers. You'll have them on hand for adding to hummus or puréed soups, or anything that could use a sweet and savory flavor boost.

Per Serving

Calories: 263; Total fat: 7g; Carbs: 43g; Fiber: 7g; Protein: 10g

Shepherd's Pie

Makes 6 large servings
Prep time: 30 minutes / Cook time: 30 minutes

NUT-FREE KID-FRIENDLY

For this Shepherd's Pie, I've replaced lamb with lentils, along with a myriad of vegetables and seasonings to make it a hearty and healthy meal. This is a great dish for when you're craving comfort food, since it's so warm and filling. If you like, you can use mashed sweet potatoes for the topping instead of white potatoes. It will give it an extra burst of sweetness and nutrition.

1 cup lentils

6 medium potatoes, scrubbed
   or peeled

¼ cup non-dairy milk (optional)

1 tablespoon coconut oil (optional)

1 yellow onion, diced

1 teaspoon olive oil

2 carrots, diced

½ cup peas, fresh or frozen

1 tablespoon thyme, fresh or dried

1 to 2 tablespoons red or white wine

Pinch freshly ground black pepper

1 to 2 teaspoons sea salt

2 tablespoons whole-grain flour

½ cup water

1. Put the lentils in a medium pot with 2 to 3 cups water, bring to a boil over high heat, and then turn down to simmer for 20 to 30 minutes, until the lentils are soft.

2. While the lentils are cooking, cut the potatoes into small chunks, put them in a large pot, and fill the pot with water until the potatoes are covered. Add a pinch sea salt, bring to a boil, and cook until the potatoes are soft, about 20 minutes. When they are cooked, pour off the cooking liquid, leaving about ½ cup in the pot. Mash or blend the potatoes until smooth, adding liquid if necessary. If you want really creamy potatoes, you can add the non-dairy milk and coconut oil. Add salt to taste.

3. Preheat the oven to 350°F.

4. Drain the cooked lentils and transfer to a 9-inch ovenproof pie plate or square baking dish.

5. Heat the now-empty lentil pot on medium, then sauté the onion in the olive oil until it softens, about 5 minutes. Add the carrots and cook until they soften, about 5 minutes. Toss the peas in to thaw, then add the thyme and the wine and stir. Add the vegetables to the dish with the lentils; add the pepper, salt, and flour, and stir to combine well. Add the water and stir once more to dissolve the flour.

6. Spread the mashed potatoes over the lentil mixture. Bake for 20 to 30 minutes, or until the potatoes start to brown on top.

Make ahead: This takes a while if you make everything from scratch, which is great for Sunday dinner if you have time. But you can easily split this up over a few nights if you prefer. Make extra mashed potatoes with the Grilled Portobello (page 183) one night, then cook extra lentils when you make the Warm Lentil Salad with Red Wine Vinaigrette (page 134). Then all you need to do to put this together is a tiny bit of cooking.

Per Serving

Calories: 344; Total fat: 4g; Carbs: 63g; Fiber: 16g; Protein: 15g

Baked Kale Chips, Five Ways page 192

chapter 10

SNACKS AND SIDES

Nori Snack Rolls 190

Tamari Toasted Almonds 191

Baked Kale Chips, Five Ways 192

Savory Roasted Chickpeas 195

Lemon Coconut Cilantro
Rolls 196

Hummus, Five Ways 197

Spicy Black Bean Dip 200

Avomame Spread 201

Greens and Beans Dip 202

Guacamole 203

Baked Sweet Potato Fries 204

Roasted Garlic Pesto
Potatoes 205

Sweet Potato Biscuits 206

Garlic Toast 207

Nori Snack Rolls

Makes 4 rolls
Prep time: 5 minutes / Cook time: 8 to 10 minutes

GLUTEN-FREE QUICK PREP ANTI-INFLAMMATORY

These nori snack rolls are the perfect chip alternative when you're craving a salty, savory snack. They're quick to put together, are super healthy, and would be fancy enough to serve as an appetizer at a dinner party. You may find it easier to roll these using your sushi rolling mat.

2 tablespoons almond, cashew, peanut, or other nut butter

2 tablespoons tamari, or soy sauce

4 standard nori sheets

1 mushroom, sliced

1 tablespoon pickled ginger

½ cup grated carrots

Options: Try variations on the fillings, such as thinly sliced red bell pepper, cucumber, grated jicama, or Baked Sweet Potato Fries (page 204).

1. Preheat the oven to 350°F.
2. Mix together the nut butter and tamari until smooth and very thick. Lay out a nori sheet, rough side up, the long way. Spread a thin line of the tamari mixture on the far end of the nori sheet, from side to side. Lay the mushroom slices, ginger, and carrots in a line at the other end (the end closest to you). Fold the vegetables inside the nori, rolling toward the tahini mixture, which will seal the roll.
3. Repeat to make 4 rolls.
4. Put on a baking sheet and bake for 8 to 10 minutes, or until the rolls are slightly browned and crispy at the ends. Let the rolls cool for a few minutes, then slice each roll into 3 smaller pieces.

Per Serving (1 roll)

Calories: 79; Total fat: 5g; Carbs: 6g; Fiber: 2g; Protein: 4g

Tamari Toasted Almonds

Makes $\frac{1}{2}$ cup

Prep time: 2 minutes / Cook time: 5 to 7 minutes

GLUTEN-FREE QUICK PREP ANTI-INFLAMMATORY

Take some ordinary raw almonds or sunflower seeds and turn them into a flavor sensation by lightly toasting them and infusing them with salty-savory tamari and sesame oil. They are a lovely snack, or use them as a topping for salads, soups, or bowls.

½ cup raw almonds, or sunflower seeds

2 tablespoons tamari, or soy sauce

1 teaspoon toasted sesame oil

1. Heat a dry skillet to medium-high heat, then add the almonds, stirring very frequently to keep them from burning.
2. Once the almonds are toasted, 7 to 8 minutes for almonds, or 3 to 4 minutes for sunflower seeds, pour the tamari and sesame oil into the hot skillet and stir to coat.
3. You can turn off the heat, and as the almonds cool the tamari mixture will stick to and dry on the nuts.

Technique: Use a skillet that is only just big enough to have a single layer of almonds or seeds, and use a stove burner that is as close to the size of the skillet as possible. This cooks them evenly and helps prevent burning as you toast them.

Per Serving (1 tablespoon)

Calories: 89; Total fat: 8g; Carbs: 3g; Fiber: 2g; Protein: 4g

Baked Kale Chips, Five Ways

Makes about 1½ cups
Prep time: 15 minutes / Cook time: 20 to 25 minutes

GLUTEN-FREE NUT-FREE QUICK PREP ANTI-INFLAMMATORY IMMUNE BOOSTER

These crunchy little chips are a great snack and the perfect way to get some nutrient-dense kale into your life. They also give you a much better snack option than potato chips when you are craving that salty crunch. They have lots of flavor to satisfy your taste buds but are much lower in calories than potato chips. Try the variations here, then branch out to make your own flavor combinations. You can also substitute Swiss chard or bok choy, or you can make chips with thin slices of zucchini or eggplant for a switch.

FOR CLASSIC BAKED KALE CHIPS

8 kale leaves, washed and
    fully dried

1 tablespoon olive oil, or coconut oil

Pinch sea salt

**FOR SALT AND VINEGAR
KALE CHIPS**

1 teaspoon apple cider vinegar

Extra sea salt

FOR SMOKY BARBECUE KALE CHIPS

½ teaspoon smoked paprika

¼ teaspoon chili powder

1 teaspoon onion powder

½ teaspoon garlic powder

FOR CURRY-SPICED KALE CHIPS

1 teaspoon curry powder

1 tablespoon nutritional yeast

FOR RANCH-STYLE KALE CHIPS

2 tablespoons almond butter,
    or sunflower seed butter

1 tablespoon apple cider vinegar

1 to 2 tablespoons water

1 tablespoon nutritional yeast

2 teaspoons onion powder

1 teaspoon garlic powder

1 teaspoon dried dill

1 teaspoon dried chives, or
    minced fresh

Sea salt

Freshly ground black pepper

TO MAKE CLASSIC BAKED KALE CHIPS

1. Preheat the oven to 300°F. Line a large baking sheet with parchment paper.
2. Tear the kale leaves off the stems, and then tear the leaves into bite-size pieces. Place in a large bowl.
3. Drizzle the kale with the oil, and rub it in with your hands. This is the only way to get the leaves fully coated. You should rub it into all the areas of the leaves. Sprinkle with the salt, and toss to combine.
4. Lay the pieces of kale out on your baking sheet. Make sure they are well spread out; if they overlap they don't bake properly.
5. Bake 20 to 25 minutes, until the chips are dry and crispy. Remove from the oven.
6. Let the chips sit for a few minutes to cool before serving.
7. Store in an airtight container, though they don't keep very well, so it's best to bake and enjoy them the same day.

TO MAKE SALT AND VINEGAR KALE CHIPS

Prepare the Classic Baked Kale Chips. After they are baked and cooled, spritz with vinegar (either use a sprayer, or flick tiny amounts with your fingertips) and sprinkle some extra salt onto the chips.

TO MAKE SMOKY BARBECUE KALE CHIPS

Prepare the Classic Baked Kale Chips. Add the extra seasonings after rubbing in the oil, and toss to combine before baking.

TO MAKE CURRY-SPICED KALE CHIPS

Prepare the Classic Baked Kale Chips. Add the extra seasonings after rubbing in the oil, and toss to combine before baking.

continued

TO MAKE RANCH-STYLE KALE CHIPS

1. In a small bowl, whisk together the almond butter and vinegar until thick. Add the water—just enough to make it smooth and creamy.

2. Add the nutritional yeast, onion powder, garlic powder, dill, chives, salt, and pepper, adding more water if necessary to make a paste. Stir to combine.

3. Prepare the Classic Baked Kale Chips, but use this dressing in place of the olive oil and salt. Bake as directed. (These may need to bake an extra few minutes.)

Technique: Make sure the kale is fully dried; this is important, because otherwise the chips won't dry out properly in the oven and will wind up chewy, soggy, or overdone as you try to dry them out while baking.

Per Serving (1 cup, Classic)

Calories: 169; Total fat: 10g; Carbs: 18g; Fiber: 3g; Protein: 6g

Savory Roasted Chickpeas

Makes 1 cup
Prep time: 5 minutes / Cook time: 20 to 25 minutes

GLUTEN-FREE NUT-FREE QUICK PREP KID-FRIENDLY ANTI-INFLAMMATORY

These are addictive, but since they're high in protein and minerals like calcium, that's a good thing. Have them as a snack, on top of a salad or soup, or as a side for lunch. Experiment with various seasonings, or try the flavor combinations listed for the Baked Kale Chips, Five Ways (page 192).

1 (14-ounce) can chickpeas, rinsed and drained, or 1½ cups cooked

2 tablespoons tamari, or soy sauce

1 tablespoon nutritional yeast

1 teaspoon smoked paprika, or regular paprika

1 teaspoon onion powder

½ teaspoon garlic powder

1. Preheat the oven to 400°F.
2. Toss the chickpeas with all the other ingredients, and spread them out on a baking sheet.
3. Bake for 20 to 25 minutes, tossing halfway through.

Technique: Bake these at a lower temperature, until fully dried and crispy, if you want to keep them longer. You can easily double the batch, and if you dry them out they will keep about a week in an airtight container.

Per Serving (¼ cup)

Calories: 121; Total fat: 2g; Carbs: 20g; Fiber: 6g; Protein: 8g

Lemon Coconut Cilantro Rolls

Makes 16 bite-size pieces
Prep time: 30 minutes / Chill time: 30 minutes

The combination of coconut, lemon, and roasted Brazil nuts makes for a rich flavor. Sprouts are one of the most nutrient-dense foods out there and are easy and cheap to grow at home through the winter. This recipe tucks sprouts away inside the roll to get them into those who think they don't like them.

½ cup fresh cilantro, chopped

1 cup sprouts (clover, alfalfa)

1 garlic clove, pressed

2 tablespoons ground Brazil nuts or almonds

2 tablespoons flaked coconut

1 tablespoon coconut oil

Pinch cayenne pepper

Pinch sea salt

Pinch freshly ground black pepper

Zest and juice of 1 lemon

2 tablespoons ground flaxseed

1 to 2 tablespoons water

2 whole-grain wraps, or corn wraps

1. Put everything but the wraps in a food processor and pulse to combine. Or combine the ingredients in a large bowl. Add the water, if needed, to help the mix come together.

2. Spread the mixture out over each wrap, roll it up, and place it in the fridge for 30 minutes to set.

3. Remove the rolls from the fridge and slice each into 8 pieces to serve as appetizers or sides with a soup or stew.

Technique: Get the best flavor by buying whole raw Brazil nuts or almonds, toasting them lightly in a dry skillet or toaster oven, and then grinding them in a coffee grinder.

Per Serving (1 piece)

Calories: 66; Total fat: 4g; Carbs: 6g; Fiber: 1g; Protein: 2g

Hummus, Five Ways

Makes 2 cups
Prep time: 10 minutes

GLUTEN-FREE NUT-FREE QUICK PREP KID-FRIENDLY

Hummus is quick and easy to make at home. Classic hummus is seasoned with lemon juice, garlic, and cumin, but you can branch off from there and make some interesting flavor combinations. I've given you five ways to spice it up, but use your imagination and create your own hummus variations.

FOR CLASSIC HUMMUS

1 (14-ounce) can chickpeas, rinsed and drained, or 1½ cups cooked

1 tablespoon tahini

Zest and juice of 1 lemon

1 to 2 garlic cloves, pressed

½ teaspoon sea salt

1 teaspoon ground cumin, plus additional for garnish

¼ cup water

Fresh parsley, chopped

Paprika

FOR ROASTED RED PEPPER HUMMUS

1 red bell pepper

½ teaspoon olive oil

Pinch sea salt

Classic Hummus

FOR CURRY HUMMUS

1 teaspoon curry powder

Classic Hummus

FOR SMOKY SWEET POTATO HUMMUS

1 sweet potato

1 teaspoon smoked paprika (optional)

Classic Hummus

FOR MINT HUMMUS

2 tablespoons fresh mint, chopped

Classic Hummus (replace lemon with lime)

FOR ZUCCHINI DILL HUMMUS

1 zucchini, coarsely chopped

2 teaspoons dried dill, or 1 tablespoon fresh dill

2 tablespoons nutritional yeast (optional)

Classic Hummus

continued

TO MAKE CLASSIC HUMMUS

1. Add the chickpeas, tahini, lemon zest and juice, garlic, salt, and cumin to a food processor (best choice) or blender (works okay). Start puréeing, adding about ¼ cup of water as it spins, with more water if necessary to get the consistency you like. You'll probably have to take the lid off and push down the mix that will fly up the sides of the processor.

2. Scoop the hummus into a serving bowl and sprinkle with parsley, paprika, and additional cumin.

TO MAKE ROASTED RED PEPPER HUMMUS

1. Preheat the oven or toaster oven to 350°F. Cut the bell pepper in half and remove the stem and seeds. Rub the oil and salt around the surface of the pepper to coat it. Put it on a baking sheet, face up, and bake until softened, about 20 minutes.

2. If you want to remove the skin from the pepper, put it into a plastic bag or a sealed container right when it comes out of the oven, so that the skin peels off easily when cooled. However, you can include the skin; there are nutrients and extra fiber in there.

3. Add the roasted pepper as you purée the Classic Hummus.

TO MAKE CURRY HUMMUS

Add 1 teaspoon or more mild or spicy curry powder as you purée the Classic Hummus.

TO MAKE SMOKY SWEET POTATO HUMMUS

1. Preheat the oven or toaster oven to 350°F. Pierce the sweet potato as deeply as you can with a fork or the tip of a paring knife. Put it on a baking sheet, and bake until softened, about 40 minutes.

2. Once the sweet potato is cooked, slice it in half and scoop out the flesh. Add the roasted sweet potato and smoked paprika (if using) as you purée the Classic Hummus.

TO MAKE MINT HUMMUS

1. Prepare the Classic Hummus, but use a lime instead of a lemon.

2. Add the fresh mint as you purée the hummus.

TO MAKE ZUCCHINI DILL HUMMUS

Add a raw zucchini (for a nutrient boost), dill, and nutritional yeast (if using) as you purée the Classic Hummus.

Leftovers: Hummus can be made in large batches to keep in the fridge, along with sliced vegetables, to be ready and waiting for those afternoon snack attacks.

Per Serving (1 cup, Classic)

Calories: 261; Total fat: 8g; Carbs: 39g; Fiber: 11g; Protein: 13g

Spicy Black Bean Dip

Makes about 2 cups
Prep time: 10 minutes

GLUTEN-FREE NUT-FREE QUICK PREP ANTI-INFLAMMATORY

This simple but flavorful dip makes a great appetizer with some steamed or raw vegetables and toasted pita chips, or it works as a base to a pizza. Make it as mild or spicy as you like by adjusting the cayenne pepper to taste. If you haven't used cayenne before, add it very carefully, as a little bit goes a long way.

1 (14-ounce) can black beans, drained and rinsed, or 1½ cups cooked

Zest and juice of 1 lime

1 tablespoon tamari, or soy sauce

¼ cup water

¼ cup fresh cilantro, chopped

1 teaspoon ground cumin

Pinch cayenne pepper

1. Put the beans in a food processor (best choice) or blender (works okay), along with the lime zest and juice, tamari, and about ¼ cup of water.
2. Blend until smooth, then blend in the cilantro, cumin, and cayenne.

Technique: If you don't have a blender or prefer a different consistency, simply transfer it to a bowl once the beans have been puréed and stir in the spices, instead of forcing the blender.

Per Serving (1 cup)

Calories: 190; Total fat: 1g; Carbs: 35g; Fiber: 12g; Protein: 13g

Avomame Spread

Makes 1½ cups
Prep time: 10 minutes

GLUTEN-FREE NUT-FREE QUICK PREP **ANTI-INFLAMMATORY** IMMUNE BOOSTER

Pair protein-rich edamame beans with healthy fat–rich avocado, and add some simple but flavorful and nutrient-dense seasonings, for a delicious and nourishing spread or dip. Serve with whole-grain pita or wraps, cut into wedges and toasted. It's also nice spread onto a pita and baked. Or use it as a dip for raw or roasted vegetables.

1 cup frozen shelled edamame beans, thawed

1 tablespoon apple cider vinegar, or lemon juice, or lime juice

1 tablespoon tamari, or soy sauce

1 teaspoon grated fresh ginger

1 avocado, coarsely chopped

¼ cup fresh cilantro, basil, mint, or parsley, chopped

½ cup alfalfa sprouts (optional)

1. Pulse the beans in a food processor with a bit of water and the apple cider vinegar until they're roughly chopped. If you don't have a food processor, thaw and then chop the beans.

2. Add the tamari, ginger, and avocado, and purée. Add the cilantro and sprouts (if using), and purée again until everything is smooth. If you don't have a food processor, mash the avocado and finely chop the rest to mix together.

Options: If you can't find edamame beans, use frozen peas, which are surprisingly high in protein and minerals such as selenium.

Per Serving (1 cup)

Calories: 343; Total fat: 22g; Carbs: 23g; Fiber: 12g; Protein: 19g

Greens and Beans Dip

Makes about 2 cups
Prep time: 20 minutes

GLUTEN-FREE NUT-FREE QUICK PREP KID-FRIENDLY ANTI-INFLAMMATORY
IMMUNE BOOSTER

This dip is packed with nutrients: protein and minerals in the beans, vitamins and antioxidants in the kale, and amino acids and minerals in the spices. It tastes delicious as a dip or as a spread in a sandwich.

1 (14-ounce) can white beans, drained and rinsed, or 1½ cups cooked

Zest and juice of 1 lemon

1 tablespoon almond butter, tahini, or other mild nut or seed butter

1 to 2 leaves kale, rinsed and stemmed

1 tablespoon nutritional yeast (optional)

1 to 2 teaspoons curry powder

1 to 2 teaspoons ground cumin

1 teaspoon smoked paprika, or regular

¼ teaspoon sea salt

1. Put everything in a food processor and pulse until it comes together. If you don't have a food processor, mash the beans and chop the kale, then mix together.

2. Taste for seasoning, adding more spices, lemon juice, or salt as desired.

Did you know? There are anti-oxidants in the zest of lemons that help offset the free radicals from cigarette smoke.

Per Serving (1 cup)

Calories: 278; Total fat: 7g; Carbs: 43g; Fiber: 13g; Protein: 17g

Guacamole

Makes 2 cups
Prep time: 10 minutes

GLUTEN-FREE NUT-FREE QUICK PREP KID-FRIENDLY ANTI-INFLAMMATORY
IMMUNE BOOSTER

This easy guacamole can add both freshness and a comfort-food vibe
to any meal—along with B vitamins, vitamins E and K, and potassium
from the avocado. Use your guacamole as a dip for red pepper slices, as
a spread in a sandwich or a wrap, stuffed into baked mushrooms, as a
topping for tacos or baked potatoes, or just eat it with a spoon.

2 ripe avocados

2 garlic cloves, pressed

Zest and juice of 1 lime

1 teaspoon ground cumin

Pinch sea salt

Pinch freshly ground black pepper

Pinch cayenne pepper (optional)

1. Mash the avocados in a large bowl.
2. Add the rest of the ingredients and
   stir to combine.

Toppings: Try adding diced tomatoes
(cherry are divine), chopped scallions or
chives, chopped fresh cilantro or basil,
lemon rather than lime, paprika, or
whatever you think would taste good!

Per Serving (1 cup)

Calories: 258; Total fat: 22g; Carbs: 18g;
Fiber: 11g; Protein: 4g

Baked Sweet Potato Fries

Makes 2 servings
Prep time: 10 minutes / Cook time: 30 to 45 minutes

GLUTEN-FREE NUT-FREE QUICK PREP KID-FRIENDLY ANTI-INFLAMMATORY
IMMUNE BOOSTER

These are easy to make and perfect to pop in the oven while you prepare some veggie burgers for a weekend meal—and you can easily double up to make enough for leftovers. These are also lovely with Avo-nnaise (page 238) as a dip, and served alongside a Grilled AHLT (page 144) for a savory brunch.

1 medium sweet potato

1 teaspoon olive oil, or 1 tablespoon vegetable broth

¼ teaspoon sea salt

1 teaspoon dried basil

½ teaspoon dried oregano

1. Preheat the oven to 350°F.
2. Peel the sweet potato and cut it into sticks. Rub the oil, salt, basil, and oregano all over them with your hands.
3. Spread the sweet potato sticks on a large baking sheet. Roast 30 to 45 minutes, or until they're soft, flipping them halfway through.

Technique: The thinner you cut your sweet potato sticks, the faster they will bake. And the faster they bake, the more they will be super soft inside, like deep-fried restaurant versions.

Per Serving (1 cup)

Calories: 258; Total fat: 22g; Carbs: 18g; Fiber: 11g; Protein: 4g

Roasted Garlic Pesto Potatoes

Makes 4 servings
Prep time: 5 minutes / Cook time: 20 to 25 minutes

GLUTEN-FREE NUT-FREE QUICK PREP

These potatoes make a perfect side dish served over fresh greens, along with one of the veggie burgers in this book or a Grilled Portobello (page 183). You can double up on oven use while you bake the burgers. They're also great to take to a summer picnic, and I guarantee they will not last long at a potluck.

6 to 8 small potatoes, scrubbed or peeled

8 garlic cloves, peeled

1 to 2 teaspoons olive oil

Pinch sea salt

¼ cup Basil Pesto (page 241)

1. Preheat the oven to 350°F.
2. Chop the potatoes into bite-size pieces. In a large bowl, toss them with the garlic cloves, oil, and salt, using your hands to make sure they all get coated.
3. Transfer everything to a rectangular baking dish. Bake for about 20 to 25 minutes, or until the potatoes are soft and lightly browned.
4. Toss with the pesto and serve.

Options: If you don't want to roast these with oil, bake the potatoes and garlic cloves whole, with the skin on, and then let them cool before chopping the potatoes and removing the garlic from the skins. Mix everything with the pesto.

Per Serving

Calories: 212; Total fat: 7g; Carbs: 35g; Fiber: 4g; Protein: 5g

Sweet Potato Biscuits

Makes 12 biscuits
Prep time: 60 minutes / Cook time: 10 minutes

NUT-FREE KID-FRIENDLY ANTI-INFLAMMATORY IMMUNE BOOSTER

These biscuits are super soft, super flavorful, and super nutrient-dense because of the sweet potato. They make a perfect side to a soup, stew, salad, or Grilled Portobello (page 183). They also freeze well, but they should be thawed before reheating.

1 medium sweet potato

3 tablespoons melted coconut oil, divided

1 tablespoon maple syrup

1 cup whole-grain flour

2 teaspoons baking powder

Pinch sea salt

Make ahead: Baking several sweet potatoes at once is a great way to have them on hand for making biscuits, puréed soups, or having a quick meal by topping the sweet potato with cooked lentils or chili.

Per Serving (1 biscuit)

Calories: 116; Total fat: 4g; Carbs: 19g; Fiber: 3g; Protein: 3g

1. Bake the sweet potato at 350°F for about 45 minutes, until tender. Allow it to cool, then remove the flesh and mash.

2. Turn the oven up to 375°F and line a baking sheet with parchment paper or lightly grease it.

3. Measure out 1 cup potato flesh. In a medium bowl, combine the mashed sweet potato with 1½ tablespoons of the coconut oil and the maple syrup.

4. Mix together the flour and baking powder in a separate medium bowl, then add the flour mixture to the potato mixture and blend well with a fork.

5. On a floured board, pat the mixture out into a ½-inch-thick circle and cut out 1-inch rounds, or simply drop spoonfuls of dough and pat them into rounds. Put the rounds onto the prepared baking sheet. Brush the top of each with some of the remaining 1½ tablespoons melted coconut oil.

6. Bake 10 minutes, or until lightly golden on top. Serve hot.

Garlic Toast

Makes 1 slice
Prep time: 5 minutes / Cook time: 5 minutes

NUT-FREE QUICK PREP KID-FRIENDLY ANTI-INFLAMMATORY

This is a super simple way to get the rich, delicious flavor of garlic bread in a plant-based way. Make just one slice to go along with your soup for dinner, or multiply it to make a whole batch for a crew, and watch them gobble it up before you tell them it's healthy.

1 teaspoon coconut oil, or olive oil

Pinch sea salt

1 to 2 teaspoons nutritional yeast

1 small garlic clove, pressed, or
   ¼ teaspoon garlic powder

1 slice whole-grain bread

1. In a small bowl, mix together the oil, salt, nutritional yeast, and garlic.
2. You can either toast the bread and then spread it with the seasoned oil, or brush the oil on the bread and put it in a toaster oven to bake for 5 minutes. If you're using fresh garlic, it's best to spread it onto the bread and then bake it.

Did you know? Garlic consumption has been shown to reduce the risk of heart attack, coronary artery disease, high blood pressure, and atherosclerosis (a buildup of cholesterol plaque in the walls of the arteries).

Per Serving (1 slice)

Calories: 138; Total fat: 6g; Carbs: 16g; Fiber: 4g; Protein: 7g

Lemon Pistachio Quinoa
Cookies page 220

chapter 11

DESSERTS

Almond-Date Energy Bites 210

Zesty Orange-Cranberry
Energy Bites 211

Tropi-Colada Frozen Pops 212

Funky Monkey Sorbet 213

Mint Chocolate Chip Sorbet 214

Lime in the Coconut Chia
Pudding 215

Chocolate Krinkles 216

Mango Coconut Cream Pie 217

Blueberry Avocado
Cheesecake 218

Banana Chocolate Cupcakes 219

Lemon Pistachio Quinoa
Cookies 220

Apple Crumble 222

Almond-Date Energy Bites

Makes 24 bites
Prep time: 5 minutes / Chill time: 15 minutes

GLUTEN-FREE QUICK PREP KID-FRIENDLY

The richness of these little bites belies their simplicity. Whip them together in just a few minutes, and they're good enough to take to a party. To make them extra fancy, dip them in a dusting of cocoa powder, ground almonds, or shredded coconut.

1 cup dates, pitted

1 cup unsweetened
   shredded coconut

¼ cup chia seeds

¾ cup ground almonds

¼ cup cocoa nibs, or non-dairy
   chocolate chips

1. Purée everything in a food processor until crumbly and sticking together, pushing down the sides whenever necessary to keep it blending. If you don't have a food processor, you can mash soft Medjool dates. But if you're using harder baking dates, you'll have to soak them (see the tip) and then try to purée them in a blender.

2. Form the mix into 24 balls and place them on a baking sheet lined with parchment or waxed paper. Put in the fridge to set for about 15 minutes.

Technique: Use the softest dates you can find. Medjool dates are the best for this purpose. The hard dates you see in the baking aisle of your supermarket are going to take a long time to blend up. If you use those, try soaking them in water for at least an hour before you start, and then draining.

Per Serving (1 bite)

Calories: 152; Total fat: 11g; Carbs: 13g; Fiber: 5g; Protein: 3g

Zesty Orange-Cranberry Energy Bites

Makes 12 bites
Prep time: 10 minutes / Chill time: 15 minutes

GLUTEN-FREE QUICK PREP KID-FRIENDLY ANTI-INFLAMMATORY

These little no-bake bites are a perfect energy booster and end-of-summer (or any time) treat. The toasted seeds give it a terrific crunch, and orange zest adds a pop of flavor. Enjoy your bites as a side to a big smoothie for breakfast, as an afternoon snack, or a healthy dessert.

2 tablespoons almond butter, or cashew or sunflower seed butter

2 tablespoons maple syrup, or brown rice syrup

¾ cup cooked quinoa

¼ cup sesame seeds, toasted

1 tablespoon chia seeds

½ teaspoon almond extract, or vanilla extract

Zest of 1 orange

1 tablespoon dried cranberries

¼ cup ground almonds

1. In a medium bowl, mix together the nut or seed butter and syrup until smooth and creamy.

2. Stir in the rest of the ingredients, and mix to make sure the consistency is holding together in a ball.

3. Form the mix into 12 balls. Place them on a baking sheet lined with parchment or waxed paper and put in the fridge to set for about 15 minutes.

Technique: If your balls aren't holding together, it's likely because of the moisture content of your cooked quinoa. Add more nut or seed butter mixed with syrup until it all sticks together.

Per Serving (1 bite)

Calories: 109; Total fat: 7g; Carbs: 11g; Fiber: 3g; Protein: 3g

Tropi-Colada Frozen Pops

Makes about 6 pops
Prep time: 5 minutes / Chill time: 4 hours

GLUTEN-FREE NUT-FREE QUICK PREP KID-FRIENDLY ANTI-INFLAMMATORY
IMMUNE BOOSTER

Enjoy all the flavor of a piña colada in ice pop form! These make a great dessert for a hot summer evening. Just watch for drips.

¾ **cup canned coconut milk**

2 cups chopped fresh pineapple

**1 cup chopped mango, fresh
   or frozen**

½ **cup unsweetened
   shredded coconut**

1. Purée everything in a food processor or blender until mostly smooth (a few chunks are nice).
2. Pour into ice pop molds, leaving a bit of room at the top for expansion, and put in the freezer until solid.

Options: This also makes a great smoothie if you don't have the patience to wait for it to freeze. Just add a frozen banana and some coconut water when you purée, and enjoy a couple of large smoothies.

Per Serving (1 ice pop)

Calories: 224; Total fat: 18g; Carbs: 17g; Fiber: 4g; Protein: 2g

Funky Monkey Sorbet

Makes 1 serving
Prep time: 5 minutes

GLUTEN-FREE QUICK PREP KID-FRIENDLY

Make a simple and delicious banana-based sorbet for a healthy treat any night of the week. You don't need to feel the slightest bit guilty diving into a bowl while you binge-watch TV. The basic sorbet, without the funky monkey extras (the walnuts and banana chocolate cupcake), can be enjoyed all on its own or can be a base for lots of other flavors. Mint Chocolate Chip Sorbet (page 214) is one example, and you can create plenty of others.

1 frozen banana

1 tablespoon almond butter, or peanut butter, or other nut or seed butter

2 to 3 tablespoons non-dairy milk, or water (only if needed)

1 tablespoon walnuts, chopped

½ Banana Chocolate Cupcake (page 219), crumbled

1. Put the banana and almond butter in a food processor or blender and purée until it's smooth. Add the non-dairy milk if needed to keep blending (but only if needed, as this will make the texture less solid).

2. Stir in the walnuts and cupcake bits, or sprinkle them on top.

3. Serve right away, or if the mixture doesn't seem firm enough, put it in the freezer for a few minutes.

Make ahead: Peel and freeze bananas when they're ripe, so you can use them to make smoothies, sorbets, or banana bread whenever you like. This is a great way to store those big bags of overripe bananas grocery stores sell at a discount.

Per Serving

Calories: 225; Total fat: 11g; Carbs: 31g; Fiber: 5g; Protein: 5g

Mint Chocolate Chip Sorbet

Makes 1 serving
Prep time: 5 minutes

GLUTEN-FREE QUICK PREP KID-FRIENDLY IMMUNE BOOSTER

Let's use fresh mint for both flavor and nutrition in this wholesome dessert. Not only good for fresh breath, mint's oils can help soothe indigestion and fight bacteria. Goji berries add a crunch reminiscent of candy cane if you're game!

1 frozen banana

1 tablespoon almond butter, or peanut butter, or other nut or seed butter

2 tablespoons fresh mint, minced

¼ cup or less non-dairy milk (only if needed)

2 to 3 tablespoons non-dairy chocolate chips, or cocoa nibs

2 to 3 tablespoons goji berries (optional)

1. Put the banana, almond butter, and mint in a food processor or blender and purée until smooth. Add the non-dairy milk if needed to keep blending (but only if needed, as this will make the texture less solid).

2. Pulse the chocolate chips and goji berries (if using) into the mix so they're roughly chopped up.

Did you know? Goji berries are a good source of vitamin A, vitamin C, iron, and dietary fiber. A ¼-cup serving of goji berries provides you with 15 percent of the daily recommended value of iron.

Per Serving

Calories: 212; Total fat: 10g; Carbs: 31g; Fiber: 4g; Protein: 3g

Lime in the Coconut Chia Pudding

Makes 3 to 4 servings
Prep time: 10 minutes / Chill time: 20 minutes

GLUTEN-FREE NUT-FREE QUICK PREP KID-FRIENDLY ANTI-INFLAMMATORY
IMMUNE BOOSTER

This is a decadent and rich dessert, and it is super healthy at the same time. It's a refreshing and beautiful way to finish off a summer meal. Chia seeds are rich in omega-3 fatty acids for brain and nerve health, protein to keep you full, calcium for bone strength, and free radical–fighting antioxidants. Try this pudding with orange instead of lime, or puréed raspberries. This can stay chilled for up to a week in the fridge. It makes a great breakfast, too.

Zest and juice of 1 lime

1 (14-ounce) can coconut milk

1 to 2 dates, or 1 tablespoon coconut or other unrefined sugar, or 1 tablespoon maple syrup, or 10 to 15 drops pure liquid stevia

2 tablespoons chia seeds, whole or ground

2 teaspoons matcha green tea powder (optional)

1. Blend all the ingredients in a blender until smooth.
2. Chill in the fridge for about 20 minutes, then serve topped with one or more of the topping ideas.

Toppings: Try blueberries, black-berries, sliced strawberries, Coconut Whipped Cream (page 231), or toasted unsweetened coconut.

Per Serving

Calories: 226; Total fat: 20g; Carbs: 13g; Fiber: 5g; Protein: 3g

Chocolate Krinkles

Makes 16 krinkles
Prep time: 20 minutes / Chill time: 30 minutes

GLUTEN-FREE KID-FRIENDLY

This is a healthy plant-based spin on a treat that my nana used to make for me when I was little. They're an easy and delicious treat that I guarantee will be gobbled up by all your guests. Cocoa powder is a rich source of antioxidants, minerals, and vitamins. When people crave chocolate, an underlying reason may be that they have a magnesium deficiency.

⅓ **cup coconut oil**

⅓ **cup maple syrup**

⅓ **cup unsweetened cocoa powder**

½ **cup natural peanut butter, or almond, cashew, or sunflower seed butter**

About 3 cups puffed whole-grain rice

Did you know? Coconut oil makes a great base for these, giving them a solid chocolate texture. Although it has saturated fat, it's a different form that doesn't have the negative impact on cardiovascular health that animal saturated fats do. Coconut oil can be helpful for vegans in maintaining healthy hormone levels.

1. Mix together the coconut oil, maple syrup, cocoa powder, and peanut butter in a large bowl until the mixture is smooth. Add the puffed rice so that it all gets coated in chocolate. If you wind up with chocolate left in the bottom of the bowl, just stir in some more puffed rice.

2. Spoon the mixture in 2-tablespoon krinkle portions onto a baking sheet lined with waxed or parchment paper. Put the baking sheet in the fridge, or in a cold room or basement, until the chocolate solidifies, about 30 minutes.

3. Keep them stored in the fridge; otherwise they tend to melt.

Per Serving (1 krinkle)

Calories: 125; Total fat: 10g; Carbs: 10g; Fiber: 1g; Protein: 3g

Mango Coconut Cream Pie

Makes 8 servings

Prep time: 20 minutes / Chill time: 30 minutes

Add a tropical theme to a no-bake, rich coconut cream pie made with
nutrient-dense plant foods so you can enjoy this guilt-free. For a quicker
option, just make the mango filling as a pudding, and sprinkle the crust
as a crumbly topping. Either way, you never have to turn your oven on
during those hot summer days.

FOR THE CRUST

½ cup rolled oats

1 cup cashews

1 cup soft pitted dates

FOR THE FILLING

1 cup canned coconut milk

½ cup water

2 large mangos, peeled and
chopped, or about 2 cups
frozen chunks

½ cup unsweetened
shredded coconut

Toppings: Top with a batch of Coconut
Whipped Cream (page 231) scooped on
top of the pie once it's set. Finish it off with
a sprinkling of toasted shredded coconut.

1. Put all the crust ingredients in a food
   processor and pulse until it holds
   together. If you don't have a food
   processor, chop everything as finely
   as possible and use ½ cup cashew
   or almond butter in place of half
   the cashews. Press the mixture
   down firmly into an 8-inch pie or
   springform pan.

2. Put the all filling ingredients in a
   blender and purée until smooth (about
   1 minute). It should be very thick, so
   you may have to stop and stir until
   it's smooth.

3. Pour the filling into the crust, use a
   rubber spatula to smooth the top, and
   put the pie in the freezer until set,
   about 30 minutes.

4. Once frozen, it should be set out for
   about 15 minutes to soften before
   serving.

Per Serving (1 slice)

Calories: 427; Total fat: 28g; Carbs: 45g;
Fiber: 6g; Protein: 8g

Blueberry Avocado Cheesecake

Makes 8 servings
Prep time: 20 minutes / Chill time: 2 hours

KID-FRIENDLY ANTI-INFLAMMATORY IMMUNE BOOSTER

This plant-based twist on cheesecake pairs flavorful, antioxidant-rich blueberries with creamy, potassium-rich avocado and a crumbly no-bake crust for a surprisingly easy and decadent frozen dessert. The lime juice is optional but adds a little zing and helps the avocado taste fresh longer. Try the fresh basil for a unique flavor.

FOR THE CRUST

1 cup rolled oats

1 cup walnuts

1 cup soft pitted dates

1 teaspoon lime zest (optional)

FOR THE FILLING

2 avocados, peeled and pitted
    (about 1½ cups)

1 cup blueberries, fresh or frozen

2 tablespoons unrefined sugar, or
    maple syrup (optional)

2 to 4 tablespoons lime juice
    (optional)

1 to 2 tablespoons fresh basil,
    minced (optional)

1. Put all the crust ingredients in a food processor and pulse until the mixture holds together. If you don't have a food processor, chop everything as finely as possible and use ½ cup cashew or almond butter in place of half the walnuts. Press the mixture down firmly into an 8-inch pie or springform pan.

2. Put all the filling ingredients in a blender and purée until smooth.

3. Pour the filling into the crust, use a rubber spatula to smooth the top, and put the cheesecake in the freezer for 2 hours.

Toppings: When serving, take the cheesecake out of the freezer 10 to 15 minutes before slicing, then scoop a spoonful of Coconut Whipped Cream (page 231) and sprinkle a few blueberries on top of each slice.

Per Serving (1 slice)

Calories: 361; Total fat: 24g; Carbs: 37g; Fiber: 7g; Protein: 6g

Banana Chocolate Cupcakes

Makes 12 cupcakes
Prep time: 20 minutes / Cook time: 20 to 25 minutes

KID-FRIENDLY **ANTI-INFLAMMATORY** IMMUNE BOOSTER

These cupcakes are not only delicious but are also packed with minerals. I chose the ingredients specifically to have lots of potassium, magnesium, and calcium to help with blood pressure balance, muscle cramps, and bone health.

3 medium bananas

1 cup non-dairy milk

2 tablespoons almond butter

1 teaspoon apple cider vinegar

1 teaspoon pure vanilla extract

1¼ cups whole-grain flour

½ cup rolled oats

¼ cup coconut sugar (optional)

1 teaspoon baking powder

½ teaspoon baking soda

½ cup unsweetened cocoa powder

¼ cup chia seeds, or sesame seeds

Pinch sea salt

¼ cup dark chocolate chips, dried cranberries, or raisins (optional)

Make ahead: These will freeze well, and if you freeze them individually they make a great addition to a packed lunch.

1. Preheat the oven to 350°F. Lightly grease the cups of two 6-cup muffin tins or line with paper muffin cups.
2. Put the bananas, milk, almond butter, vinegar, and vanilla in a blender and purée until smooth. Or stir together in a large bowl until smooth and creamy.
3. Put the flour, oats, sugar (if using), baking powder, baking soda, cocoa powder, chia seeds, salt, and chocolate chips in another large bowl, and stir to combine.
4. Mix together the wet and dry ingredients, stirring as little as possible.
5. Spoon into muffin cups, and bake for 20 to 25 minutes.
6. Take the cupcakes out of the oven and let them cool fully before taking out of the muffin tins, since they'll be very moist.

Per Serving (1 cupcake)

Calories: 215; Total fat: 6g; Carbs: 39g; Fiber: 9g; Protein: 6g

Lemon Pistachio Quinoa Cookies

Makes 12 to 16 cookies
Prep time: 10 minutes / Cook time: 20 minutes

GLUTEN-FREE QUICK PREP KID-FRIENDLY ANTI-INFLAMMATORY

Using cooked quinoa in cookies creates such great texture and adds so much nutrition. This recipe goes to show it *is* possible to make healthy cookies. Quinoa is much talked about because it has essential amino acids (a.k.a. complete proteins) and is gluten-free. It's also high in folate, magnesium, phosphorus, and manganese.

2 tablespoons ground flaxseed

3 tablespoons water

1 large banana

½ cup unrefined sugar

½ cup almond butter, or sunflower seed butter

2 cups cooked quinoa

3 tablespoons freshly squeezed lemon juice

1 teaspoon lemon zest (optional)

1 teaspoon pure vanilla extract

½ teaspoon baking soda

1 teaspoon baking powder

1¼ cups coconut flour, brown rice flour, or ground almonds

½ cup shelled and chopped pistachios

¼ cup non-dairy chocolate chips

1. Preheat the oven to 400°F. Line a large baking sheet with parchment paper.

2. In a small bowl, mix the ground flaxseed with 3 tablespoons water and let it sit until it turns into a jelly-like texture (we call this a flax egg).

3. Mash the banana in a large bowl, then mix in the sugar and almond butter until it's smooth and creamy. Add the quinoa and the flax egg, along with the lemon juice, lemon zest (if using), and vanilla. Mix until everything is combined well.

4. Add the baking soda, baking powder, and flour, and stir gently until all the dry ingredients are incorporated. Fold in the pistachios and chocolate chips.

5. Form the dough into 12 to 16 balls. Place on the baking sheet and press them down flat with your hand. Bake for 20 minutes.

6. Take them out of the oven, and let them cool for a few minutes before transferring them to a cooling rack and letting them cool completely. They will be a bit delicate until they're fully cooled, so try to keep yourself— and your family—from diving in too soon.

Make ahead: Cook the quinoa in advance by putting 1 cup in a pot with 2 cups water, bringing to a boil, then simmering 25 minutes.

Per Serving (1 cookie)

Calories: 330; Total fat: 17g; Carbs: 38g; Fiber: 12g; Protein: 10g

Apple Crumble

Makes 6 servings

Prep time: 20 minutes / Cook time: 25 minutes

KID-FRIENDLY ANTI-INFLAMMATORY IMMUNE BOOSTER

Apple crumble is easily made plant based. The fiber and phytonutrients in apples can help you regulate your blood sugar and blood fat. Leave the peels on for maximum nutrient density. Serve this crumble warm and topped with the Funky Monkey Sorbet (page 213) for plant-based à la mode.

FOR THE FILLING

4 to 5 apples, cored and chopped (about 6 cups)

½ cup unsweetened applesauce, or ¼ cup water

2 to 3 tablespoons unrefined sugar (coconut, date, sucanat, maple syrup)

1 teaspoon ground cinnamon

Pinch sea salt

FOR THE CRUMBLE

2 tablespoons almond butter, or cashew or sunflower seed butter

2 tablespoons maple syrup

1½ cups rolled oats

½ cup walnuts, finely chopped

½ teaspoon ground cinnamon

2 to 3 tablespoons unrefined granular sugar (coconut, date, sucanat)

1. Preheat the oven to 350°F.

2. Put the apples and applesauce in an 8-inch-square baking dish, and sprinkle with the sugar, cinnamon, and salt. Toss to combine.

3. In a medium bowl, mix together the nut butter and maple syrup until smooth and creamy. Add the oats, walnuts, cinnamon, and sugar and stir to coat, using your hands if necessary. (If you have a small food processor, pulse the oats and walnuts together before adding them to the mix.)

4. Sprinkle the topping over the apples, and put the dish in the oven. Bake for 20 to 25 minutes, or until the fruit is soft and the topping is lightly browned.

Options: Try adding cranberries (dried, fresh, or frozen) to the apples, or replace the apples with peaches.

Per Serving

Calories: 356; Total fat: 17g; Carbs: 49g; Fiber: 7g; Protein: 7g

Fresh Mango Salsa *page 240*

chapter 12

HOMEMADE BASICS, SAUCES, AND CONDIMENTS

Easy-Peasy Almond Milk 226

Buckwheat Sesame Milk 227

Sunflower Hemp Milk 228

Cheesy Sprinkle 229

Cashew Sour Cream 230

Coconut Whipped Cream 231

Herbed Millet Pizza Crust 232

Easy DIY Pizza Crust 234

Green Goddess Dressing 235

Creamy Balsamic Dressing 236

Toasted Sesame Miso Dressing 237

Avo-nnaise 238

Peanut Sauce 239

Fresh Mango Salsa 240

Basil Pesto 241

Marinara Sauce 242

Easy-Peasy Almond Milk

Makes 2 cups
Prep time: 10 minutes

GLUTEN-FREE QUICK PREP KID-FRIENDLY

Most homemade almond milk recipes tell you to soak whole raw almonds overnight, and then blend. You can certainly do that, but here's a shortcut: Use raw almond butter. This milk is perfect to make in small batches, so it doesn't go bad if you're the only one using it. It also doesn't require a high-powered blender.

2 to 3 tablespoons raw almond butter

2 cups water

Pinch sea salt

1 to 2 dates, or 10 drops pure stevia (or vanilla stevia), or 1 to 2 tablespoons unrefined sugar

¼ teaspoon pure vanilla extract (optional)

1. Put everything in a blender and purée until smooth.
2. Strain the fiber from the almonds through a piece of cheesecloth or a fine-mesh sieve.
3. Keep in an airtight container in the fridge for up to 5 days.

Technique: Use a raw almond butter, not roasted, for a more neutral flavor. If you can't find it, see if you can find a raw cashew or sunflower seed butter.

Per Serving (1 cup)

Calories: 140; Total fat: 10g; Carbs: 14g; Fiber: 2g; Protein: 3g

Buckwheat Sesame Milk

Makes 4 cups
Prep time: 10 minutes

GLUTEN-FREE NUT-FREE QUICK PREP **ANTI-INFLAMMATORY**

When making your own non-dairy milks, try branching out to use different grains, seeds, and nuts for different flavors and nutrients. Buckwheat gives a rich, nutty flavor, and calcium-rich tahini for added creaminess is a perfect pairing.

1 cup cooked buckwheat

1 tablespoon tahini, or other nut or seed butter

1 teaspoon pure vanilla extract (optional)

2 to 3 dates, or 15 drops pure stevia (or vanilla stevia), or 2 to 3 tablespoons unrefined sugar

3 cups water

1. Put everything in a blender, and purée until smooth.
2. Strain the fiber through a piece of cheesecloth or a fine-mesh sieve.
3. Keep in an airtight container in the fridge for up to 5 days.

Make ahead: Cook the buckwheat in advance, or put ½ cup untoasted buckwheat (or any other whole grain, like quinoa or millet or rice) in a pot with 1 cup water. Bring it to a boil then leave to simmer, covered, until it's soft. Buckwheat takes about 20 minutes to cook.

Per Serving (1 cup)

Calories: 107; Total fat: 3g; Carbs: 19g; Fiber: 3g; Protein: 3g

Sunflower Hemp Milk

Makes 2 cups
Prep time: 10 minutes

GLUTEN-FREE NUT-FREE QUICK PREP KID-FRIENDLY IMMUNE BOOSTER

This non-dairy milk is a combination of sunflower and hemp seeds for a boost of zinc, selenium, and omega-3s. It can be difficult to get enough selenium, which is important for your immune system, as well as healthy hair, skin, and nails.

2 cups water

3 tablespoons sunflower seeds

2 tablespoons hemp seeds, or other seed

1 to 2 dates, or 10 drops pure stevia (or vanilla stevia), or 1 to 2 tablespoons unrefined sugar

¼ teaspoon pure vanilla extract (optional)

1. Put everything in a blender, and purée until smooth.
2. Strain the fiber through a piece of cheesecloth or a fine-mesh sieve.
3. Keep in an airtight container in the fridge for up to 5 days.

Did you know? Hemp seeds, or hemp hearts, are a soft and easily digested source of omega-3 fatty acids, as well as magnesium and protein.

Per Serving (1 cup)

Calories: 224; Total fat: 16g; Carbs: 17g; Fiber: 4g; Protein: 8g

Cheesy Sprinkle

Makes ½ cup
Prep time: 10 minutes

This is a salty, savory, and nutritious sprinkle to enjoy as a Parmesan-like dusting over spaghetti, or make it into a crumble for topping a pizza with the addition of a little olive oil. You could also add a splash of lemon juice to get a tangy feta-like taste for a Greek salad.

½ cup ground sunflower seeds, or Brazil nuts, or macadamia nuts

2 teaspoons sea salt

1 to 2 tablespoons nutritional yeast

1 tablespoon olive oil (optional)

1. Place the sunflower seeds in a small bowl, then add the salt and nutritional yeast. Mix to combine.
2. Leave as is for a dry sprinkle, or add just enough olive oil to bring the mixture together into a crumbly texture.

Did you know? Sunflower seeds have 47 percent of your daily vitamin E requirements, and 21 percent of your daily selenium requirements in just 2 tablespoons. Brazil nuts have 137 percent of your daily selenium requirements in just one nut.

Per Serving (1 tablespoon)

Calories: 106; Total fat: 9g; Carbs: 5g; Fiber: 2g; Protein: 4g

Cashew Sour Cream

Makes 1½ cups

Soak time: 1 to 8 hours / Prep time: 5 minutes

GLUTEN-FREE QUICK PREP KID-FRIENDLY ANTI-INFLAMMATORY IMMUNE BOOSTER

Use this like you would dairy-based sour cream: on baked potatoes, on fajitas, as a dip for chips or veggies, or even as a creamy swirl in your chili. Cashews are the perfect base to make creamy things, because they're so soft and have a mild flavor. They're also rich in magnesium, which works with calcium to build strong bones and prevent muscle cramps, and may even help reduce migraines. Make sure you use raw cashews, not roasted or toasted, which would give a very different flavor and texture.

1 cup raw cashews

½ cup water

Juice of ½ lemon (about 2 to 3 tablespoons)

1 teaspoon apple cider vinegar, or more lemon juice

¼ teaspoon sea salt

1 tablespoon nutritional yeast (optional)

Make ahead: This is best made ahead of time not only for soaking the cashews but also for the cream to thicken in the fridge if you chill it. Keep it in a small airtight container in the fridge, and it will last for about one week.

1. Place the cashews in a medium bowl and cover with water. Soak overnight (about 8 hours). If you don't have that long, you can cover them with boiling water and they should soften in about 1 hour. Rinse and drain.
2. Put the nuts in a blender. Add the water, lemon juice, vinegar, salt, and nutritional yeast (if using). Blend on high until the mixture is completely smooth and creamy, about 2 minutes. Add more water if needed to keep it blending.

Per Serving (1 cup)

Calories: 860; Total fat: 66g; Carbs: 54g; Fiber: 7g; Protein: 31g

Coconut Whipped Cream

Makes just under 1 cup

Chill time: 24 hours / Prep time: 10 minutes

GLUTEN-FREE NUT-FREE QUICK PREP KID-FRIENDLY

This is easy to make, as long as you choose the right can of coconut milk. See the box below. It's important to grind the coconut sugar before you use it, so it's a fine powder, or else it will be too heavy and cause the coconut cream to lose its fluffiness. This is a great topping for fresh-cut fruit or any dessert, or to scoop on top of a rich homemade latte.

1 (14-ounce) can full-fat coconut milk, or ¾ cup coconut cream

2 tablespoons coconut sugar

1 tablespoon arrowroot powder, or cornstarch

1 teaspoon pure vanilla extract (optional)

Technique: Some cans of coconut milk won't separate, particularly if they use guar gum, since it prevents separation. If yours hasn't formed a somewhat hard mass on the top after 24 hours in the fridge, you'll need to try another brand. There are some brands of full-fat, pure coconut cream, which won't need to be separated and can be used as is.

1. Refrigerate the can of coconut milk for at least 24 hours. When you open the can, it should have a hardened mass on the top. Scoop this off into a large bowl, and reserve the rest to use in smoothies.

2. In a small blender, food processor, or clean coffee grinder, purée the coconut sugar and arrowroot powder until fine.

3. Whip the coconut cream with electric beaters until soft and fluffy, sprinkling with sugar and vanilla (if using) as you continue to whip.

Per Serving (1 cup)

Calories: 455; Total fat: 36g; Carbs: 34g; Fiber: 1g; Protein: 4g

Herbed Millet Pizza Crust

Makes 1 large thin-crust pizza crust
Prep time: 30 minutes / Cook time: 20 minutes

GLUTEN-FREE NUT-FREE KID-FRIENDLY ANTI-INFLAMMATORY

This pizza crust is made of cooked millet, seasoned with herbs for flavor. You could also make this crust with polenta, buckwheat, or short-grain brown rice. All are gluten-free.

½ cup coarsely ground millet

1½ cups water

1 tablespoon mixed dried
    Italian herbs

¼ teaspoon sea salt

1 to 2 tablespoons nutritional yeast

1. Preheat the oven to 350°F. Line an 8-inch-round pie dish or springform pan with parchment paper so that you can lift the crust out after it's cooked. The crust will be a bit fragile until it cools and tends to stick unless you use a nonstick pan.

2. Put the millet in a small pot with the water and a pinch salt, bring it to a boil, then cover and simmer for 15 to 20 minutes. Stir it occasionally to keep it from sticking to the bottom of the pot. You can add the dried herbs to cook with the millet for a more intense flavor, or just stir them in after the millet is cooked.

3. Once the millet is cooked, add the salt and nutritional yeast. Spread the cooked and seasoned millet out in an even layer in your pan, all the way to the edges.

4. Put the crust in the oven for 20 minutes, or until lightly browned around the edges.

Technique: While the crust bakes, you can prepare the sauce and veggies to use as toppings for your pizza. Then you just take it out, top it, and put it back in the oven to finish.

Per Serving (1 crust)

Calories: 800; Total fat: 9g; Carbs: 152g; Fiber: 20g; Protein: 28g

Easy DIY Pizza Crust

Makes 2 medium pizza crusts
Prep time: 10 minutes / Cook time: 10 to 15 minutes

NUT-FREE QUICK PREP KID-FRIENDLY

It's easier than you might think to make your own pizza crust. This doesn't need to rise, as bread does; you can simply make the dough and put it in the oven to bake. The best pizza crusts are baked in wood-fired ovens, which get incredibly hot, so feel free to turn your oven up as high as it will go. Just keep an eye on the crust, as it will obviously cook faster in a hotter oven.

1 cup whole-grain flour

1 tablespoon dry active yeast

1 teaspoon unrefined sugar

½ teaspoon sea salt

1 tablespoon olive oil

1 cup water

Toppings: The crusts will only be half-cooked at this point. You then put your toppings on, and put the pizza back into the oven to finish cooking. You could cook it all at once, but in my experience the pizza crust doesn't bake through in the center when the sauce and toppings are on it right from the start.

Per Serving (1 crust)

Calories: 465; Total fat: 9g; Carbs: 85g; Fiber: 15g; Protein: 18g

1. Preheat the oven to 400°F. Sprinkle some coarsely ground millet or corn flour on 1 large or 2 small baking sheets.

2. Combine the flour, yeast, sugar, and salt in a large bowl. Make a well in the center and add the oil, then the water. Stir the dough together with a spoon until it's too dry to stir, then bring it together with your hands. Add more water or flour as necessary to make a soft dough that doesn't stick to your fingers.

3. Knead for 5 minutes on a lightly floured board. Press or roll out into two pizza crusts.

4. Lay the crusts on the baking sheets, and put them in the oven for 10 minutes, or until they start to get a light color around the edges.

Green Goddess Dressing

Makes 1 cup
Prep time: 10 minutes

GLUTEN-FREE NUT-FREE QUICK PREP **ANTI-INFLAMMATORY** IMMUNE BOOSTER

This dressing is an essential, and it's easy to make plant based. Serve it as a dip, or toss with your salad greens before putting the salad together, with an extra drizzle on top. It should keep 5 to 6 days in the fridge in an airtight container.

½ cup tahini

2 tablespoons apple cider vinegar

Juice of 1 lemon

¼ cup tamari, or soy sauce

2 garlic cloves, minced or pressed

½ cup water

½ cup fresh basil, minced

½ cup fresh parsley, minced

½ cup scallions, or chives, minced

¼ teaspoon sea salt

Pinch freshly ground black pepper
   (optional)

1 tablespoon maple syrup (optional)

Put all the ingredients in a blender or food processor and blend until smooth, 30 to 45 seconds. Add more water if needed to get a thick, creamy dressing.

Options: If you can find fresh tarragon, replace part of the basil or parsley with that. You could also throw some fresh spinach in the blender.

Per Serving (1 tablespoon)

Calories: 54; Total fat: 4g; Carbs: 3g; Fiber: 1g; Protein: 2g

Creamy Balsamic Dressing

Makes ¾ cup

Prep time: 10 minutes

GLUTEN-FREE NUT-FREE QUICK PREP KID-FRIENDLY

This is a perfect all-purpose salad dressing to have on hand always, so you can throw together a quick salad or bowl. It's delicious as an even simpler version without the fresh basil, if you don't have any. This keeps for about a week in an airtight bottle.

¼ **cup tahini**

¼ **cup balsamic vinegar**

¼ **cup fresh basil, minced**

⅛ **cup water**

1 **tablespoon maple syrup (optional)**

1 **garlic clove, pressed**

Pinch sea salt

Pinch freshly ground black pepper (optional)

Put all the ingredients in a blender or food processor and blend until smooth. You could whisk this together without a blender, if you mince the basil very fine.

Options: Make it even creamier and slightly sweeter by using cashew butter instead of tahini.

Per Serving (1 tablespoon)

Calories: 39; Total fat: 3g; Carbs: 7g; Fiber: 0g; Protein: 1g

Toasted Sesame Miso Dressing

Makes $\frac{1}{3}$ cup
Prep time: 5 minutes

GLUTEN-FREE NUT-FREE QUICK PREP ANTI-INFLAMMATORY IMMUNE BOOSTER

This salty, delicious dressing is based on miso, which is a fermented soybean paste, and flavored with toasted sesame oil. It makes a great dip for vegetables or spring rolls, or can be used as a dressing for many different salads. This keeps for a long time in an airtight bottle, so you could double or triple the recipe and make this in large batches. It's great to have on hand to drizzle on quick stir-fries, salads, and bowls.

2 tablespoons miso

2 tablespoons apple cider vinegar, or rice vinegar

1 tablespoon tamari, or soy sauce

1 tablespoon water

½ teaspoon toasted sesame oil

½-inch piece ginger, grated

½ teaspoon maple syrup (optional)

1 tablespoon sesame seeds (optional)

Put all the ingredients together in a bowl and stir together until smooth and creamy.

Options: If you can't find or don't like miso, use tahini instead to make a creamy sesame ginger dressing.

Per Serving (1 tablespoon)

Calories: 35; Total fat: 2g; Carbs: 3g; Fiber: 1g; Protein: 1g

Avo-nnaise

Makes 1 cup
Prep time: 10 minutes

GLUTEN-FREE NUT-FREE QUICK PREP KID-FRIENDLY ANTI-INFLAMMATORY

Get all the flavor of egg-based mayo, and more nutrients. Spread this on a burger or a sandwich, or use it as a dip for Baked Sweet Potato Fries (page 204). Because this is avocado-based, it won't keep for too long. The lemon juice helps minimize oxidation, but you'll want to use this up in about three days.

1 avocado, peeled

1 tablespoon freshly squeezed lemon juice

1 tablespoon nutritional yeast

1 garlic clove, or 1 teaspoon garlic powder

Pinch sea salt

1 teaspoon Dijon mustard (optional)

1 teaspoon paprika (optional)

Put all the ingredients in a blender or food processor and blend until smooth, adding a little water if necessary for consistency.

Options: You could make this with a tahini or cashew butter base instead of the avocado, with a more bit lemon juice or apple cider vinegar.

Per Serving (1 tablespoon)

Calories: 19; Total fat: 1g; Carbs: 1g; Fiber: 1g; Protein: 1g

Peanut Sauce

Makes ¾ cup
Prep time: 10 minutes

GLUTEN-FREE QUICK PREP KID-FRIENDLY

This rich, flavorful sauce is lovely to toss with rice noodles and vegetables in a Pad Thai Bowl (page 150), to dip with Vietnamese Summer Rolls (page 164), or to toss with some simple stir-fried vegetables over cooked quinoa. Make it once and have it on hand for cravings during the week.

⅓ cup natural peanut butter, or almond, cashew, or sunflower seed butter

3 tablespoons brown rice vinegar, or apple cider vinegar

2 tablespoons freshly squeezed lime juice

2 tablespoons tamari, or soy sauce

1 tablespoon toasted sesame oil

1 tablespoon maple syrup (optional)

Pinch red pepper flakes

¼ cup water

1. Put the peanut butter, vinegar, and lime juice in a medium mixing bowl and whisk to combine until thickened.

2. Add the tamari, sesame oil, maple syrup (if using), and red pepper flakes and stir to mix. Add the water a little at a time and whisk until you get a thick, creamy sauce, slightly thinner for a dressing and slightly thicker for a dip. Or you could purée everything in a blender or food processor until smooth and creamy.

Technique: Taste and adjust seasonings as needed, adding more maple syrup for sweetness, chili sauce (chili or red pepper) for heat, lime juice for acidity, or tamari for saltiness.

Per Serving (1 tablespoon)

Calories: 56; Total fat: 5g; Carbs: 3g; Fiber: 0g; Protein: 2g

Fresh Mango Salsa

Makes 2 cups
Prep time: 15 minutes

GLUTEN-FREE NUT-FREE QUICK PREP KID-FRIENDLY IMMUNE BOOSTER

This salsa is a lovely, summery addition to meals. You can put some on top of a Grilled Portobello (page 183) at a barbecue, on a Black Bean Taco Salad Bowl (page 154), Blackeye Pea Burritos (page 182), or Hearty Chili (page 115), or have it with Hummus (page 197) on a rice cake or toasted pita.

1 large mango, diced

1 medium tomato, diced

1 garlic clove, pressed

Juice of ½ lime

1 scallion, chopped

1 tablespoon chopped jalapeño
    pepper (optional)

¼ cup fresh cilantro, parsley, mint,
    and/or basil, chopped

Pinch sea salt

Mix everything together in a bowl, or pulse in a food processor if you want a smoother texture.

Options: If fresh mangos are not in season, this salsa is also really nice with fresh peaches, nectarines, cantaloupe, or just more tomatoes.

Per Serving (1 cup)

Calories: 135; Total fat: 1g; Carbs: 35g; Fiber: 5g; Protein: 2g

Basil Pesto

Makes about 1½ cups
Prep time: 15 minutes

GLUTEN-FREE QUICK PREP KID-FRIENDLY ANTI-INFLAMMATORY IMMUNE BOOSTER

Fresh basil pesto is a wonderful way to use the basil leaves that mature in late summer all at once, and it's a healthy alternative to store-bought pesto. Freeze it in ice cube trays, then keep them in a freezer bag to use through the winter. Fresh basil is fantastically nutritious, full of vitamin K for healthy bones, and has antibacterial and DNA-protective qualities. Pine nuts (which are actually seeds) are a natural appetite suppressant, which might help keep you from overeating this amazingly delicious pesto.

1 cup fresh basil, chopped

½ cup pine nuts, or walnuts, or sunflower seeds

1 to 2 garlic cloves, pressed

Zest and juice of 1 small lemon

2 tablespoons nutritional yeast (optional)

¼ cup avocado, or 2 tablespoons tahini (optional)

⅛ teaspoon sea salt

Options: Try fresh parsley, arugula, mint, or oregano instead of basil. Add some white beans to make a pesto bean dip.

1. To get the sweetest flavor from fresh basil, submerge the leaves in a large bowl of ice water for about 5 minutes before chopping.

2. For a richer flavor, you can toast the nuts lightly by putting them in a small skillet on medium heat, stirring often. Or put them in an oven at 300°F for 8 to 10 minutes. Watch them carefully, because small nuts and seeds will burn quickly. You can also skip this step and go right to step 3.

3. Purée all the ingredients in a food processor or blender until smooth, then taste and add more salt or seasonings if necessary.

Per Serving (1 tablespoon)

Calories: 58; Total fat: 5g; Carbs: 2g; Fiber: 1g; Protein: 2g

Marinara Sauce

Makes 4 cups
Prep time: 15 minutes / Cook time: 20 minutes

GLUTEN-FREE NUT-FREE QUICK PREP KID-FRIENDLY IMMUNE BOOSTER

This classic tomato sauce has so many potential uses: with Spaghetti and Buckwheat Meatballs (page 174), as a base sauce for pizzas, made into a quick Weeknight Chickpea Tomato Soup (page 114), or simply tossed with whole-wheat penne. Make it a spicy arrabiata, or add some chunky vegetables. Many marinara recipes will include a tiny bit of sugar to cut the acidity of the tomatoes, but the traditional source of that sugar is carrots, which bring that lovely beta-carotene along with them. Make this sauce in batches and freeze it in individual servings so you can pull it out for a quick meal.

½ tablespoon olive oil

1 small onion, chopped

1 to 3 garlic cloves, minced
    or pressed

1 carrot, finely diced or grated

1 tablespoon dried basil

1 teaspoon dried oregano

1 teaspoon dried marjoram, or more
    basil, or oregano

1 to 2 tablespoons red wine, or
    balsamic vinegar

1 (28-ounce) can diced tomatoes

1 to 2 tablespoons capers, or
    chopped olives (optional)

¼ teaspoon sea salt

1. Heat the oil in a large skillet on medium-high, and sauté the onion and garlic. Once the onion has softened, about 5 minutes, add the carrot, basil, oregano, and marjoram.

2. Once the carrot has softened, about 5 minutes, add the wine, and let it sizzle and deglaze the pan.

3. Then add the tomatoes, capers (if using), and salt, stir, and leave to simmer for 20 minutes (or longer if you like).

Options: Make this an arrabiata by adding red pepper flakes to taste when you add the herbs. Or make a chunky vegetable sauce: When you sauté the onion and garlic, add about 2 cups cubed eggplant. When it's soft, add 1 diced red bell pepper and 1 diced carrot.

Per Serving (1 cup)

Calories: 71; Total fat: 3g; Carbs: 11g; Fiber: 3g; Protein: 3g

Strawberry-Kiwi Spritzer page 249

chapter 13

DRINKS

Infused Water 246

Morning Ginger-Lemon
Elixir 247

Hibiscus Lemon Iced Tea 248

Strawberry-Kiwi Spritzer 249

Tropical Mocktail 250

London Fog 251

Chai Latte 252

Matcha Latte 253

Iced Mocha Latte 254

Spiced Hot Chocolate 255

Infused Water

Makes 3 cups
Prep time: 10 minutes

NUT-FREE GLUTEN-FREE QUICK PREP KID-FRIENDLY

Our bodies are more than 60 percent water. It makes up most of our blood, digestive juices, and all other fluids. It's involved in almost all our essential functions, from digestion to absorption. Although water is so important, many people just don't get enough. Let's make it tastier, to inspire drinking more through the day. All these variations start with 3 cups water. But you can make a bigger batch so that it can infuse over a couple of days.

FOR FRUITY WATER

2 tablespoons blueberries

2 tablespoons raspberries

2 tablespoons watermelon cubes

FOR CITRUS WATER

2 slices fresh lemon and/or lime

2 slices fresh orange

4 thin slices fresh ginger (optional)

FOR CUCUMBER-MINT WATER

3 to 4 cucumber slices

2 tablespoons fresh mint, chopped

2 tablespoons freshly squeezed lime juice (optional)

1. Put 3 cups water in a pitcher or resealable bottle, and add your choice of fruit, vegetables, and fresh herbs. Crush the produce a bit so that its flavors seep into the water, either with a wooden spoon or a bottle that has a crushing mechanism.

2. This water will last about 3 days in the fridge. Be sure to replace the fruit, vegetables, or herbs at that point.

Did you know? You may think you don't need to drink anything because you're not thirsty. Don't be fooled; the thirst sensation only kicks in if you're actually dehydrated.

Per Serving (1 cup) for fruity water, if you eat the fruit

Calories: 8; Total fat: 0g; Carbs: 2g; Fiber: 0.5g; Protein: 0g

Morning Ginger-Lemon Elixir

Makes 1 mug
Prep time: 10 minutes

NUT-FREE GLUTEN-FREE QUICK PREP ANTI-INFLAMMATORY

Start your day with a digestion- and metabolism-boosting elixir. Cinnamon is optional, but it's been shown to improve insulin sensitivity, blood lipid levels, inflammation, blood pressure, and body weight. The smell of cinnamon may also boost brain activity. Have this first thing in the morning, before breakfast, as a powerful start to your day.

1½ to 2 cups boiling water

4 thin slices fresh ginger

1 lemon wedge

Pinch ground cinnamon (optional)

1 teaspoon maple syrup, or coconut sugar (optional)

1. Pour the water into a mug. Add the ginger, squeeze in the juice from the lemon, sprinkle in the cinnamon, and stir in the maple syrup (if using).

2. You could also grate the ginger, and just squeeze the juice into the mug for more ginger infusion.

Did you know? Ginger is a well-known digestive aid, helping curb nausea and trapped gas. It also has very potent anti-inflammatory compounds called *gingerols*, which may reduce pain and improve mobility for those with osteoarthritis or rheumatoid arthritis.

Per Serving (1 mug, with maple syrup)

Calories: 25; Total fat: 0g; Carbs: 6g; Fiber: 0g; Protein: 0g

Hibiscus Lemon Iced Tea

Makes 8 cups
Prep time: 5 to 10 minutes

This is a refreshing and beautifully colored drink, perfect to have stocked in the fridge all summer long. Hibiscus tea is caffeine-free, made from a part of the roselle flower, and its rich color means it's high in anthocyanins—the same compounds that make blueberries blue and eggplant purple. Hibiscus may help reduce blood pressure and relieve constipation.

2 cups boiling water

6 to 8 bags hibiscus tea, or 2 to 4 tablespoons loose

3 cups ice

Juice of ½ lemon

2 tablespoons maple syrup (optional)

2 tablespoons fresh mint

3 cups cold water

Technique: The strength of teas can vary greatly, so experiment with the quantity of tea you need for your pitcher. Bagged tea can sometimes be very weak, so you may need to add more bags. Loose tea can sometimes be very strong, so you may need to use less or dilute with more water.

1. Put the boiling water in a large mug with all the tea and leave to steep for 3 to 5 minutes. It should be strong and very dark red. If not, add more tea and steep longer. You could also cold brew by simply putting an extra 2 cups cold water in the pitcher with the tea to steep overnight.

2. Put the ice in a large pitcher and add the lemon juice, maple syrup, mint (which you can crush slightly before adding to bring out the flavor), and cold water. Pour the hot tea over the ice, which will melt but chill the tea. If you've used loose tea, pour it through a strainer.

Per Serving (1 cup)

Calories: 15; Total fat: 0g; Carbs: 4g; Fiber: 0g; Protein: 0g

Strawberry-Kiwi Spritzer

Makes 3 cups
Prep time: 5 minutes

NUT-FREE GLUTEN-FREE QUICK PREP KID-FRIENDLY

Instead of reaching for a sugary, chemical-laden soda, try this alternative. This is a super simple idea, so you can easily branch out, but these measurements should help you get started. When you're buying the fizzy water, naturally sparkling water is lovely, but soda water is usually easier to find. If you get hooked, you may want to invest in a home carbonation machine.

½ cup strawberries

½ cup chopped kiwi

Juice of ¼ lemon (optional)

2 tablespoons fresh mint, chopped (optional)

½ cup uncarbonated water

2 cups sparkling water

1. Purée the strawberries, kiwi, lemon juice, and mint (if using) with the uncarbonated water in a blender until smooth.
2. Pour the sparkling water in a cup, and add the puréed fruit to it. This prevents too much fizzing and pressure inside the blender with the sparkling water.

Options: If you don't want to blend anything, try this with pure cranberry juice instead of the strawberry-kiwi purée.

Per Serving (1 cup)

Calories: 29; Total fat: 0g; Carbs: 7g; Fiber: 2g; Protein: 1g

Tropical Mocktail

Makes 7½ to 8 cups
Prep time: 10 minutes

NUT-FREE GLUTEN-FREE QUICK PREP KID-FRIENDLY

When it starts getting hot, it's nice to have some refreshing drink ideas.
You can make this mocktail with any type of juice, but this one is all about
the tropical flavors. When you buy juice, look for pure juice with no added
sugar or refined syrups.

3 cups ice

**1 liter sparkling water, or
soda water**

¼ cup guava juice

¼ cup mango juice

¼ cup pineapple juice

¼ cup fresh melon balls

1. Combine the ice, water, and all the
   juices in a large pitcher.
2. Scoop balls out of a fresh melon, or
   chop up some cubes if you don't have
   a melon baller.
3. Find some fun glasses (martini, wine,
   etc.) and head out to the patio with
   your sunglasses, some tunes, and
   maybe a good book.

Options: Try different juices, and pair
them with things like citrus slices, berries,
and cucumber slices. You can also add
muddled fresh herbs to your pitcher, like
mint, basil, lemon balm—or even thyme
or lavender for a different flavor.

Per Serving (1 cup)

Calories: 13; Total fat: 0g; Carbs: 3g;
Fiber: 0g; Protein: 0g

London Fog

Makes 1 serving
Prep time: 5 minutes

NUT-FREE GLUTEN-FREE QUICK PREP

A London fog is Earl Grey tea with milk and vanilla. In a coffee shop, that usually means vanilla syrup. You can make a healthier version at home, using non-dairy milk and coconut sugar and pure vanilla extract. Or, if you can find vanilla stevia drops, they are good too—use 6 drops in place of the sugar and vanilla.

¾ cup water

1 bag Earl Grey tea

½ cup unsweetened non-dairy milk

½ teaspoon pure vanilla extract

1½ teaspoons unrefined sugar

1. Boil the water, and place your teabag in a large mug. Pour the boiling water over the Earl Grey tea (fill the mug about halfway, leaving room for milk). Steep for 2 to 3 minutes.

2. While that steeps, heat up the non-dairy milk in a small pot. Add the vanilla and sugar, stirring to dissolve in the milk. Pour the milk into the tea.

Toppings: Try this topped off with Coconut Whipped Cream (page 231).

Per Serving

Calories: 48; Total fat: 1g; Carbs: 8g; Fiber: 1g; Protein: 1g

Chai Latte

Makes 1 serving
Prep time: 5 minutes

NUT-FREE GLUTEN-FREE QUICK PREP

Chai lattes in coffee shops are made with chai-flavored syrup. You can make a more flavorful and wholesome version by using actual chai tea. Bump it up a notch by adding some fresh ginger juice.

¾ cup water

1 bag chai tea, or 1 tablespoon loose

½ cup unsweetened non-dairy milk

1½ teaspoons unrefined sugar

½ teaspoon pure vanilla extract

1. Boil the water, and place your teabag in a large mug. Pour the boiling water over the chai tea (fill the mug about halfway, leaving room for milk). Steep for 2 to 3 minutes.

2. While that steeps, heat up the non-dairy milk in a small pot. Add the sugar and vanilla, stirring to dissolve in the milk. Pour the milk into the tea.

Options: If you can find vanilla stevia drops, you can use 6 drops in place of the sugar and vanilla.

Per Serving

Calories: 48; Total fat: 1g; Carbs: 8g; Fiber: 1g; Protein: 1g

Matcha Latte

Makes 1 serving
Prep time: 5 minutes

NUT-FREE GLUTEN-FREE QUICK PREP

This latte is packed with age-defying antioxidants, brain-boosting amino acids, and fat-burning compounds called EGCG thanks to the matcha green tea powder. If you can't find any matcha at a local grocery or tea store, you can easily order it online. For lattes, get the ceremonial or smoothie-grade—the food-grade is a bit more bitter.

¾ cup water

1 teaspoon matcha green
   tea powder

½ cup non-dairy milk

½ teaspoon pure vanilla extract

1½ teaspoons unrefined sugar

1. Boil the water, and fill a large mug halfway. Let it cool a minute or two, then add the matcha powder and whisk until smooth and frothy.

2. Heat up the non-dairy milk in a small pot. Add the vanilla and sugar, stirring to dissolve in the milk.

3. Pour the milk into the mug with the tea. Stir to blend.

Did you know? Matcha green tea powder is packed with age-defying antioxidants, brain-boosting amino acids, and fat-burning compounds called ECGCs.

Per Serving

Calories: 48; Total fat: 1g; Carbs: 8g; Fiber: 1g; Protein: 1g

Iced Mocha Latte

Makes 2 servings
Prep time: 5 minutes

NUT-FREE GLUTEN-FREE QUICK PREP

Creamy, rich, icy, frothy ... this homemade iced mocha latte really hits the spot when you want a coffee shop treat without leaving the house.

3 to 5 tablespoons pure maple syrup, divided

3 tablespoons unsweetened cocoa powder

2 cups brewed coffee

1 cup non-dairy milk

1 cup ice

1. In a small bowl, mix together 3 tablespoons of the maple syrup with the cocoa powder, until it makes a syrup.

2. Put that syrup, along with everything else, in a blender and purée for 30 to 60 seconds, until smooth and creamy, adding the other 2 tablespoons maple syrup if you wish.

Leftovers: Brew the coffee stronger than usual. This is a great use for leftover coffee, if you brew a whole pot or French press in the morning.

Per Serving

Calories: 152; Total fat: 2g; Carbs: 35g; Fiber: 3g; Protein: 2g

Spiced Hot Chocolate

Makes 1 serving
Prep time: 5 minutes

NUT-FREE GLUTEN-FREE QUICK PREP KID-FRIENDLY

Here's my trick for making hot chocolate rich and creamy without milk: mix the cocoa powder with maple syrup. You can sweeten this with unrefined granulated sugar, but you won't get the same creaminess unless you use a liquid sweetener.

1 tablespoon unsweetened cocoa powder

1 tablespoon maple syrup, or brown rice syrup

¼ teaspoon ground cinnamon (optional)

Pinch ground cardamom (optional)

Pinch ground cloves (optional)

1 teaspoon minced fresh ginger, or ground (optional)

¾ cup boiling water

½ cup non-dairy milk

1. Put the cocoa and maple syrup in a large mug and stir until it makes a paste. Stir in whatever spices you want to add, and then pour in the boiling water until the mug is half full.

2. Heat up the non-dairy milk in a small pot and add to the mug. Stir to mix.

Did you know? Hot chocolate originated in South America, where it was made with plain chocolate, water, and spicy chilies, without milk. If you're game for the spices, they add rich flavor and a nutritional boost.

Per Serving

Calories: 97; Total fat: 2g; Carbs: 21g; Fiber: 3g; Protein: 2g

APPENDIX A:
THE DIRTY DOZEN AND THE CLEAN FIFTEEN™

A nonprofit environmental watchdog organization called Environmental Working Group (EWG) looks at data supplied by the U.S. Department of Agriculture (USDA) and the Food and Drug Administration (FDA) about pesticide residues. Each year it compiles a list of the best and worst pesticide loads found in commercial crops. You can use these lists to decide which fruits and vegetables to buy organic to minimize your exposure to pesticides and which produce is considered safe enough to buy conventionally. This does not mean they are pesticide-free, though, so wash these fruits and vegetables thoroughly.

Dirty Dozen

- Apples
- Celery
- Cherries
- Grapes
- Nectarines
- Peaches
- Pears
- Potatoes
- Spinach
- Strawberries
- Sweet Bell Peppers
- Tomatoes

In addition to the Dirty Dozen, the EWG added one type of produce contaminated with highly toxic organophosphate insecticides:

- Hot peppers

Clean Fifteen

- Asparagus
- Avocados
- Cabbage
- Cantaloupes (domestic)
- Cauliflower
- Eggplants
- Grapefruits
- Honeydew
- Kiwis
- Mangoes
- Onions
- Papayas
- Pineapples
- Sweet Corn
- Sweet peas (frozen)

APPENDIX B:
CONVERSION SHEET

VOLUME EQUIVALENTS (Liquid)

US Standard (ounces)	US Standard (approximate)	Metric
2 tablespoons	1 fl. oz.	30 mL
¼ cup	2 fl. oz.	60 mL
½ cup	4 fl. oz.	120 mL
1 cup	8 fl. oz.	240 mL
1½ cups	12 fl. oz	355 mL
2 cups or 1 pint	16 fl. oz.	475 mL
4 cups or 1 quart	32 fl. oz.	1 L
1 gallon	128 fl. oz.	4 L

OVEN TEMPERATURES

Fahrenheit (F)	Celsius (C) (approximate)
250°F	120°C
300°F	150°C
325°F	165°C
350°F	180°C
375°F	190°C
400°F	200°C
425°F	220°C
450°F	230°C

VOLUME EQUIVALENTS (Dry)

US Standard	Metric (approximate)
1/8 teaspoon	0.5 mL
¼ teaspoon	1 mL
½ teaspoon	2 mL
¾ teaspoon	4 mL
1 teaspoon	5 mL
1 tablespoon	15 mL
¼ cup	59 mL
1/3 cup	79 mL
½ cup	118 mL
2/3 cup	156 mL
¾ cup	177 mL
1 cup	235 mL
2 cups or 1 pint	475 mL
3 cups	700 mL
4 cups or 1 quart	1 L

WEIGHT EQUIVALENTS

US Standard	Metric (approximate)
½ ounce	15 g
1 ounce	30 g
2 ounces	60 g
4 ounces	115 g
8 ounces	225 g
12 ounces	340 g
16 ounces or 1 pound	455 g

APPENDIX C:
BLANK SHOPPING LIST

vegetables
_____

beans/legumes
_____

fruit
_____

nuts/seeds
_____

whole-grains
_____

other
_____

APPENDIX D: BLANK MEAL PLANNER

	Sunday	Monday	Tuesday
Breakfast			
Lunch			
Dinner			

Wednesday	Thursday	Friday	Saturday

RESOURCES

Becoming Vegan, by Brenda Davis and Vesanto Melina, Book Publishing Co., 2014.

The Complete Idiot's Guide to Plant-Based Nutrition, by Julieanna Hever, Alpha Books, 2011.

The Food Revolution, by John Robbins, Conari Press, 2010.

How Not to Die, by Michael Greger with Gene Stone, Flatiron Books, 2015.

Vegan for Her, by Virginia Messina with JL Fields, Da Capo, 2013.

Vegan for Life, by Jack Norris and Virginia Messina, Da Capo, 2011.

Veganomicon, by Isa Chandra Moskowitz and Terry Hope Romero, Da Capo Lifelong Books, 2007.

Vegan Pregnancy Survival Guide, by Sayward Rebhal, Herbivore Books, 2011.

Whole Foods Plant-Based Cookbooks

The Main Street Vegan Academy Cookbook, by Victoria Moran and JL Fields, BenBella Books, 2017.

Minimalist Baker's Everyday Cooking, by Dana Shultz, Avery, 2016.

The Oh She Glows Cookbook, by Angela Liddon, Avery, 2014.

Plant-Powered Families, by Dreena Burton, BenBella Books, 2015.

Radiant Health, Inner Wealth, by Quintessence Challis, Quintessential Health Publishing, 2009.

Vegan Bowl Attack! by Jackie Sobon, Fair Winds Press, 2016.

Vegan Richa's Everyday Kitchen, by Richa Hingle, Vegan Heritage Press, 2017.

Websites

HappyCow Vegan and Vegetarian Restaurant Finder: www.happycow.net

Jack Norris, RD: www.jacknorrisrd.com

NutritionFacts.org: www.nutritionfacts.org

People for the Ethical Treatment of Animals: www.peta.org

Physicans Committee for Responsible Medicine: www.pcrm.org

The Vegan RD: www.theveganrd.com

The Vegan Society: www.vegansociety.com

Vegan Health.org: www.veganhealth.org

Vegan.com: www.vegan.com

REFERENCES

Adam, O., et al. "Anti-Inflammatory Effects of a Low Arachinodonic Acid Diet and Fish Oil in Patients with Rheumatoid Arthritis." *Rheumatology International* 23, no. 1 (January 2003): 27–36. doi:10.1007/s00296-002-0234-7.

Barclay, Eliza. "How Plastic in the Ocean Is Contaminating Your Seafood." NPR. December 13, 2013. http://www.npr.org/sections/thesalt/2013/12/12 /250438904/how-plastic-in-the-ocean-is-contaminating-your-seafood.

Bradbury, K. E., et al. "Serum Concentrations of Cholesterol, Apolipoprotein A-I and Apolipoprotein B in a Total of 1694 Meat-Eaters, Fish-Eaters, Vegetarians, and Vegans." *European Journal of Clinical Nutrition* 69 (2015): 1,180. http://www.ncbi.nlm.nih.gov/pubmed/24346473.

Carteron, Nancy. "Foods to Avoid with Arthritis." Healthline. October 2, 2017. https://www.healthline.com/health-slideshow/foods-to-avoid-with-arthritis.

Centers for Disease Control and Prevention. "Heart Disease Facts." Accessed October 30, 2017. http://www.cdc.gov/heartdisease/facts.htm.

Chan, J., K. Jaceldo-Siegl, and G. E. Fraser. "Serum 25-Hydroxyvitamin D Status of Vegetarians, Partial Vegetarians, and Nonvegetarians: The Adventist Health Study-2." *American Journal of Clinical Nutrition* 89, no. 5 (May 2009): 1,686S–1,692S. doi:10.3945/ajcn.2009.26736X.

Clinton, Chelsea M., et al. "Whole-Foods, Plant-Based Diet Alleviates the Symptoms of Osteoarthritis." *Arthritis* 2015 (October 30, 2015): Article ID 708152. http://dx.doi.org/10.1155/2015/708152.

Craig, Winston J. "Health Effects of Vegan Diets." *American Journal of Clinical Nutrition* 89, no. 5 (May 2009): 1,627S–1,633S. http://ajcn.nutrition.org /content/89/5/1627S.full.

Greger, Michael. "Vitamin B12 Recommendation Change." NutritionFacts.org. Accessed October 30, 2017. http://nutritionfacts.org/videos/vitamin-b12 -recommendation-change.

Harvard Health Publishing. "Foods That Fight Inflammation." Harvard Medical School. Last modified August 13, 2017. https://www.health.harvard.edu /staying-healthy/foods-that-fight-inflammation.

Icahn School of Medicine at Mount Sinai. "Study Shows That Reducing Processed and Fried Food Intake Lowers Related Health Risks and Restores Body's Defenses." November 4, 2009. http://icahn.mssm.edu/about-us/news-and -events/study-shows-that-reducing-processed-and-fried-food-intake-lowers -related-health-risks-and-restores-bodys-defenses.

Kjeldsen-Kragh, J., et al. "Changes in Laboratory Variables in Rheumatoid Arthritis Patients During a Trial of Fasting and One-Year Vegetarian Diet." *Scandinavian Journal of Rheumatology* 24, no. 2 (1995): 85–93. https://www.ncbi.nlm.nih.gov /pubmed/7747149.

Kjeldsen-Kragh, J. "Rheumatoid Arthritis Treated with Vegetarian Diets." *American Journal of Clinical Nutrition* 70, no. 3 (September 1999): 594S–600S. https://www.ncbi.nlm.nih.gov/pubmed/10479237.

Knapton, Sarah. "Seafood Eaters Ingest up to 11,000 Tiny Pieces of Plastic Every Year, Study Shows." *The Telegraph.* January 24, 2017. http://www.telegraph. co.uk/science/2017/01/24/seafood-eaters-ingest-11000-tiny-pieces-plastic-every- year-study.

Norris, Jack. "Calcium and Vitamin D." VeganHealth.org. Last modified October 2013. http://www.veganhealth.org/articles/bones#recvitd.

NutritionFacts.org. "Plant-Based Diets." Accessed October 30, 2017. https:// nutritionfacts.org/topics/plant-based-diets.

Physicians Committee for Responsible Medicine. "Foods and Arthritis." Accessed October 30, 2017. http://www.pcrm.org/health/health-topics/foods-and-arthritis.

Physicians Committee for Responsible Medicine. "Vegetarian Foods: Powerful for Health." Accessed October 30, 2017. http://www.pcrm.org/health/diets/vegdiets/vegetarian-foods-powerful-for-health.

Shaw, Jonathan. "A Diabetes Link to Meat." *Harvard Magazine*. January–February 2012. http://www.harvardmagazine.com/2012/01/a-diabetes-link-to-meat.

Uribarri, Jaime, et al. "Advanced Glycation End Products in Foods and a Practical Guide to Their Reduction in the Diet." *Journal of the American Dietetic Association* 110, no. 6 (June 2010): 911–916. doi:10.1016/j.jada.2010.03.018.

RECIPE INDEX

A

Almond-Date Energy
    Bites, 210
Apple Crumble, 222–223
Applesauce Crumble
    Muffins, 90–91
Avocado Red Pepper Sushi
    Rolls, 158–159
Avomame Spread, 201
Avo-nnaise, 238

B

Baked Banana French Toast
    with Raspberry
    Syrup, 92–93
Baked Kale Chips, Five
    Ways, 192–194
Baked Sweet Potato
    Fries, 204
Banana Chocolate
    Cupcakes, 219
Banana Nut Smoothie, 83
Basil Mango Jicama
    Salad, 120
Basil Pesto, 241
Bibimbap Bowl, 156–157
Black Bean Taco Salad
    Bowl, 154–155
Blackeye Pea Burritos, 182
Blueberry Avocado
    Cheesecake, 218
Buckwheat Sesame Milk, 227
Build Your Own Mushroom
    Fajitas, 180–181

C

Cajun Burgers, 142–143
Cashew-Ginger Soba
    Noodle Bowl, 152–153

Cashew Sour Cream, 230
Chai Chia Smoothie, 77
Chai Latte, 252
Cheesy Sprinkle, 229
Chickpea Scramble, 100–101
Chocolate Krinkles, 216
Chocolate PB Smoothie, 81
Chocolate Quinoa Breakfast
    Bowl, 96
Cinnamon Apple Toast, 94
Coconut Watercress
    Soup, 107
Coconut Whipped
    Cream, 231
Creamy Avocado-Dressed
    Kale Salad, 122–123
Creamy Balsamic
    Dressing, 236
Creamy Mint-Lime
    Spaghetti Squash, 170–171
Creamy Pumpkin and
    Toasted Walnut Soup, 111
Curried Mango Chickpea
    Wrap, 147
Curry Spiced Lentil
    Burgers, 138–139

D

Dill Potato Salad, 128

E

Easy DIY Pizza Crust, 234
Easy-Peasy Almond
    Milk, 226

F

Falafel Wrap, 148–149
Forbidden Black Rice and
    Edamame Salad, 132–133

Fresh Mango Salsa, 240
Fruit Salad with Zesty Citrus
    Couscous, 97
Fruity Granola, 98–99
Funky Monkey Sorbet, 213

G

Garlic Toast, 207
Ginger Carrot Soup, 106
Green Goddess
    Dressing, 235
Greens and Beans
    Dip, 202
Grilled AHLT, 144
Grilled Portobello with
    Mashed Potatoes and
    Green Beans, 183–185
Guacamole, 203

H

Hearty Chili, 115
Herbed Millet Pizza
    Crust, 232–233
Hibiscus Lemon Iced
    Tea, 248
Hummus, Five Ways, 197–199
Hydration Station, 79

I

Iced Mocha Latte, 254
Indian Red Split Lentil
    Soup, 116–117
Infused Water, 246

L

Lemon Coconut Cilantro
    Rolls, 196

Lemon Pistachio Quinoa
    Cookies, 220–221
Lime in the Coconut Chia
    Pudding, 215
Loaded Black Bean
    Pizza, 145
London Fog, 251

M

Mango Coconut Cream
    Pie, 217
Mango Madness, 80
Maple Dijon Burgers, 140–141
Marinara Sauce, 242–243
Matcha Latte, 253
Max Power Smoothie, 76
Mediterranean Hummus
    Pizza, 146
Mint Chocolate Chip
    Sorbet, 214
Minty Beet and Sweet
    Potato Soup, 108–109
Miso-Coconut Dragon
    Bowl, 151
Miso Noodle Soup, 110
Morning Ginger-Lemon
    Elixir, 247
Moroccan Aubergine
    Salad, 126–127
Muesli and Berries Bowl, 95

N

Nori Snack Rolls, 190

O

Oatmeal Breakfast
    Cookies, 86–87
Olive and White Bean
    Pasta, 173

Orange Walnut
    Pasta, 176–177
Overnight Oats On the
    Go, 84–85

P

Pad Thai Bowl, 150
Peanut Sauce, 239
Pink Panther Smoothie, 82
Potato Skin
    Samosas, 166–167

Roasted Beet and Avocado
    Salad, 121
Roasted Cauliflower
    Tacos, 178–179
Roasted Garlic Pesto
    Potatoes, 205
Roasted Red Pepper and
    Butternut Squash
    Soup, 112–113
Roasted Veg with Creamy
    Avocado Dip, 102–103

S

Savory Roasted
    Chickpeas, 195
Savory Split Pea
    Soup, 118–119
Shepherd's Pie, 186–187
Simple Sesame
    Stir-Fry, 168–169
Spaghetti and Buckwheat
    Meatballs, 174–175
Spiced Hot Chocolate, 255
Spicy Black Bean Dip, 200
Spicy Chickpea Sushi
    Rolls, 160–161
Strawberry-Kiwi
    Spritzer, 249

Sun-dried Tomato and
    Pesto Quinoa, 172
Sunflower Hemp Milk, 228
Sunshine Muffins, 88–89
Sushi Bowl, 162
Sweet Potato Biscuits, 206
Sweet Potato Patties, 163

T

Tabbouleh Salad, 130–131
Tamari Toasted
    Almonds, 191
Toasted Sesame Miso
    Dressing, 237
Tropical Mocktail, 250
Tropi-Colada Frozen
    Pops, 212
Tropi-Kale Breeze, 78
Tuscan White Bean
    Salad, 129

V

Vietnamese Summer
    Rolls, 164–165

W

Warm Lentil Salad with Red
    Wine Vinaigrette, 134–135
Weeknight Chickpea
    Tomato Soup, 114
Wilted Sesame-Miso Kale
    Salad, 124–125

Z

Zesty Orange-Cranberry
    Energy Bites, 211

INDEX

A

Advanced glycation end
  products (AGEs), 5
Alfalfa sprouts
  Avocado Red Pepper
    Sushi Rolls, 158–159
  Avomame Spread, 201
  Chai Chia Smoothie, 77
  Chocolate PB
    Smoothie, 81
  Lemon Coconut Cilantro
    Rolls, 196
Almond butter
  Apple Crumble, 222–223
  Baked Kale Chips, Five
    Ways, 192–194
  Banana Chocolate
    Cupcakes, 219
  Banana Nut Smoothie, 83
  Buckwheat Sesame
    Milk, 227
  Cashew-Ginger Soba
    Noodle Bowl, 152–153
  Chocolate PB
    Smoothie, 81
  Chocolate Quinoa
    Breakfast Bowl, 96
  Easy-Peasy Almond
    Milk, 226
  Falafel Wrap, 148–149
  Funky Monkey Sorbet, 213
  Greens and Beans
    Dip, 202
  Lemon Pistachio Quinoa
    Cookies, 220–221
  Mint Chocolate Chip
    Sorbet, 214
  Nori Snack Rolls, 190
  Oatmeal Breakfast
    Cookies, 86–87
  Peanut Sauce, 239

  Sunshine Muffins, 88–89
  Zesty Orange-Cranberry
    Energy Bites, 211
Alzheimer's disease, 3–4
Amaranth, 17, 19
Anti-inflammatory foods, 5
Anti-inflammatory recipes
  Apple Crumble, 222–223
  Avocado Red Pepper
    Sushi Rolls, 158–159
  Avomame Spread, 201
  Avo-nnaise, 238
  Baked Kale Chips, Five
    Ways, 192–194
  Baked Sweet Potato
    Fries, 204
  Banana Chocolate
    Cupcakes, 219
  Basil Mango Jicama
    Salad, 120
  Basil Pesto, 241
  Bibimbap Bowl, 156–157
  Blackeye Pea
    Burritos, 182
  Blueberry Avocado
    Cheesecake, 218
  Cajun Burgers, 142–143
  Cashew Sour Cream, 230
  Chai Chia Smoothie, 77
  Chickpea Scramble,
    100–101
  Coconut Watercress
    Soup, 107
  Creamy
    Avocado-Dressed
    Kale Salad, 122–123
  Creamy Pumpkin and
    Toasted Walnut
    Soup, 111
  Curried Mango Chickpea
    Wrap, 147
  Curry Spiced Lentil
    Burgers, 138–139

  Forbidden Black Rice
    and Edamame
    Salad, 132–133
  Fruit Salad with Zesty
    Citrus Couscous, 97
  Fruity Granola, 98–99
  Garlic Toast, 207
  Green Goddess
    Dressing, 235
  Greens and Beans
    Dip, 202
  Grilled AHLT, 144
  Guacamole, 203
  Herbed Millet Pizza
    Crust, 232–233
  Indian Red Split Lentil
    Soup, 116–117
  Lemon Coconut Cilantro
    Rolls, 196
  Lemon Pistachio Quinoa
    Cookies, 220–221
  Lime in the Coconut Chia
    Pudding, 215
  Mango Coconut Cream
    Pie, 217
  Maple Dijon
    Burgers, 140–141
  Max Power Smoothie, 76
  Mediterranean Hummus
    Pizza, 146
  Minty Beet and Sweet
    Potato Soup, 108–109
  Miso-Coconut Dragon
    Bowl, 151
  Miso Noodle Soup, 110
  Morning Ginger-Lemon
    Elixir, 247
  Moroccan Aubergine
    Salad, 126–127
  Nori Snack Rolls, 190
  Pink Panther Smoothie, 82
  Roasted Cauliflower
    Tacos, 178–179

Anti-inflammatory recipes
(*continued*)
 Roasted Red Pepper and
  Butternut Squash
  Soup, 112–113
 Roasted Veg with Creamy
  Avocado Dip, 102–103
 Savory Roasted
  Chickpeas, 195
 Savory Split Pea
  Soup, 118–119
 Simple Sesame
  Stir-Fry, 168–169
 Spaghetti and Buckwheat
  Meatballs, 174–175
 Spicy Black Bean Dip, 200
 Spicy Chickpea Sushi
  Rolls, 160–161
 Sunshine Muffins, 88–89
 Sweet Potato
  Biscuits, 206
 Tabbouleh Salad, 130–131
 Tamari Toasted
  Almonds, 191
 Toasted Sesame Miso
  Dressing, 237
 Tropi-Colada Frozen
  Pops, 212
 Tropi-Kale Breeze, 78
 Tuscan White Bean
  Salad, 129
 Warm Lentil Salad with
  Red Wine
  Vinaigrette, 134–135
 Wilted Sesame-Miso Kale
  Salad, 124–125
 Zesty Orange-Cranberry
  Energy Bites, 211
Antioxidants, 2–3, 5, 9, 17
Apples and applesauce
 Apple Crumble, 222–223
 Applesauce Crumble
  Muffins, 90–91
 Cinnamon Apple
  Toast, 94
 Muesli and Berries
  Bowl, 95
Arachidonic acid, 5, 24
Arthritis, 4–5
Arugula
 Miso-Coconut Dragon
  Bowl, 151
Asparagus
 Bibimbap Bowl, 156–157

Avocados
 about, 20
 Avocado Red Pepper
  Sushi Rolls, 158–159
 Avomame Spread, 201
 Avo-nnaise, 238
 Basil Pesto, 241
 Black Bean Taco Salad
  Bowl, 154–155
 Blueberry Avocado
  Cheesecake, 218
 Cashew-Ginger Soba
  Noodle Bowl, 152–153
 Creamy
  Avocado-Dressed
  Kale Salad, 122–123
 Grilled AHLT, 144
 Guacamole, 203
 Loaded Black Bean
  Pizza, 145
 Minty Beet and Sweet
  Potato Soup, 108–109
 Roasted Beet and
  Avocado Salad, 121
 Roasted Veg with
  Creamy Avocado
  Dip, 102–103
 Sushi Bowl, 162
 Tropi-Kale Breeze, 78

B

Balance, 70–71
Bananas
 Baked Banana French
  Toast with Raspberry
  Syrup, 92–93
 Banana Chocolate
  Cupcakes, 219
 Banana Nut Smoothie, 83
 Chai Chia Smoothie, 77
 Chocolate PB
  Smoothie, 81
 Chocolate Quinoa
  Breakfast Bowl, 96
 Funky Monkey Sorbet, 213
 Hydration Station, 79
 Lemon Pistachio Quinoa
  Cookies, 220–221
 Mango Madness, 80
 Max Power Smoothie, 76
 Mint Chocolate Chip
  Sorbet, 214

 Oatmeal Breakfast
  Cookies, 86–87
Basil
 Avomame Spread, 201
 Basil Mango Jicama
  Salad, 120
 Basil Pesto, 241
 Blueberry Avocado
  Cheesecake, 218
 Creamy Balsamic
  Dressing, 236
 Fresh Mango Salsa, 240
 Green Goddess
  Dressing, 235
 Max Power Smoothie, 76
 Miso Noodle Soup, 110
 Tuscan White Bean
  Salad, 129
 Vietnamese Summer
  Rolls, 164–165
Beans. *See also* Chickpeas;
 Green beans
 Black Bean Taco Salad
  Bowl, 154–155
 and gas, 57
 Ginger Carrot Soup, 106
 Greens and Beans
  Dip, 202
 Hearty Chili, 115
 Loaded Black Bean
  Pizza, 145
 Miso Noodle Soup, 110
 Olive and White Bean
  Pasta, 173
 Spicy Black Bean Dip, 200
 Tuscan White Bean
  Salad, 129
Bean sprouts
 Bibimbap Bowl, 156–157
 Pad Thai Bowl, 150
 Vietnamese Summer
  Rolls, 164–165
Beets
 Minty Beet and Sweet
  Potato Soup, 108–109
 Roasted Beet and
  Avocado Salad, 121
 Roasted Veg with Creamy
  Avocado Dip, 102–103
 Wilted Sesame-Miso Kale
  Salad, 124–125
Bell peppers
 Avocado Red Pepper
  Sushi Rolls, 158–159

Black Bean Taco Salad
    Bowl, 154–155
Blackeye Pea
    Burritos, 182
Build Your Own
    Mushroom
    Fajitas, 180–181
Cashew-Ginger Soba
    Noodle Bowl, 152–153
Creamy
    Avocado-Dressed
    Kale Salad, 122–123
Creamy Mint-Lime
    Spaghetti
    Squash, 170–171
Curried Mango Chickpea
    Wrap, 147
Dill Potato Salad, 128
Forbidden Black Rice
    and Edamame
    Salad, 132–133
Hummus, Five
    Ways, 197–199
Maple Dijon
    Burgers, 140–141
Mediterranean Hummus
    Pizza, 146
Miso-Coconut Dragon
    Bowl, 151
Olive and White Bean
    Pasta, 173
Pad Thai Bowl, 150
Roasted Red Pepper and
    Butternut Squash
    Soup, 112–113
Sushi Bowl, 162
Berries
    Baked Banana French
    Toast with Raspberry
    Syrup, 92–93
    blueberries, 20
    Blueberry Avocado
    Cheesecake, 218
    Chocolate Quinoa
    Breakfast Bowl, 96
    Fruit Salad with Zesty
    Citrus Couscous, 97
    Hydration Station, 79
    Infused Water, 246
    Mango Madness, 80
    Max Power Smoothie, 76
    Muesli and Berries
    Bowl, 95
    Pink Panther Smoothie, 82

Strawberry-Kiwi
    Spritzer, 249
Zesty Orange-Cranberry
    Energy Bites, 211
Beverages. See Drinks
Blenders, 36
Bowls
    Bibimbap Bowl, 156–157
    Black Bean Taco Salad
    Bowl, 154–155
    builder, 34–35
    Cashew-Ginger Soba
    Noodle Bowl, 152–153
    Chocolate Quinoa
    Breakfast Bowl, 96
    Miso-Coconut Dragon
    Bowl, 151
    Muesli and Berries
    Bowl, 95
    Pad Thai Bowl, 150
    Sushi Bowl, 162
Breakfasts. See also
    Smoothies
    Applesauce Crumble
    Muffins, 90–91
    Baked Banana French
    Toast with Raspberry
    Syrup, 92–93
    Chickpea Scramble,
    100–101
    Chocolate Quinoa
    Breakfast Bowl, 96
    Cinnamon Apple
    Toast, 94
    Fruit Salad with Zesty
    Citrus Couscous, 97
    Fruity Granola, 98–99
    Muesli and Berries
    Bowl, 95
    Oatmeal Breakfast
    Cookies, 86–87
    Overnight Oats On the
    Go, 84–85
    Roasted Veg with Creamy
    Avocado Dip, 102–103
    Sunshine Muffins, 88–89
Broccoli
    Forbidden Black Rice
    and Edamame
    Salad, 132–133
    Simple Sesame
    Stir-Fry, 168–169
    Wilted Sesame-Miso Kale
    Salad, 124–125

Buckwheat
    about, 19
    Buckwheat Sesame
    Milk, 227
    Cajun Burgers, 142–143
    Spaghetti and Buckwheat
    Meatballs, 174–175
Bulbs, 14–15. See also
    specific

C

Cabbage
    Pad Thai Bowl, 150
Calcium, 28
Calorie density, 6–7
Cancer, 3
Capers
    Marinara Sauce, 242–243
    Moroccan Aubergine
    Salad, 126–127
Carbohydrates, 22
Cardiovascular disease, 2
Carrots
    Bibimbap Bowl, 156–157
    Build Your Own
    Mushroom
    Fajitas, 180–181
    Cajun Burgers, 142–143
    Cashew-Ginger Soba
    Noodle Bowl, 152–153
    Curry Spiced Lentil
    Burgers, 138–139
    Ginger Carrot Soup, 106
    Loaded Black Bean
    Pizza, 145
    Mango Madness, 80
    Marinara Sauce, 242–243
    Max Power Smoothie, 76
    Nori Snack Rolls, 190
    Pad Thai Bowl, 150
    Potato Skin
    Samosas, 166–167
    Roasted Cauliflower
    Tacos, 178–179
    Roasted Veg with
    Creamy Avocado
    Dip, 102–103
    Savory Split Pea
    Soup, 118–119
    Shepherd's Pie, 186–187
    Sunshine Muffins, 88–89

Carrots (continued)
    Tuscan White Bean
        Salad, 129
    Vietnamese Summer
        Rolls, 164–165
    Warm Lentil Salad with
        Red Wine
        Vinaigrette, 134–135
Cashew butter
    Apple Crumble, 222–223
    Cashew-Ginger Soba
        Noodle Bowl, 152–153
    Chocolate Krinkles, 216
    Falafel Wrap, 148–149
    Nori Snack Rolls, 190
    Peanut Sauce, 239
    Zesty Orange-Cranberry
        Energy Bites, 211
Cauliflower
    Roasted Cauliflower
        Tacos, 178–179
Celery
    Dill Potato Salad, 128
Chewing, 25–26, 57
Chia seeds
    about, 19
    Almond-Date Energy
        Bites, 210
    Banana Chocolate
        Cupcakes, 219
    Banana Nut Smoothie, 83
    Chai Chia Smoothie, 77
    Chocolate PB
        Smoothie, 81
    Chocolate Quinoa
        Breakfast Bowl, 96
    Lime in the Coconut Chia
        Pudding, 215
    Max Power Smoothie, 76
    Overnight Oats On the
        Go, 84–85
    Pink Panther Smoothie, 82
    Spaghetti and Buckwheat
        Meatballs, 174–175
    Zesty Orange-Cranberry
        Energy Bites, 211
Chickpeas
    about, 21
    Bibimbap Bowl, 156–157
    Chickpea Scramble,
        100–101
    Curried Mango Chickpea
        Wrap, 147
    Falafel Wrap, 148–149

Hummus, Five
    Ways, 197–199
Maple Dijon
    Burgers, 140–141
Savory Roasted
    Chickpeas, 195
Spicy Chickpea Sushi
    Rolls, 160–161
Weeknight Chickpea
    Tomato Soup, 114
Chives
    Baked Kale Chips, Five
        Ways, 192–194
    Dill Potato Salad, 128
    Green Goddess
        Dressing, 235
    Tuscan White Bean
        Salad, 129
Chlorophyll, 14, 18
Chocolate. See also
    Cocoa powder
    Almond-Date Energy
        Bites, 210
    Banana Chocolate
        Cupcakes, 219
    Lemon Pistachio Quinoa
        Cookies, 220–221
    Mint Chocolate Chip
        Sorbet, 214
    Muesli and Berries
        Bowl, 95
    Oatmeal Breakfast
        Cookies, 86–87
Chronic disease, 1–4
Cilantro
    Avomame Spread, 201
    Black Bean Taco Salad
        Bowl, 154–155
    Build Your Own
        Mushroom
        Fajitas, 180–181
    Curried Mango Chickpea
        Wrap, 147
    Forbidden Black Rice
        and Edamame
        Salad, 132–133
    Fresh Mango Salsa, 240
    Hearty Chili, 115
    Lemon Coconut Cilantro
        Rolls, 196
    Miso Noodle Soup, 110
    Pad Thai Bowl, 150
    Potato Skin
        Samosas, 166–167

Spicy Black Bean Dip, 200
Sushi Bowl, 162
Vietnamese Summer
    Rolls, 164–165
Cinnamon, 85
Citrus zesters, 36
Cocoa powder
    about, 216
    Banana Chocolate
        Cupcakes, 219
    Chocolate Krinkles, 216
    Chocolate PB
        Smoothie, 81
    Chocolate Quinoa
        Breakfast Bowl, 96
    Iced Mocha Latte, 254
    Spiced Hot
        Chocolate, 255
Coconut
    Almond-Date Energy
        Bites, 210
    Fruit Salad with Zesty
        Citrus Couscous, 97
    Fruity Granola, 98–99
    Lemon Coconut Cilantro
        Rolls, 196
    Mango Coconut Cream
        Pie, 217
    Muesli and Berries
        Bowl, 95
    Tropi-Colada Frozen
        Pops, 212
Coconut milk
    Baked Banana French
        Toast with Raspberry
        Syrup, 92–93
    Chai Chia Smoothie, 77
    Coconut Watercress
        Soup, 107
    Coconut Whipped
        Cream, 231
    Lime in the Coconut Chia
        Pudding, 215
    Mango Coconut Cream
        Pie, 217
    Miso-Coconut Dragon
        Bowl, 151
    Pink Panther
        Smoothie, 82
    Tropi-Colada Frozen
        Pops, 212
    Tropi-Kale Breeze, 78
Coffee
    Iced Mocha Latte, 254

Collard greens
   Max Power Smoothie, 76
Complexion, 8
Condiments. *See also*
   Dressings
   Avo-nnaise, 238
   Basil Pesto, 241
   Fresh Mango Salsa, 240
Corn
   Black Bean Taco Salad
      Bowl, 154–155
Couscous
   Fruit Salad with Zesty
      Citrus Couscous, 97
   Tabbouleh Salad, 130–131
Cucumbers
   Falafel Wrap, 148–149
   Hydration Station, 79
   Infused Water, 246
   Spicy Chickpea Sushi
      Rolls, 160–161
   Tabbouleh Salad, 130–131
   Vietnamese Summer
      Rolls, 164–165
Cutting boards, 33

D

Dairy products, 5, 24
Dates
   Almond-Date Energy
      Bites, 210
   Banana Nut Smoothie, 83
   Blueberry Avocado
      Cheesecake, 218
   Buckwheat Sesame
      Milk, 227
   Chai Chia Smoothie, 77
   Easy-Peasy Almond
      Milk, 226
   Lime in the Coconut Chia
      Pudding, 215
   Mango Coconut Cream
      Pie, 217
   Sunflower Hemp Milk, 228
Dehydration, 79, 246
Dementia, 3–4
Desserts
   Almond-Date Energy
      Bites, 210
   Apple Crumble, 222–223
   Banana Chocolate
      Cupcakes, 219

   Blueberry Avocado
      Cheesecake, 218
   Chocolate Krinkles, 216
   Funky Monkey Sorbet, 213
   Lemon Pistachio Quinoa
      Cookies, 220–221
   Lime in the Coconut Chia
      Pudding, 215
   Mango Coconut Cream
      Pie, 217
   Mint Chocolate Chip
      Sorbet, 214
   Tropi-Colada Frozen
      Pops, 212
   Zesty Orange-Cranberry
      Energy Bites, 211
DHA, 29
Diabetes, 4
Digestion, 8, 57
Digestive enzymes, 29, 57
Dill
   Creamy Avocado-
      Dressed Kale
      Salad, 122–123
   Dill Potato Salad, 128
   Hummus, Five
      Ways, 197–199
   Roasted Veg with Creamy
      Avocado Dip, 102–103
   Sweet Potato Patties, 163
Dining out, 71
Dips and spreads
   Avomame Spread, 201
   Greens and Beans
      Dip, 202
   Guacamole, 203
   Hummus, Five
      Ways, 197–199
   Spicy Black Bean Dip, 200
Dressings
   Creamy Balsamic
      Dressing, 236
   Green Goddess
      Dressing, 235
   Toasted Sesame Miso
      Dressing, 237
Drinks. *See also* Smoothies
   Buckwheat Sesame
      Milk, 227
   Chai Latte, 252
   Easy-Peasy Almond
      Milk, 226
   Hibiscus Lemon Iced
      Tea, 248

   Iced Mocha Latte, 254
   Infused Water, 246
   London Fog, 251
   Matcha Latte, 253
   Morning Ginger-Lemon
      Elixir, 247
   Spiced Hot
      Chocolate, 255
   Strawberry-Kiwi
      Spritzer, 249
   Sunflower Hemp Milk, 228
   Tropical Mocktail, 250

E

Edamame
   Avomame Spread, 201
   Forbidden Black Rice
      and Edamame
      Salad, 132–133
   Simple Sesame
      Stir-Fry, 168–169
   Sushi Bowl, 162
Eggplants
   Moroccan Aubergine
      Salad, 126–127
Eggs, replacing, 25
Empty calories, 6, 25
Equipment, 33, 36–37
Exercise, *57*, 69–70

F

Fats, 18, 20, 22, 23, 41
Fiber, 22
Flavonols, 81
Flavor-enhancement, 13,
   37–41
Flaxseed
   Applesauce Crumble
      Muffins, 90–91
   Banana Nut Smoothie, 83
   Chocolate PB Smoothie, 81
   Chocolate Quinoa
      Breakfast Bowl, 96
   Lemon Coconut Cilantro
      Rolls, 196
   Lemon Pistachio Quinoa
      Cookies, 220–221
   Max Power Smoothie, 76
   Oatmeal Breakfast
      Cookies, 86–87

Flaxseed (*continued*)
    Overnight Oats On the
        Go, 84–85
    Spaghetti and Buckwheat
        Meatballs, 174–175
    Sunshine Muffins, 88–89
Flexitarianism, 12
Flowers, 15. *See also specific*
Folic acid, 4
Food processors, 36
Fruits, 16. *See also specific*

G

Garlic
    about, 177, 207
    Basil Pesto, 241
    Bibimbap Bowl, 156–157
    Blackeye Pea
        Burritos, 182
    Cajun Burgers, 142–143
    Creamy
        Avocado-Dressed
        Kale Salad, 122–123
    Creamy Balsamic
        Dressing, 236
    Creamy Mint-Lime
        Spaghetti Squash,
        170–171
    Fresh Mango Salsa, 240
    Garlic Toast, 207
    Green Goddess
        Dressing, 235
    Grilled Portobello with
        Mashed Potatoes and
        Green Beans, 183–185
    Guacamole, 203
    Hearty Chili, 115
    Hummus, Five
        Ways, 197–199
    Lemon Coconut Cilantro
        Rolls, 196
    Maple Dijon
        Burgers, 140–141
    Marinara Sauce, 242–243
    Minty Beet and Sweet
        Potato Soup, 108–109
    Moroccan Aubergine
        Salad, 126–127
    Orange Walnut
        Pasta, 176–177
    Potato Skin
        Samosas, 166–167

    Roasted Garlic Pesto
        Potatoes, 205
    Roasted Red Pepper and
        Butternut Squash
        Soup, 112–113
    Savory Split Pea
        Soup, 118–119
    Sun-dried Tomato and
        Pesto Quinoa, 172
    Tabbouleh Salad, 130–131
    Tuscan White Bean
        Salad, 129
    Warm Lentil Salad with
        Red Wine
        Vinaigrette, 134–135
    Weeknight Chickpea
        Tomato Soup, 114
Garlic presses, 36
Gas, 57
Ginger
    about, 21, 247
    Avomame Spread, 201
    Cashew-Ginger Soba
        Noodle Bowl, 152–153
    Chai Chia Smoothie, 77
    Ginger Carrot Soup, 106
    graters, 36–37
    Indian Red Split Lentil
        Soup, 116–117
    Infused Water, 246
    Max Power Smoothie, 76
    Morning Ginger-Lemon
        Elixir, 247
    Nori Snack Rolls, 190
    Potato Skin
        Samosas, 166–167
    Spiced Hot
        Chocolate, 255
    Toasted Sesame Miso
        Dressing, 237
Gluten-free recipes
    Almond-Date Energy
        Bites, 210
    Avocado Red Pepper
        Sushi Rolls, 158–159
    Avomame Spread, 201
    Avo-nnaise, 238
    Baked Kale Chips, Five
        Ways, 192–194
    Baked Sweet Potato
        Fries, 204
    Banana Nut Smoothie, 83
    Basil Mango Jicama
        Salad, 120

    Basil Pesto, 241
    Bibimbap Bowl, 156–157
    Black Bean Taco Salad
        Bowl, 154–155
    Blackeye Pea
        Burritos, 182
    Buckwheat Sesame
        Milk, 227
    Build Your Own
        Mushroom
        Fajitas, 180–181
    Cajun Burgers, 142–143
    Cashew-Ginger Soba
        Noodle Bowl, 152–153
    Cashew Sour Cream, 230
    Chai Chia Smoothie, 77
    Chai Latte, 252
    Cheesy Sprinkle, 229
    Chickpea Scramble,
        100–101
    Chocolate Krinkles, 216
    Chocolate Quinoa
        Breakfast Bowl, 96
    Coconut Watercress
        Soup, 107
    Coconut Whipped
        Cream, 231
    Creamy
        Avocado-Dressed
        Kale Salad, 122–123
    Creamy Balsamic
        Dressing, 236
    Creamy Mint-Lime
        Spaghetti Squash,
        170–171
    Creamy Pumpkin and
        Toasted Walnut
        Soup, 111
    Curry Spiced Lentil
        Burgers, 138–139
    Dill Potato Salad, 128
    Easy-Peasy Almond
        Milk, 226
    Forbidden Black Rice
        and Edamame
        Salad, 132–133
    Fresh Mango Salsa, 240
    Funky Monkey
        Sorbet, 213
    Ginger Carrot Soup, 106
    Green Goddess
        Dressing, 235
    Greens and Beans
        Dip, 202

Grilled Portobello with Mashed Potatoes and Green Beans, 183–185
Guacamole, 203
Hearty Chili, 115
Herbed Millet Pizza Crust, 232–233
Hibiscus Lemon Iced Tea, 248
Hummus, Five Ways, 197–199
Hydration Station, 79
Iced Mocha Latte, 254
Indian Red Split Lentil Soup, 116–117
Infused Water, 246
Lemon Pistachio Quinoa Cookies, 220–221
Lime in the Coconut Chia Pudding, 215
Loaded Black Bean Pizza, 145
London Fog, 251
Mango Madness, 80
Marinara Sauce, 242–243
Matcha Latte, 253
Max Power Smoothie, 76
Mediterranean Hummus Pizza, 146
Mint Chocolate Chip Sorbet, 214
Minty Beet and Sweet Potato Soup, 108–109
Miso-Coconut Dragon Bowl, 151
Miso Noodle Soup, 110
Morning Ginger-Lemon Elixir, 247
Moroccan Aubergine Salad, 126–127
Nori Snack Rolls, 190
Orange Walnut Pasta, 176–177
Overnight Oats On the Go, 84–85
Pad Thai Bowl, 150
Peanut Sauce, 239
Pink Panther Smoothie, 82
Potato Skin Samosas, 166–167
Roasted Beet and Avocado Salad, 121

Roasted Garlic Pesto Potatoes, 205
Roasted Red Pepper and Butternut Squash Soup, 112–113
Roasted Veg with Creamy Avocado Dip, 102–103
Savory Roasted Chickpeas, 195
Savory Split Pea Soup, 118–119
Simple Sesame Stir-Fry, 168–169
Spiced Hot Chocolate, 255
Spicy Black Bean Dip, 200
Spicy Chickpea Sushi Rolls, 160–161
Strawberry-Kiwi Spritzer, 249
Sun-dried Tomato and Pesto Quinoa, 172
Sunflower Hemp Milk, 228
Sushi Bowl, 162
Sweet Potato Patties, 163
Tamari Toasted Almonds, 191
Toasted Sesame Miso Dressing, 237
Tropical Mocktail, 250
Tropi-Colada Frozen Pops, 212
Tropi-Kale Breeze, 78
Tuscan White Bean Salad, 129
Vietnamese Summer Rolls, 164–165
Warm Lentil Salad with Red Wine Vinaigrette, 134–135
Weeknight Chickpea Tomato Soup, 114
Wilted Sesame-Miso Kale Salad, 124–125
Zesty Orange-Cranberry Energy Bites, 211
Goji berries
  about, 214
  Fruity Granola, 98–99
  Mint Chocolate Chip Sorbet, 214
  Pink Panther Smoothie, 82

Grain-free recipes
  Chickpea Scramble, 100–101
  Chocolate Quinoa Breakfast Bowl, 96
  Creamy Pumpkin and Toasted Walnut Soup, 111
  Roasted Beet and Avocado Salad, 121
  Weeknight Chickpea Tomato Soup, 114
  Wilted Sesame-Miso Kale Salad, 124–125
Graters, 36–37
Green beans
  Creamy Avocado-Dressed Kale Salad, 122–123
  Grilled Portobello with Mashed Potatoes and Green Beans, 183–185
Greens. See also specific
  Black Bean Taco Salad Bowl, 154–155
  Falafel Wrap, 148–149
  Roasted Beet and Avocado Salad, 121

H

Heart disease, 2
Hemp seeds
  about, 228
  Banana Nut Smoothie, 83
  Chai Chia Smoothie, 77
  Chocolate Quinoa Breakfast Bowl, 96
  Overnight Oats On the Go, 84–85
  Sunflower Hemp Milk, 228
Herbs, 18. See also specific
High blood pressure, 2–3, 14
Homemade basics
  Buckwheat Sesame Milk, 227
  Cashew Sour Cream, 230
  Cheesy Sprinkle, 229
  Coconut Whipped Cream, 231
  Easy DIY Pizza Crust, 234
  Easy-Peasy Almond Milk, 226

Homemade basics
(*continued*)
  Herbed Millet Pizza
    Crust, 232–233
  Sunflower Hemp Milk, 228

I

Immersion blenders, 36
Immune booster recipes
  Apple Crumble, 222–223
  Avocado Red Pepper
    Sushi Rolls, 158–159
  Avomame Spread, 201
  Baked Kale Chips, Five
    Ways, 192–194
  Baked Sweet Potato
    Fries, 204
  Banana Chocolate
    Cupcakes, 219
  Basil Mango Jicama
    Salad, 120
  Basil Pesto, 241
  Bibimbap Bowl, 156–157
  Black Bean Taco Salad
    Bowl, 154–155
  Blackeye Pea
    Burritos, 182
  Blueberry Avocado
    Cheesecake, 218
  Cashew-Ginger Soba
    Noodle Bowl, 152–153
  Cashew Sour Cream, 230
  Cheesy Sprinkle, 229
  Chickpea Scramble,
    100–101
  Coconut Watercress
    Soup, 107
  Creamy Avocado-
    Dressed Kale
    Salad, 122–123
  Creamy Mint-Lime
    Spaghetti Squash,
    170–171
  Creamy Pumpkin and
    Toasted Walnut
    Soup, 111
  Curry Spiced Lentil
    Burgers, 138–139
  Falafel Wrap, 148–149
  Forbidden Black Rice
    and Edamame
    Salad, 132–133

Fresh Mango Salsa, 240
Fruit Salad with Zesty
  Citrus Couscous, 97
Green Goddess
  Dressing, 235
Greens and Beans
  Dip, 202
Grilled Portobello with
  Mashed Potatoes and
  Green Beans, 183–185
Guacamole, 203
Hearty Chili, 115
Hydration Station, 79
Indian Red Split Lentil
  Soup, 116–117
Lemon Coconut Cilantro
  Rolls, 196
Lime in the Coconut Chia
  Pudding, 215
Loaded Black Bean
  Pizza, 145
Mango Coconut Cream
  Pie, 217
Mango Madness, 80
Maple Dijon
  Burgers, 140–141
Marinara Sauce, 242–243
Max Power Smoothie, 76
Mediterranean Hummus
  Pizza, 146
Mint Chocolate Chip
  Sorbet, 214
Minty Beet and Sweet
  Potato Soup, 108–109
Miso-Coconut Dragon
  Bowl, 151
Moroccan Aubergine
  Salad, 126–127
Orange Walnut
  Pasta, 176–177
Pad Thai Bowl, 150
Pink Panther
  Smoothie, 82
Potato Skin
  Samosas, 166–167
Roasted Cauliflower
  Tacos, 178–179
Roasted Red Pepper and
  Butternut Squash
  Soup, 112–113
Roasted Veg with Creamy
  Avocado Dip, 102–103
Spicy Chickpea Sushi
  Rolls, 160–161

Sun-dried Tomato and
  Pesto Quinoa, 172
Sunflower Hemp Milk, 228
Sunshine Muffins, 88–89
Sweet Potato
  Biscuits, 206
Tabbouleh Salad, 130–131
Toasted Sesame Miso
  Dressing, 237
Tropi-Colada Frozen
  Pops, 212
Tropi-Kale Breeze, 78
Tuscan White Bean
  Salad, 129
Vietnamese Summer
  Rolls, 164–165
Warm Lentil Salad with
  Red Wine
  Vinaigrette, 134–135
Weeknight Chickpea
  Tomato Soup, 114
Wilted Sesame-Miso Kale
  Salad, 124–125
Immune system, 8
Inflammation, 4–5

J

Jalapeño peppers
  Fresh Mango Salsa, 240
Jicama
  Basil Mango Jicama
    Salad, 120
Juices
  Tropical Mocktail, 250

K

Kale
  Baked Kale Chips, Five
    Ways, 192–194
  Cashew-Ginger Soba
    Noodle Bowl, 152–153
  Creamy
    Avocado-Dressed
    Kale Salad, 122–123
  Greens and Beans
    Dip, 202
  Max Power Smoothie, 76
  Tropi-Kale Breeze, 78
  Weeknight Chickpea
    Tomato Soup, 114

Wilted Sesame-Miso Kale Salad, 124–125

Kid-friendly recipes
Almond-Date Energy Bites, 210
Apple Crumble, 222–223
Applesauce Crumble Muffins, 90–91
Avocado Red Pepper Sushi Rolls, 158–159
Avo-nnaise, 238
Baked Banana French Toast with Raspberry Syrup, 92–93
Baked Sweet Potato Fries, 204
Banana Chocolate Cupcakes, 219
Banana Nut Smoothie, 83
Basil Mango Jicama Salad, 120
Basil Pesto, 241
Blackeye Pea Burritos, 182
Blueberry Avocado Cheesecake, 218
Build Your Own Mushroom Fajitas, 180–181
Cashew Sour Cream, 230
Cheesy Sprinkle, 229
Chickpea Scramble, 100–101
Chocolate Krinkles, 216
Chocolate PB Smoothie, 81
Chocolate Quinoa Breakfast Bowl, 96
Cinnamon Apple Toast, 94
Coconut Whipped Cream, 231
Creamy Balsamic Dressing, 236
Curried Mango Chickpea Wrap, 147
Dill Potato Salad, 128
Easy DIY Pizza Crust, 234
Easy-Peasy Almond Milk, 226
Falafel Wrap, 148–149
Fresh Mango Salsa, 240
Fruit Salad with Zesty Citrus Couscous, 97
Fruity Granola, 98–99

Funky Monkey Sorbet, 213
Garlic Toast, 207
Greens and Beans Dip, 202
Grilled AHLT, 144
Grilled Portobello with Mashed Potatoes and Green Beans, 183–185
Guacamole, 203
Herbed Millet Pizza Crust, 232–233
Hummus, Five Ways, 197–199
Hydration Station, 79
Infused Water, 246
Lemon Coconut Cilantro Rolls, 196
Lemon Pistachio Quinoa Cookies, 220–221
Lime in the Coconut Chia Pudding, 215
Loaded Black Bean Pizza, 145
Mango Coconut Cream Pie, 217
Mango Madness, 80
Maple Dijon Burgers, 140–141
Marinara Sauce, 242–243
Max Power Smoothie, 76
Mediterranean Hummus Pizza, 146
Mint Chocolate Chip Sorbet, 214
Minty Beet and Sweet Potato Soup, 108–109
Moroccan Aubergine Salad, 126–127
Muesli and Berries Bowl, 95
Oatmeal Breakfast Cookies, 86–87
Orange Walnut Pasta, 176–177
Overnight Oats On the Go, 84–85
Peanut Sauce, 239
Potato Skin Samosas, 166–167
Roasted Cauliflower Tacos, 178–179
Roasted Red Pepper and Butternut Squash Soup, 112–113

Savory Roasted Chickpeas, 195
Shepherd's Pie, 186–187
Spaghetti and Buckwheat Meatballs, 174–175
Spiced Hot Chocolate, 255
Spicy Chickpea Sushi Rolls, 160–161
Strawberry-Kiwi Spritzer, 249
Sunflower Hemp Milk, 228
Sunshine Muffins, 88–89
Sweet Potato Biscuits, 206
Sweet Potato Patties, 163
Tropical Mocktail, 250
Tropi-Colada Frozen Pops, 212
Tropi-Kale Breeze, 78
Vietnamese Summer Rolls, 164–165
Weeknight Chickpea Tomato Soup, 114
Zesty Orange-Cranberry Energy Bites, 211

Kiwis
Strawberry-Kiwi Spritzer, 249

Knives, 33

Leaves, 14. *See also specific*
Leftovers, 65
Legumes, 17, 22. *See also specific*
Lemons and lemon juice
Avomame Spread, 201
Avo-nnaise, 238
Basil Pesto, 241
Cashew Sour Cream, 230
Creamy Avocado-Dressed Kale Salad, 122–123
Falafel Wrap, 148–149
Green Goddess Dressing, 235
Greens and Beans Dip, 202
Hibiscus Lemon Iced Tea, 248

Lemons and lemon juice
(*continued*)
Hummus, Five
Ways, 197–199
Infused Water, 246
Lemon Coconut Cilantro
Rolls, 196
Lemon Pistachio Quinoa
Cookies, 220–221
Maple Dijon
Burgers, 140–141
Morning Ginger-Lemon
Elixir, 247
Moroccan Aubergine
Salad, 126–127
Strawberry-Kiwi
Spritzer, 249
Tabbouleh Salad, 130–131
Lentils
Curry Spiced Lentil
Burgers, 138–139
Indian Red Split Lentil
Soup, 116–117
Shepherd's Pie, 186–187
Warm Lentil Salad
with Red Wine
Vinaigrette, 134–135
Lettuce
Cashew-Ginger Soba
Noodle Bowl, 152–153
Curried Mango Chickpea
Wrap, 147
Roasted Cauliflower
Tacos, 178–179
Vietnamese Summer
Rolls, 164–165
Warm Lentil Salad
with Red Wine
Vinaigrette, 134–135
Lifestyle changes, 69–71
Limes and lime juice
Avomame Spread, 201
Black Bean Taco Salad
Bowl, 154–155
Blueberry Avocado
Cheesecake, 218
Creamy Mint-Lime
Spaghetti
Squash, 170–171
Curried Mango Chickpea
Wrap, 147
Fresh Mango Salsa, 240
Guacamole, 203
Infused Water, 246

Lime in the Coconut Chia
Pudding, 215
Pad Thai Bowl, 150
Peanut Sauce, 239
Roasted Cauliflower
Tacos, 178–179
Roasted Red Pepper and
Butternut Squash
Soup, 112–113
Spicy Black Bean Dip, 200

M

Macronutrients, 18, 22
Main dishes. *See also* Bowls
Avocado Red Pepper
Sushi Rolls, 158–159
Blackeye Pea
Burritos, 182
Build Your Own
Mushroom
Fajitas, 180–181
Cajun Burgers, 142–143
Creamy Mint-Lime
Spaghetti
Squash, 170–171
Curried Mango Chickpea
Wrap, 147
Curry Spiced Lentil
Burgers, 138–139
Falafel Wrap, 148–149
Grilled AHLT, 144
Grilled Portobello with
Mashed Potatoes and
Green Beans, 183–185
Loaded Black Bean
Pizza, 145
Maple Dijon
Burgers, 140–141
Mediterranean Hummus
Pizza, 146
Olive and White Bean
Pasta, 173
Orange Walnut
Pasta, 176–177
Potato Skin
Samosas, 166–167
Roasted Cauliflower
Tacos, 178–179
Shepherd's Pie, 186–187
Simple Sesame
Stir-Fry, 168–169

Spaghetti and Buckwheat
Meatballs, 174–175
Spicy Chickpea Sushi
Rolls, 160–161
Sun-dried Tomato and
Pesto Quinoa, 172
Sweet Potato Patties, 163
Vietnamese Summer
Rolls, 164–165
Mangos
Basil Mango Jicama
Salad, 120
Curried Mango Chickpea
Wrap, 147
Fresh Mango Salsa, 240
Mango Coconut Cream
Pie, 217
Mango Madness, 80
Max Power Smoothie, 76
Tropi-Colada Frozen
Pops, 212
Tropi-Kale Breeze, 78
Vietnamese Summer
Rolls, 164–165
Maple syrup
Apple Crumble, 222–223
Baked Banana French
Toast with Raspberry
Syrup, 92–93
Banana Nut Smoothie, 83
Blueberry Avocado
Cheesecake, 218
Build Your Own Mushroom
Fajitas, 180–181
Chocolate Krinkles, 216
Chocolate PB
Smoothie, 81
Cinnamon Apple
Toast, 94
Creamy Balsamic
Dressing, 236
Forbidden Black Rice
and Edamame
Salad, 132–133
Fruit Salad with Zesty
Citrus Couscous, 97
Green Goddess
Dressing, 235
Hibiscus Lemon Iced
Tea, 248
Iced Mocha Latte, 254
Lime in the Coconut Chia
Pudding, 215

Maple Dijon
    Burgers, 140–141
Miso-Coconut Dragon
    Bowl, 151
Morning Ginger-Lemon
    Elixir, 247
Oatmeal Breakfast
    Cookies, 86–87
Overnight Oats On the
    Go, 84–85
Peanut Sauce, 239
Spiced Hot
    Chocolate, 255
Sweet Potato
    Biscuits, 206
Toasted Sesame Miso
    Dressing, 237
Zesty Orange-Cranberry
    Energy Bites, 211
Matcha green tea powder
    about, 253
    Chocolate PB Smoothie, 81
    Lime in the Coconut Chia
        Pudding, 215
    Matcha Latte, 253
    Tropi-Kale Breeze, 78
Meal plans
    about, 42
    week one, 45–51
    week two, 53–59
    week three, 61–67
Measuring cups and
    spoons, 33
Meats, replacing, 24
Melons
    Fruit Salad with Zesty
        Citrus Couscous, 97
    Infused Water, 246
    Pink Panther Smoothie, 82
    Tropical Mocktail, 250
Micronutrients, 18
Microplanes, 36
Millet
    Bibimbap Bowl, 156–157
    Black Bean Taco Salad
        Bowl, 154–155
    Creamy
        Avocado-Dressed
        Kale Salad, 122–123
    Herbed Millet Pizza
        Crust, 232–233
    Miso-Coconut Dragon
        Bowl, 151
    Sushi Bowl, 162

Mint
    Avomame Spread, 201
    Coconut Watercress
        Soup, 107
    Creamy Mint-Lime
        Spaghetti
        Squash, 170–171
    Fresh Mango Salsa, 240
    Fruit Salad with Zesty
        Citrus Couscous, 97
    Hibiscus Lemon Iced
        Tea, 248
    Hummus, Five
        Ways, 197–199
    Hydration Station, 79
    Infused Water, 246
    Mint Chocolate Chip
        Sorbet, 214
    Minty Beet and Sweet
        Potato Soup, 108–109
    Miso-Coconut Dragon
        Bowl, 151
    Moroccan Aubergine
        Salad, 126–127
    Pad Thai Bowl, 150
    Pink Panther Smoothie, 82
    Strawberry-Kiwi
        Spritzer, 249
    Tabbouleh Salad, 130–131
    Vietnamese Summer
        Rolls, 164–165
Miso
    Miso-Coconut Dragon
        Bowl, 151
    Miso Noodle Soup, 110
    Savory Split Pea
        Soup, 118–119
    Toasted Sesame Miso
        Dressing, 237
Molasses
    Sunshine Muffins, 88–89
Muesli
    Muesli and Berries owl, 95
Mushrooms
    about, 16
    Build Your Own
        Mushroom
        Fajitas, 180–181
    Chickpea Scramble,
        100–101
    Grilled Portobello with
        Mashed Potatoes and
        Green Beans, 183–185

Miso-Coconut Dragon
    Bowl, 151
Nori Snack Rolls, 190
Tuscan White Bean
    Salad, 129
Weeknight Chickpea
    Tomato Soup, 114
Wilted Sesame-Miso Kale
    Salad, 124–125

N

Non-dairy milk. See also
    Coconut milk
    Applesauce Crumble
        Muffins, 90–91
    Banana Chocolate
        Cupcakes, 219
    Banana Nut Smoothie, 83
    Basil Mango Jicama
        Salad, 120
    Chai Latte, 252
    Chocolate PB
        Smoothie, 81
    Chocolate Quinoa
        Breakfast Bowl, 96
    Creamy Pumpkin and
        Toasted Walnut
        Soup, 111
    Dill Potato Salad, 128
    Funky Monkey Sorbet, 213
    Grilled Portobello with
        Mashed Potatoes and
        Green Beans, 183–185
    Iced Mocha Latte, 254
    London Fog, 251
    Matcha Latte, 253
    Max Power Smoothie, 76
    Mint Chocolate Chip
        Sorbet, 214
    Muesli and Berries
        Bowl, 95
    Pink Panther Smoothie, 82
    Shepherd's Pie, 186–187
    Spiced Hot Chocolate, 255
    Sunshine Muffins, 88–89
Nori
    Avocado Red Pepper
        Sushi Rolls, 158–159
    Nori Snack Rolls, 190
    Spicy Chickpea Sushi
        Rolls, 160–161
    Sushi Bowl, 162

Nut butters. *See also specific*
Applesauce Crumble Muffins, 90–91
Buckwheat Sesame Milk, 227
Chocolate Quinoa Breakfast Bowl, 96
Funky Monkey Sorbet, 213
Mint Chocolate Chip Sorbet, 214
Nori Snack Rolls, 190
Nut-free recipes
Avocado Red Pepper Sushi Rolls, 158–159
Avomame Spread, 201
Avo-nnaise, 238
Baked Banana French Toast with Raspberry Syrup, 92–93
Baked Kale Chips, Five Ways, 192–194
Baked Sweet Potato Fries, 204
Basil Mango Jicama Salad, 120
Bibimbap Bowl, 156–157
Black Bean Taco Salad Bowl, 154–155
Blackeye Pea Burritos, 182
Buckwheat Sesame Milk, 227
Build Your Own Mushroom Fajitas, 180–181
Cajun Burgers, 142–143
Chai Chia Smoothie, 77
Chai Latte, 252
Cheesy Sprinkle, 229
Chickpea Scramble, 100–101
Cinnamon Apple Toast, 94
Coconut Watercress Soup, 107
Coconut Whipped Cream, 231
Creamy Avocado-Dressed Kale Salad, 122–123
Creamy Balsamic Dressing, 236

Creamy Mint-Lime Spaghetti Squash, 170–171
Curried Mango Chickpea Wrap, 147
Curry Spiced Lentil Burgers, 138–139
Dill Potato Salad, 128
Easy DIY Pizza Crust, 234
Falafel Wrap, 148–149
Forbidden Black Rice and Edamame Salad, 132–133
Fresh Mango Salsa, 240
Fruit Salad with Zesty Citrus Couscous, 97
Garlic Toast, 207
Green Goddess Dressing, 235
Greens and Beans Dip, 202
Grilled AHLT, 144
Grilled Portobello with Mashed Potatoes and Green Beans, 183–185
Guacamole, 203
Hearty Chili, 115
Herbed Millet Pizza Crust, 232–233
Hibiscus Lemon Iced Tea, 248
Hummus, Five Ways, 197–199
Hydration Station, 79
Iced Mocha Latte, 254
Indian Red Split Lentil Soup, 116–117
Infused Water, 246
Lime in the Coconut Chia Pudding, 215
Loaded Black Bean Pizza, 145
London Fog, 251
Mango Madness, 80
Marinara Sauce, 242–243
Matcha Latte, 253
Max Power Smoothie, 76
Mediterranean Hummus Pizza, 146
Minty Beet and Sweet Potato Soup, 108–109
Miso Noodle Soup, 110
Morning Ginger-Lemon Elixir, 247

Moroccan Aubergine Salad, 126–127
Olive and White Bean Pasta, 173
Overnight Oats On the Go, 84–85
Pink Panther Smoothie, 82
Potato Skin Samosas, 166–167
Roasted Cauliflower Tacos, 178–179
Roasted Garlic Pesto Potatoes, 205
Roasted Red Pepper and Butternut Squash Soup, 112–113
Roasted Veg with Creamy Avocado Dip, 102–103
Savory Roasted Chickpeas, 195
Savory Split Pea Soup, 118–119
Shepherd's Pie, 186–187
Simple Sesame Stir-Fry, 168–169
Spaghetti and Buckwheat Meatballs, 174–175
Spiced Hot Chocolate, 255
Spicy Black Bean Dip, 200
Spicy Chickpea Sushi Rolls, 160–161
Strawberry-Kiwi Spritzer, 249
Sunflower Hemp Milk, 228
Sushi Bowl, 162
Sweet Potato Biscuits, 206
Sweet Potato Patties, 163
Tabbouleh Salad, 130–131
Toasted Sesame Miso Dressing, 237
Tropical Mocktail, 250
Tropi-Colada Frozen Pops, 212
Tropi-Kale Breeze, 78
Tuscan White Bean Salad, 129
Vietnamese Summer Rolls, 164–165
Warm Lentil Salad with Red Wine Vinaigrette, 134–135
Weeknight Chickpea Tomato Soup, 114

Nutrient density, 6
Nutrients, 21–22
Nuts
about, 17
Almond-Date Energy
Bites, 210
Apple Crumble, 222–223
Applesauce Crumble
Muffins, 90–91
Basil Pesto, 241
Blueberry Avocado
Cheesecake, 218
Brazil, 21
Cashew-Ginger Soba
Noodle Bowl, 152–153
Cashew Sour Cream, 230
Cheesy Sprinkle, 229
Chocolate Quinoa
Breakfast Bowl, 96
Creamy Pumpkin and
Toasted Walnut
Soup, 111
Fruity Granola, 98–99
Funky Monkey Sorbet, 213
Lemon Coconut Cilantro
Rolls, 196
Lemon Pistachio Quinoa
Cookies, 220–221
Mango Coconut Cream
Pie, 217
Maple Dijon
Burgers, 140–141
Miso-Coconut Dragon
Bowl, 151
Muesli and Berries
Bowl, 95
Orange Walnut
Pasta, 176–177
Roasted Beet and
Avocado Salad, 121
Tamari Toasted
Almonds, 191
Wilted Sesame-Miso Kale
Salad, 124–125
Zesty Orange-Cranberry
Energy Bites, 211

O

Oats
Apple Crumble, 222–223
Banana Chocolate
Cupcakes, 219

Blueberry Avocado
Cheesecake, 218
Chocolate PB
Smoothie, 81
Fruity Granola, 98–99
Mango Coconut Cream
Pie, 217
Maple Dijon
Burgers, 140–141
Max Power Smoothie, 76
Muesli and Berries
Bowl, 95
Oatmeal Breakfast
Cookies, 86–87
Overnight Oats On the
Go, 84–85
Sunshine Muffins, 88–89
Oils, 23
Oil sprayers, 37
Olives
Falafel Wrap, 148–149
Marinara Sauce, 242–243
Mediterranean Hummus
Pizza, 146
Moroccan Aubergine
Salad, 126–127
Olive and White Bean
Pasta, 173
Orange Walnut
Pasta, 176–177
Savory Split Pea
Soup, 118–119
Omega-3 fatty acids, 3,
28–29
Omega-6 fatty acids, 28–29
Onions. See also Scallions
Blackeye Pea
Burritos, 182
Build Your Own
Mushroom
Fajitas, 180–181
Coconut Watercress
Soup, 107
Creamy Pumpkin and
Toasted Walnut
Soup, 111
Curry Spiced Lentil
Burgers, 138–139
Ginger Carrot Soup, 106
Hearty Chili, 115
Indian Red Split Lentil
Soup, 116–117
Loaded Black Bean
Pizza, 145

Marinara Sauce, 242–243
Mediterranean Hummus
Pizza, 146
Minty Beet and Sweet
Potato Soup, 108–109
Miso-Coconut Dragon
Bowl, 151
Potato Skin
Samosas, 166–167
Roasted Red Pepper and
Butternut Squash
Soup, 112–113
Savory Split Pea
Soup, 118–119
Shepherd's Pie, 186–187
Sun-dried Tomato and
Pesto Quinoa, 172
Sweet Potato Patties, 163
Warm Lentil Salad with
Red Wine
Vinaigrette, 134–135
Weeknight Chickpea
Tomato Soup, 114
Oranges and orange juice
Forbidden Black Rice
and Edamame
Salad, 132–133
Fruit Salad with Zesty
Citrus Couscous, 97
Hydration Station, 79
Infused Water, 246
Orange Walnut
Pasta, 176–177
Sunshine Muffins, 88–89
Zesty Orange-Cranberry
Energy Bites, 211
Oregano
Tuscan White Bean
Salad, 129

P

Parsley
about, 19
Avomame Spread, 201
Black Bean Taco Salad
Bowl, 154–155
Cajun Burgers, 142–143
Chickpea Scramble,
100–101
Falafel Wrap, 148–149
Fresh Mango Salsa, 240

Parsley (*continued*)
    Green Goddess
        Dressing, 235
    Hearty Chili, 115
    Hummus, Five
        Ways, 197–199
    Max Power Smoothie, 76
    Orange Walnut
        Pasta, 176–177
    Potato Skin
        Samosas, 166–167
    Sweet Potato Patties, 163
    Tabbouleh Salad, 130–131
    Vietnamese Summer
        Rolls, 164–165
Parsnips
    Minty Beet and Sweet
        Potato Soup, 108–109
Pasta
    Olive and White Bean
        Pasta, 173
    Orange Walnut
        Pasta, 176–177
    Spaghetti and Buckwheat
        Meatballs, 174–175
Peaches
    Mango Madness, 80
Peanut butter
    Chocolate Krinkles, 216
    Chocolate PB
        Smoothie, 81
    Funky Monkey Sorbet, 213
    Mint Chocolate Chip
        Sorbet, 214
    Overnight Oats On
        the Go, 84–85
    Peanut Sauce, 239
Peanuts
    Pad Thai Bowl, 150
Peas
    Blackeye Pea
        Burritos, 182
    Cashew-Ginger Soba
        Noodle Bowl, 152–153
    Coconut Watercress
        Soup, 107
    Potato Skin
        Samosas, 166–167
    Savory Split Pea
        Soup, 118–119
    Shepherd's Pie, 186–187
    Simple Sesame
        Stir-Fry, 168–169

Pescatarianism, 12
Phytochemicals, 1–2
Pineapple
    Tropi-Colada Frozen
        Pops, 212
    Tropi-Kale Breeze, 78
Plant-based diets
    benefits of, 8–9
    beyond three
        weeks, 68–71
    cooking equipment, 33,
        36–37
    fast food at home, 34–35
    food groups, 13–18
    freezer staples, 32–33
    and health, 1–4
    ideal plate, 27
    and inflammation, 4–5
    nutrients in, 11, 21–22
    nutrition guidelines, 24–29
    nutritionist's culinary
        guide to
        enjoying, 40–41
    pantry staples, 31–32
    refrigerator staples, 32
    seasonings, 37–39
    superfoods, 19–21
    types of, 12
    week one meal
        plan, 45–51
    week two meal
        plan, 53–59
    week three meal
        plan, 61–67
    for weight loss, 6–8
Portion size, 7, 26–27
Positive energy, 71
Potassium, 2, 13–14, 39
Potatoes. *See also* Sweet
    potatoes
    Dill Potato Salad, 128
    Grilled Portobello with
        Mashed Potatoes and
        Green Beans, 183–185
    Potato Skin Samosas,
        166–167
    Roasted Garlic Pesto
        Potatoes, 205
    Shepherd's Pie, 186–187
Pots and pans, 33
Probiotics, 29
Processed foods, 25
Protein, 22–23

Pumpkin
    Creamy Pumpkin and
        Toasted Walnut
        Soup, 111
Pumpkin seeds
    Fruity Granola, 98–99
    Minty Beet and Sweet
        Potato Soup, 108–109
    Roasted Beet and
        Avocado Salad, 121
    Wilted Sesame-Miso Kale
        Salad, 124–125

Q

Quick prep recipes
    Almond-Date Energy
        Bites, 210
    Applesauce Crumble
        Muffins, 90–91
    Avomame Spread, 201
    Avo-nnaise, 238
    Baked Banana French
        Toast with Raspberry
        Syrup, 92–93
    Baked Kale Chips, Five
        Ways, 192–194
    Baked Sweet Potato
        Fries, 204
    Banana Nut Smoothie, 83
    Basil Mango Jicama
        Salad, 120
    Basil Pesto, 241
    Bibimbap Bowl, 156–157
    Black Bean Taco Salad
        Bowl, 154–155
    Blackeye Pea
        Burritos, 182
    Buckwheat Sesame
        Milk, 227
    Cashew-Ginger Soba
        Noodle Bowl, 152–153
    Cashew Sour Cream, 230
    Chai Chia Smoothie, 77
    Chai Latte, 252
    Cheesy Sprinkle, 229
    Chickpea Scramble,
        100–101
    Chocolate PB
        Smoothie, 81
    Chocolate Quinoa
        Breakfast Bowl, 96

Cinnamon Apple
    Toast, 94
Coconut Watercress
    Soup, 107
Coconut Whipped
    Cream, 231
Creamy
    Avocado-Dressed
    Kale Salad, 122–123
Creamy Balsamic
    Dressing, 236
Creamy Mint-Lime
    Spaghetti
    Squash, 170–171
Creamy Pumpkin and
    Toasted Walnut
    Soup, 111
Curried Mango Chickpea
    Wrap, 147
Dill Potato Salad, 128
Easy DIY Pizza Crust, 234
Easy-Peasy Almond
    Milk, 226
Forbidden Black Rice
    and Edamame
    Salad, 132–133
Fresh Mango Salsa, 240
Fruit Salad with Zesty
    Citrus Couscous, 97
Fruity Granola, 98–99
Funky Monkey Sorbet, 213
Garlic Toast, 207
Ginger Carrot Soup, 106
Green Goddess
    Dressing, 235
Greens and Beans
    Dip, 202
Grilled AHLT, 144
Guacamole, 203
Hearty Chili, 115
Hibiscus Lemon Iced
    Tea, 248
Hummus, Five
    Ways, 197–199
Hydration Station, 79
Iced Mocha Latte, 254
Indian Red Split Lentil
    Soup, 116–117
Infused Water, 246
Lemon Pistachio Quinoa
    Cookies, 220–221
Lime in the Coconut Chia
    Pudding, 215

Loaded Black Bean
    Pizza, 145
London Fog, 251
Mango Madness, 80
Marinara Sauce, 242–243
Matcha Latte, 253
Max Power Smoothie, 76
Mediterranean Hummus
    Pizza, 146
Mint Chocolate Chip
    Sorbet, 214
Minty Beet and Sweet
    Potato Soup, 108–109
Miso-Coconut Dragon
    Bowl, 151
Miso Noodle Soup, 110
Morning Ginger-Lemon
    Elixir, 247
Muesli and Berries
    Bowl, 95
Nori Snack Rolls, 190
Oatmeal Breakfast
    Cookies, 86–87
Olive and White Bean
    Pasta, 173
Overnight Oats On the
    Go, 84–85
Pad Thai Bowl, 150
Peanut Sauce, 239
Pink Panther Smoothie, 82
Roasted Beet and
    Avocado Salad, 121
Roasted Cauliflower
    Tacos, 178–179
Roasted Garlic Pesto
    Potatoes, 205
Roasted Red Pepper and
    Butternut Squash
    Soup, 112–113
Roasted Veg with Creamy
    Avocado Dip, 102–103
Savory Roasted
    Chickpeas, 195
Savory Split Pea
    Soup, 118–119
Simple Sesame
    Stir-Fry, 168–169
Spiced Hot
    Chocolate, 255
Spicy Black Bean Dip, 200
Strawberry-Kiwi
    Spritzer, 249
Sun-dried Tomato and
    Pesto Quinoa, 172

Sunflower Hemp Milk, 228
Sunshine Muffins, 88–89
Sweet Potato Patties, 163
Tabbouleh Salad, 130–131
Tamari Toasted
    Almonds, 191
Toasted Sesame Miso
    Dressing, 237
Tropical Mocktail, 250
Tropi-Colada Frozen
    Pops, 212
Tropi-Kale Breeze, 78
Tuscan White Bean
    Salad, 129
Warm Lentil Salad
    with Red Wine
    Vinaigrette, 134–135
Weeknight Chickpea
    Tomato Soup, 114
Zesty Orange-Cranberry
    Energy Bites, 211
Quinoa
    about, 19
    Bibimbap Bowl, 156–157
    Black Bean Taco Salad
        Bowl, 154–155
    Chocolate Quinoa
        Breakfast Bowl, 96
    Creamy
        Avocado-Dressed
        Kale Salad, 122–123
    Falafel Wrap, 148–149
    Lemon Pistachio Quinoa
        Cookies, 220–221
    Miso-Coconut Dragon
        Bowl, 151
    Muesli and Berries
        Bowl, 95
    Overnight Oats On the
        Go, 84–85
    Simple Sesame
        Stir-Fry, 168–169
    Sun-dried Tomato and
        Pesto Quinoa, 172
    Sushi Bowl, 162
    Zesty Orange-Cranberry
        Energy Bites, 211

R

Raisins
    Banana Chocolate
        Cupcakes, 219

Raisins (*continued*)
    Fruity Granola, 98–99
    Muesli and Berries
        Bowl, 95
    Oatmeal Breakfast
        Cookies, 86–87
    Overnight Oats On the
        Go, 84–85
    Sunshine Muffins, 88–89
Recovery, post-workout, 8
Refined foods, 25
Restaurants, 71
Rice
    Avocado Red Pepper
        Sushi Rolls, 158–159
    Bibimbap Bowl, 156–157
    black, 133
    Black Bean Taco Salad
        Bowl, 154–155
    Creamy
        Avocado-Dressed
        Kale Salad, 122–123
    Forbidden Black Rice
        and Edamame
        Salad, 132–133
    Miso-Coconut Dragon
        Bowl, 151
    Spicy Chickpea Sushi
        Rolls, 160–161
    Sushi Bowl, 162
    Sweet Potato Patties, 163
Rice noodles
    Pad Thai Bowl, 150
Roots, 14. *See also specific*
Rosemary
    Tuscan White Bean
        Salad, 129

S

Salads
    Basil Mango Jicama
        Salad, 120
    Creamy
        Avocado-Dressed
        Kale Salad, 122–123
    Dill Potato Salad, 128
    Forbidden Black Rice
        and Edamame
        Salad, 132–133
    Fruit Salad with Zesty
        Citrus Couscous, 97

Moroccan Aubergine
    Salad, 126–127
Roasted Beet and
    Avocado Salad, 121
Tabbouleh Salad, 130–131
Tuscan White Bean
    Salad, 129
Warm Lentil Salad with
    Red Wine
    Vinaigrette, 134–135
Wilted Sesame-Miso Kale
    Salad, 124–125
Salt, 39, 40–41
Sauces
    Marinara Sauce, 242–243
    Peanut Sauce, 239
Scallions
    Basil Mango Jicama
        Salad, 120
    Bibimbap Bowl, 156–157
    Black Bean Taco Salad
        Bowl, 154–155
    Build Your Own
        Mushroom
        Fajitas, 180–181
    Cashew-Ginger Soba
        Noodle Bowl, 152–153
    Creamy
        Avocado-Dressed
        Kale Salad, 122–123
    Dill Potato Salad, 128
    Falafel Wrap, 148–149
    Forbidden Black Rice
        and Edamame
        Salad, 132–133
    Fresh Mango Salsa, 240
    Green Goddess
        Dressing, 235
    Miso Noodle Soup, 110
    Pad Thai Bowl, 150
    Savory Split Pea
        Soup, 118–119
    Simple Sesame
        Stir-Fry, 168–169
    Spicy Chickpea Sushi
        Rolls, 160–161
    Sushi Bowl, 162
    Tabbouleh Salad, 130–131
    Tuscan White Bean
        Salad, 129
    Vietnamese Summer
        Rolls, 164–165
Seafood, replacing, 24

Seasonings, 37–39, 41
Seed butters. *See also*
    specific
    Applesauce Crumble
        Muffins, 90–91
    Buckwheat Sesame
        Milk, 227
    Chocolate Quinoa
        Breakfast Bowl, 96
    Funky Monkey
        Sorbet, 213
    Mint Chocolate Chip
        Sorbet, 214
Seeds, 17. *See also specific*
Sesame seeds
    Banana Chocolate
        Cupcakes, 219
    Bibimbap Bowl, 156–157
    Forbidden Black Rice
        "and Edamame
        Salad, 132–133
    Indian Red Split Lentil
        Soup, 116–117
    Simple Sesame
        Stir-Fry, 168–169
    Sushi Bowl, 162
    Toasted Sesame Miso
        Dressing, 237
    Zesty Orange-Cranberry
        Energy Bites, 211
Shopping, 46
Sides
    Baked Sweet Potato
        Fries, 204
    Garlic Toast, 207
    Lemon Coconut Cilantro
        Rolls, 196
    Roasted Garlic Pesto
        Potatoes, 205
    Sweet Potato
        Biscuits, 206
Sleep, 69
Smoothies
    Banana Nut Smoothie, 83
    builder, 34
    Chai Chia Smoothie, 77
    Chocolate PB
        Smoothie, 81
    Hydration Station, 79
    Mango Madness, 80
    Max Power Smoothie, 76
    Pink Panther Smoothie, 82
    Tropi-Kale Breeze, 78

Snacks. *See also* Dips and
spreads
 Baked Kale Chips, Five
 Ways, 192–194
 Lemon Coconut Cilantro
 Rolls, 196
 Nori Snack Rolls, 190
 Savory Roasted
 Chickpeas, 195
 Tamari Toasted
 Almonds, 191
Soba noodles
 Cashew-Ginger Soba
 Noodle Bowl, 152–153
 Miso Noodle Soup, 110
Sodium, 2, 39, 40–41
Soups
 Coconut Watercress
 Soup, 107
 Creamy Pumpkin and
 Toasted Walnut
 Soup, 111
 Ginger Carrot Soup, 106
 Hearty Chili, 115
 Indian Red Split Lentil
 Soup, 116–117
 Minty Beet and Sweet
 Potato Soup, 108–109
 Miso Noodle Soup, 110
 Roasted Red Pepper and
 Butternut Squash
 Soup, 112–113
 Savory Split Pea
 Soup, 118–119
 Weeknight Chickpea
 Tomato Soup, 114
Spices, 18, 37–38
Spinach
 Bibimbap Bowl, 156–157
 Cashew-Ginger Soba
 Noodle Bowl, 152–153
 Chocolate PB
 Smoothie, 81
 Grilled AHLT, 144
 Hydration Station, 79
 Indian Red Split Lentil
 Soup, 116–117
 Maple Dijon B
 urgers, 140–141
 Max Power Smoothie, 76
 Miso-Coconut Dragon
 Bowl, 151
 Moroccan Aubergine
 Salad, 126–127

Olive and White Bean
 Pasta, 173
Sun-dried Tomato and
 Pesto Quinoa, 172
Sushi Bowl, 162
Sprouting jars, 37
Squash. *See also* Zucchini
 about, 20
 Creamy Mint-Lime
 Spaghetti
 Squash, 170–171
 Orange Walnut
 Pasta, 176–177
 Roasted Red Pepper and
 Butternut Squash
 Soup, 112–113
 Spaghetti and Buckwheat
 Meatballs, 174–175
Staples, 31–32. *See also*
 Homemade basics
Starches, 14
Stems, 15. *See also specific*
Stress, 6, 70
Strokes, 3
Sun-dried tomatoes
 Savory Split Pea
 Soup, 118–119
 Sun-dried Tomato and
 Pesto Quinoa, 172
Sunflower seed butter
 Apple Crumble, 222–223
 Baked Kale Chips, Five
 Ways, 192–194
 Banana Nut Smoothie, 83
 Cashew-Ginger Soba
 Noodle Bowl, 152–153
 Chocolate Krinkles, 216
 Chocolate PB
 Smoothie, 81
 Falafel Wrap, 148–149
 Lemon Pistachio Quinoa
 Cookies, 220–221
 Oatmeal Breakfast
 Cookies, 86–87
 Peanut Sauce, 239
 Sunshine Muffins, 88–89
 Zesty Orange-Cranberry
 Energy Bites, 211
Sunflower seeds
 about, 21, 229
 Cheesy Sprinkle, 229
 Fruity Granola, 98–99
 Muesli and Berries
 Bowl, 95

Roasted Beet and
 Avocado Salad, 121
Sunflower Hemp Milk, 228
Sunshine Muffins, 88–89
Tabbouleh Salad, 130–131
Tamari Toasted
 Almonds, 191
Superfoods, 19–21
Supplements, 26, 28–29
Sweet potatoes
 Baked Sweet Potato
 Fries, 204
 Forbidden Black Rice and
 Edamame
 Salad, 132–133
 Hummus, Five
 Ways, 197–199
 Indian Red Split Lentil
 Soup, 116–117
 Minty Beet and Sweet
 Potato Soup, 108–109
 Roasted Veg with
 Creamy Avocado
 Dip, 102–103
 Sweet Potato
 Biscuits, 206
 Sweet Potato Patties, 163
Swiss chard
 Simple Sesame
 Stir-Fry, 168–169
 Warm Lentil Salad with
 Red Wine
 Vinaigrette, 134–135

T

Tahini
 Basil Mango Jicama
 Salad, 120
 Buckwheat Sesame
 Milk, 227
 Cajun Burgers, 142–143
 Creamy Balsamic
 Dressing, 236
 Creamy Mint-Lime
 Spaghetti
 Squash, 170–171
 Curried Mango Chickpea
 Wrap, 147
 Falafel Wrap, 148–149
 Green Goddess
 Dressing, 235

Tahini (*continued*)
    Greens and Beans
        Dip, 202
    Hummus, Five
        Ways, 197–199
    Roasted Red Pepper and
        Butternut Squash
        Soup, 112–113
Tamari
    Avocado Red Pepper
        Sushi Rolls, 158–159
    Avomame Spread, 201
    Bibimbap Bowl, 156–157
    Cashew-Ginger Soba
        Noodle Bowl, 152–153
    Green Goddess
        Dressing, 235
    Nori Snack Rolls, 190
    Peanut Sauce, 239
    Savory Roasted
        Chickpeas, 195
    Savory Split Pea
        Soup, 118–119
    Simple Sesame
        Stir-Fry, 168–169
    Spaghetti and Buckwheat
        Meatballs, 174–175
    Spicy Black Bean Dip, 200
    Spicy Chickpea Sushi
        Rolls, 160–161
    Sushi Bowl, 162
    Tamari Toasted
        Almonds, 191
    Toasted Sesame Miso
        Dressing, 237
    Wilted Sesame-Miso Kale
        Salad, 124–125
Teas
    Chai Latte, 252
    Hibiscus Lemon Iced
        Tea, 248
    London Fog, 251
    Matcha Latte, 253
Teff, 19
Thirst sensation, 246
Thyme
    Minty Beet and Sweet
        Potato Soup, 108–109

Shepherd's Pie, 186–187
Tomatoes. *See also*
    Sun-dried tomatoes
    Black Bean Taco Salad
        Bowl, 154–155
    Blackeye Pea
        Burritos, 182
    Chickpea Scramble,
        100–101
    Creamy Avocado-
        Dressed Kale
        Salad, 122–123
    Creamy Mint-Lime
        Spaghetti
        Squash, 170–171
    Falafel Wrap, 148–149
    Fresh Mango Salsa, 240
    Grilled AHLT, 144
    Hearty Chili, 115
    Loaded Black Bean
        Pizza, 145
    Marinara Sauce, 242–243
    Roasted Cauliflower
        Tacos, 178–179
    Savory Split Pea
        Soup, 118–119
    Sun-dried Tomato and
        Pesto Quinoa, 172
    Tabbouleh Salad, 130–131
    Weeknight Chickpea
        Tomato Soup, 114

U

Utensils, 36

V

Veganism, 12
Vegetables, 13–15. *See also*
    specific
Vegetarianism, 12
Vines, 15. *See also specific*
Vitamin A, 19–20, 113
Vitamin B12, 4, 26
Vitamin D, 28

W

Watercress
    Coconut Watercress
        Soup, 107
Weight loss, 6–8
Whole foods, 22, 25
Whole grains, 17, 22. *See also*
    specific

Y

Yams, 117

Z

Zesters, 36
Zucchini
    Blackeye Pea
        Burritos, 182
    Build Your Own Mushroom
        Fajitas, 180–181
    Chickpea Scramble,
        100–101
    Dill Potato Salad, 128
    Falafel Wrap, 148–149
    Hummus, Five
        Ways, 197–199
    Indian Red Split Lentil
        Soup, 116–117
    Mediterranean Hummus
        Pizza, 146
    Olive and White Bean
        Pasta, 173
    Savory Split Pea
        Soup, 118–119
    Sun-dried Tomato and
        Pesto Quinoa, 172
    Tuscan White Bean
        Salad, 129

ACKNOWLEDGMENTS

I am so grateful to all the pioneers of plant-based nutrition who've paved the way for me to learn and share this compassionate, sustainable, peaceful way of life.

Thank you to Mary, who was my only vegan friend before I went vegan, and who patiently steered me in the right direction to learn what it means and that it's much more than what you eat.

Thank you to my family for being so supportive and even making some big changes in their lives without any push, which is the highest compliment a girl could ask for.

Thank you to all the amazing people I've met online through this work—there are too many to name, and I hope you know who you are. A few who I'd specifically like to thank for being such wonderful influences:

Dreena Burton, you are such a beautiful presence and create such a bounty of delicious recipes. I'm sure that several in this book are inspired by your work. You are the queen of veggie burgers and cookies!

Jack Norris, your dedication to research and solid information is such an important resource for me and so many others.

Michael Greger, your personality and knowledge make nutrition research exciting and fun.

To Alex, you are both the anchor grounding me and the parasail lifting me in the air. Thank you for putting up with all the time I spend in front of the computer, agonizing over words and spreadsheets, and for knowing how to get me out of the house when I go stir-crazy. You are the best.

ABOUT THE AUTHOR

 **Heather Nicholds** is a Certified Holistic Nutritionist who helps newly minted vegans (or the veg-curious) fully nourish their bodies so they have the energy to enjoy their lives. Her focus is on making it happen—clarifying practical strategies, making healthy meals that taste phenomenal, and showing you how it can all work, even when you're busy. Her goal is to inspire and motivate you to take control of your own health and energy levels through conscious choices about what you eat. Heather is a YouTube video personality and has been a speaker at BlogHer Food and Toronto Veg Food Fest. She has been featured on Shape.com, *One Green Planet*, *Huffington Post*, and *Greatist*.

CPSIA information can be obtained
at www.ICGtesting.com
Printed in the USA
BVHW06s0000290818
525536BV00001B/1/P

9 781939 754